THE
CASTLE STORY

THE
CASTLE STORY
SHEILA SANCHA

HarperCollins*Publishers*

THE CASTLE STORY

First published 1991 by Kestrel Books
This edition published 1991 by William Collins Sons & Co Ltd
Reprinted 1993 by Collins

Collins is an imprint of HarperCollins Publishers Ltd,
77-85 Fulham Palace Road, Hammersmith,
London W6 8JB

Copyright © Sheila Sancha 1979

Designed by the author and Treld Bicknell

A CIP record for this title is available from the British Library

ISBN 0 00 196336 8 (HB)
0 00 184177 7 (PB)

Printed and bound in Hong Kong

CONTENTS

Preface   7

Bibliography   7

1   A Glance at Early Fortifications   11

2   Digging in Behind Earth and Timber Defences   21

3   A Quiet Life in Hall and Chamber   34

4   Great Square Towers and How to Take Them   45

5   Siegecraft, Chivalry and Sheer Brute Force   63

6   Changing Times   79

7   The Rise of the Gatehouse and Decline of the Keep   101

8   Gothic Arches and Painted Chambers   116

9   Trouble in Wales and Other Matters   128

10 The Heyday of English Military Architecture   141

11 Castles Begin to Lose Their Importance   162

12 The Return of the Great Square Keep   183

13 Ending the Story   201

    Maps   214

    Glossary and Chronological Table   216

    Index   223

TO
CARLOS

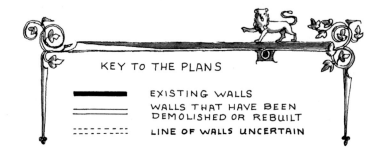

KEY TO THE PLANS

———— EXISTING WALLS

━━━━ WALLS THAT HAVE BEEN
DEMOLISHED OR REBUILT

- - - - - - LINE OF WALLS UNCERTAIN

PREFACE TO NEW EDITION

It has long been my ambition to have a new edition of *The Castle Story* and I am delighted to see it back in print. The book is the result of many years' research and exploration: an obsessive desire to find out why the castles were built, who lived in them, and how the rooms were used. The ruins are a haunting link with people of the past who saw the same walls and arches we see today, although much is missing. Half the fun of exploring a castle is to try to summon up those knights, ladies, squires and servants; to try to imagine them holding court, sitting at table, or withstanding a siege. But the vision is blurred because medieval history and archaeology are so extremely complicated. I found the best way to clarify the mass of information was to slot the castles into their historical context, then photograph the ruins and draw over the photographs. The photographs are of the existing buildings, while the drawings show the parts that are missing: the shape of the people, furniture, and other objects lifted from contemporary illuminated manuscripts.

BIBLIOGRAPHY

Architecture

Ella Armitage, *The Early Norman Castles of the British Isles*, Murray, 1912. R. Allen Brown, *English Castles*, B.T. Batsford, 1954. R. Allen Brown, H.M. Colvin and A. J. Taylor, *The History of the King's Works*, HMSO, two vols., 1963. Fred H. Crossley, *Timber Building in England*, B.T. Batsford, 1951. Sir Banister Fletcher, *A History of Architecture on the Comparative Method*, B.T. Batsford. D.F. Renn, *Norman Castles in Britain*, John Baker, Humanities Press, 1968. Sidney Toy, *The Castles of Great Britain*, Heinemann,1953. Margaret Wood, *The English Mediaeval House*, Phoenix House, 1965; *Norman Domestic Architecture*, Royal Archaeological Institute, 1974.

The reconstruction of Cadbury Castle on pages 10 and 15 was taken from Leslie Alcock, *By South Cadbury is That Camelot... Excavations at Cadbury Castle 1966-70*, Thames and Hudson, 1972.

The reconstruction of Tamworth is based on reports published by the South Staffordshire Archaeological and Historical Society on excavations at Tamworth in 1967 on the western entrance to the Saxon borough by J.Gould and on the excavation of a Saxon water-mill in Bolebridge Street Tamworth by Philip Rahtz and Ken Sheridan in 1971.

The reconstruction of Hereford town is taken from M.O. Lobel, ed., *Historic Towns*, London, 1969.

For the details of each individual castle I have relied upon the Department of the Environment Official Guidebooks, HMSO, and other relevant guidebooks where the castles are privately owned.

History
R. Allen Brown, *The Normans and the Norman Conquest*, Constable 1969. Sir George Clark, ed, *The Oxford History of England,* vols IV, V and VI, Clarendon Press, Oxford, 1953-61. William Croft Dickinson, *Scotland from the Earliest Times to 1603*, Nelson, 1961. John E. Morris, *The Welsh Wars of Edward I,* Clarendon Press, Oxford, 1901. Sir Maurice Powicke, *King Henry III and the Lord Edward*, Oxford University Press.

Armour
Claude Blair, *European Armour.* B. T. Batsford, 1958. Vesey Norman, *Arms and Armour,* Weidenfeld & Nicolson, 1964; *The Medieval Soldier*, Arthur Barker Ltd, 1971.

Literature
Aucassin and Nicolette and Other Tales, translated by Pauline Matarasso, Penguin Books, 1971. Bede, *A History of the English Church and People*, translated by Leo Sherley-Price, Penguin Books, 1955. *A Choice of Chaucer's Verse,* translated by Nevill Coghill, Faber. David C. Douglas, ed, *English Historical Documents*, Vols II, III and IV, Eyre & Spottiswoode. Jean Froissart, *Chronicles*, translated by Geoffrey Brereton, Penguin Books. *Gesta Stephani: The Deeds of Stephen*, translated by K. R. Potter, Thomas Nelson & Sons. William of Malmesbury, *The Historia Nouvella*, translated by K. R. Potter, Thomas Nelson & Sons.

The letter on page 160 from Master James of St George to the barons of the exchequer is taken from page 398 of *The History of the King's Works* (see above under Architecture) and is translated by Dr Arnold Taylor, Inspector of Ancient Monuments, and quoted by permission of the Controller of HM Stationery Office.

All the translators in the above list have been most kind in giving me permission to quote excerpts from their work. It has been fascinating to be able to read these books and then relate them to the buildings; and I am most grateful to be able to use these voices from the past to enliven my text.

Other excerpts are as follows:

Page 52. Ordericus Vitalis, *The Ecclesiastical History of England and Normandy*, translated by Thomas Forester, Henry H. Bohn, 1854.
Page 116. Close Roll 30 Henry III, taken from Turner, *Architecture of England,* vol I, page 261, 1877.
Page 180. Adam of Domerham, Monk of Glastonbury, taken from Geoffrey Ashe, *Quest for Arthur's Britain*, page 125.
The excerpt on page 135 is quoted by kind permission of the Society for Promoting Christian Knowledge: that on page 174 by kind permission of the Selden Society.

ACKNOWLEDGMENTS

Most of the information for this book came from the individual guidebooks bought at the ticket offices each time I visited a castle. I owe much to the various authors. The guidebooks supplied the history and archaeology of the buildings, but I needed a wealth of background material to fill in the gaps, both historical and architectural, between one castle and the next, and most of this was discovered in the extensive Kensington Library. More specialized books could be found in the superb library of the Society of Antiquaries. Whenever I failed to understand a particular problem, there was no difficulty in finding the right authority to explain it. I welcome this opportunity to thank all those who have taken time and trouble to reply to my letters and answer my questions verbally. In particular, I would like to thank Brian Davison, Inspector of Ancient Monuments for English Heritage, who advised me in the early stages of the project. Armour is a particularly complicated subject and it was extremely kind of Vesey Norman, then Master of the Armouries, HM Tower of London, to explain so much on the telephone. Finally, I am very grateful to Derek Renn, whose book *Norman Castles in Britain* is a veritable mine of information. I was delighted when he volunteered to read and comment on the first draft of my text, which allowed me to assess the accuracy of the work, and gave me the confidence to go ahead and finish it.

The author and publishers wish to thank the following for their kind permission to reproduce the photographs in this book: Caisse Nationale des Monuments et des Sites, Paris, for the photograph on page 22. The Irish Tourist Board for the photographs on pages 97 and 199. The National Monuments Record Office for the photographs on pages 49 and 74. The Photographic Library of the Department of the Environment for the photographs on pages 91, 126 and 140. Hallam Ashley for the photograph at the bottom of page 209. They would also like to thank the following for their kind permission to take photographs: The Castle Museum, Norwich, page 53. The Singleton Open Air Museum, pages 36 and 37. Finally they would like to thank the Ordnance Survey for permission to base the following plans on their maps: pages 10, 18 and 32.

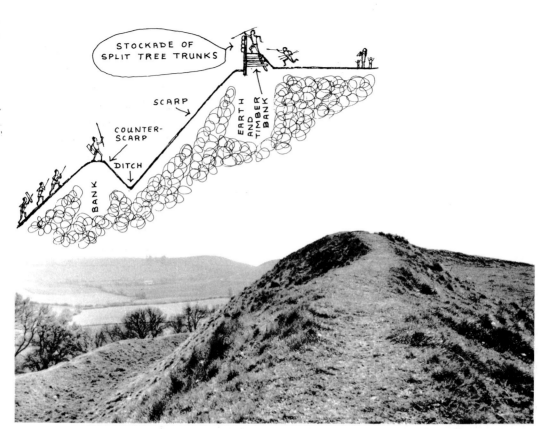

STOCKADE OF SPLIT TREE TRUNKS

SCARP

COUNTER-SCARP

DITCH

BANK

EARTH AND TIMBER BANK

A steep hill became harder for an enemy to climb if banks and ditches were dug round the sides. This is the east bank – or rampart – of Cadbury Castle (Somerset), an Iron Age hill-fort occupied from before 600 B.C. until the Romans massacred the inhabitants in the late first century A.D. The original banks lie under later defences (see page 15). Fine parallel lines indicate banks and ditches: the four banks surrounding Cadbury Castle rise one above the other up the hill.

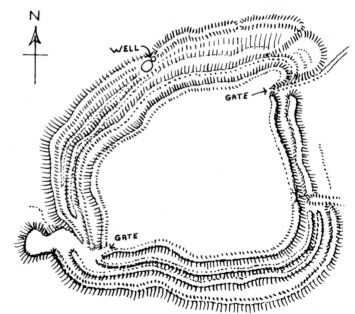

N

WELL

GATE

GATE

I A GLANCE AT EARLY FORTIFICATIONS

Iron Age Celtic warriors wore gold ornaments round their necks and arms and often fought naked, painting their bodies and greasing their hair into spikes to frighten the enemy. They used swords and spears, either held in the hand or hurled like a javelin; while their men also wielded spears and flung sling-stones.

PRIMITIVE MEN FOUND THAT THE BEST WAY TO AVOID being eaten by wolves or knocked on the head by their enemies was to live in places that were extremely difficult to get at. So they built their rough shelters in savage remote country: on rocky headlands jutting into the sea, on firm land surrounded by dangerous swamps, on cliff edges, or on high flat-topped hills. However, these natural strongholds usually had some vulnerable spot, some area of fairly level ground where the enemy could come rushing in, and steep hillsides had to be made even harder for enemies to climb. Primitive men decided, therefore, to defend their settlements by throwing up great banks and ditches, often several lines of them – and the first fortifications had been dug.

The man on the top of the bank had an outstanding advantage over the enemy who had just slithered to the bottom of the ditch, and who then had to struggle up an almost vertical slope, dodging the hail of rocks, throwing-spears, sling-stones and arrows aimed from above. When the defender built a stockade or wall on top of his bank, he was in an even stronger position. Stockades were made of any material that lay close at hand: split tree trunks, a wattle of interlaced branches, or briar hedges. Sometimes the banks of Iron Age forts were boxed in with stout timber walls and the entrances were defended by huge wooden gates. Stone walls were used in districts where stone was available.

The Romans wore the same types of armour as the later medieval knights but, without stirrups, their cavalry were not as securely seated in the saddle. The javelin ended in an iron shaft that could not be hacked away when it stuck in a wooden shield. This soldier is standing outside the west gate of Pevensey Castle, a Roman fort which later became a Norman fortress.

Iron Age warriors fought their fierce battles on foot or by hurling spears from two-horse chariots, but their defences were not strong enough to keep the Romans out; and soon most of Britain had become just another of Rome's far-flung colonies.

The Romans had good facilities for transporting stone, and were able to fortify their towns and military camps with massive walls, towers and gateways. Earthenware tiles were often used as well as stone, which is interesting, because bricks were not made extensively in this country until about the fourteenth century; medieval builders often tore down the old Roman walls to pick out the tiles and use them again. It was easier to fell trees than to haul heavy loads of stone along the long straight roads or row them up the rivers, so the Romans used timber to defend less important places. The fundamental banks and ditches, laid out in rectangular shapes with rounded corners, kept the enemy away from the base of the walls, whatever material they were made of. Enemies came from all quarters: there were the Picts to the north; Scots to the west; and, from the end of the third century A.D., the Saxons started raiding the shores on both sides of the Channel. The Romans built a series of seaside forts to keep them at bay and these are called the Forts of the Saxon Shore.

Many Iron Age and Roman sites are marked as castles on the maps when they are really defended settlements or military camps, while the fortlets on Hadrian's Wall are called milecastles. This is confusing, because the word should not apply to them at all. The difference between these early places and the later medieval castles is that castles were both military and residential buildings, housing a family and a garrison as well: a Roman fort defended the soldiers within its walls and was a purely military affair; while an Iron Age fort was a place of refuge for the people who farmed the land round about, or a protection for the huts of a village. A medieval castle was the fortified residence of a king or powerful baron, his family, soldiers and dependants.

THIS SOLDIER WIELDS A HEAVY JAVELIN AND A SHORT SWORD

12

The Romans had trouble at home and marched their legions away, leaving the Britons to face the Picts and Scots alone, while the Saxon raids finally turned into full-scale invasions. The Saxons settled in Essex, Sussex and other eastern parts of Britain, but they seem to have met some kind of organized resistance from the west. History towards the end of the fifth century is full of mystery – glorified by the names of two heroes: Ambrosius Aurelianus and the elusive Arthur. Ambrosius rallied the Britons and led them in battle against the Saxons; he was a Roman and there is no doubt as to his existence. It has never been conclusively proved that Arthur ever really lived at all, though it seems likely that there is more than a grain of truth in all the myths and legends that surround him. Archaeologists are still trying to dig up more information about this fascinating period.

Roman forts were usually rectangular with rounded towers, or bastions, jutting away from the walls towards the ditch. Portchester, built at the end of the third century A.D., was one of the forts that defended the coast against Saxon raiders. The harbour was still in use in medieval times and the Normans built a castle to defend it inside the old Roman walls.

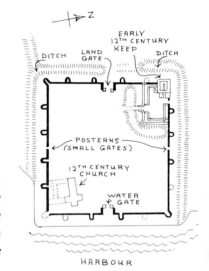

HEAVY ROMAN MERCHANT SHIPS

(THE HARBOUR MUST HAVE BEEN DEEPER THAN IT IS NOW)

Arthur is thought to have lived between A.D. 480 and 540. Little is known about this period; he may have worn some kind of Roman armour with a touch of the Celt about it — an iron-framed helmet, a warm woollen cloak, cross-gartered hose, a round shield and a spear.

In order to defend themselves against the fierce Saxons, some of the British warriors went back and refortified their ancient strongholds; the Iron Age hill-fort Cadbury Castle, in Somerset, is an outstanding example of this. The original inhabitants had been massacred by the Romans about A.D. 70, after which the fort lay abandoned. Recent evidence has shown that the place was reoccupied at the time when Arthur is thought to have been active, soon after A.D. 480, so it could have been Arthur himself who organized the building of the new defences. Arthur was not a king (if he was anything), but he would have been the war leader commanding the combined British forces against the Saxons. Cadbury Castle is larger than most of the fortified places which have been found in the west country, and there was enough space to accommodate several armies at once. In the 'Arthurian period' the top bank was crowned with a stone-and-timber wall, and traces have been discovered of the square timber tower that defended the south-west entrance; while, on the crest of the hill, there is evidence of a large rectangular feasting hall. All these wooden structures have rotted away, but they have left the marks of their post-holes printed in the soil.

Almost all Dark Age buildings were timber, and there was plenty of timber about. England must have been a fairy-tale country: the magnificent oak forests alive with bears, wolves, wild boar and other less dangerous animals. The Anglo-Saxon invaders did not live behind the stone walls of the Roman towns, but chopped down the forest trees and built their huts and mead halls in country districts. We know very little about

14

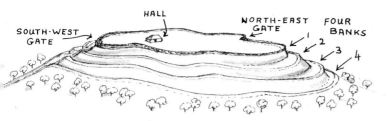

early Saxon fortifications but, in general, they must have defended their settlements against neighbouring war bands, robbers and wolves by surrounding them with banks and ditches topped with palisades and hedgeworks. There would have been stone walls as well – in stony districts – but these are hard to find because they often lie buried under later fortifications.

When archaeological evidence is missing, clues can sometimes be found in documents. In 547 King Ida built defences of some kind round his royal town, perched high on the rock at Bamburgh on the coast of Northumberland. According to *The Anglo-Saxon Chronicle* this was 'first enclosed by a stockade and thereafter by a rampart'. Bamburgh was attacked in 633 by the pagan King Penda of Mercia, and the great historian St Bede, who was born only forty years after the event and lived not far away in the monastery of Jarrow, gives a vivid description of the siege:

Cadbury Castle – destroyed by the Romans – was re-occupied some time between A.D. 470 and 500, and Arthur himself may have organized the new defences. Excavation has revealed traces of a stone and timber wall on the top bank, a gatehouse at

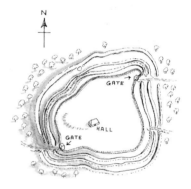

the south-west entrance (likely reconstruction shown left), and post-holes of a large timber hall where Arthur and his warriors may have feasted.

The Normans built a castle high on the rock at Bamburgh, the site of King Ida's fortified town. The existing stonework belongs to many different periods, and it is hard to say if the lower parts of the wall were built by Saxon or Norman hands.

Saxon warriors fought with spears, axes, single-edged knives, and swords. This round wooden shield was covered with leather and the hand-grip protected by the central boss. The helmet was of iron and horn.

THE ROCK ITSELF, AND PERHAPS A FEW STONES BUILT INTO THE BASE OF THE NORMAN CASTLE, ARE ALL THAT REMAIN OF KING IDA'S STRONGHOLD

BRONZE BOAR
HORN
IRON BANDS
IRON BOSS
WOODEN SHIELD, COVERED WITH LEATHER AND DECORATED WITH GILT BRONZE

Penda and his enemy army of Mercians spread ruin far and wide throughout the lands of the Northumbrians and reached the very gates of the royal city . . . Unable to enter it either by force or after a siege, Penda attempted to set fire to it. Pulling down all the neighbouring villages, he carried to Bamburgh a vast quantity of beams, rafters, wattled walls and thatched roofs, piling it high around the city wall on the landward side. Directly the wind became favourable, he set fire to this mass, intending to destroy the city. Now, while all this was happening, the most reverend Bishop Aidan was living on Farne Island, which lies nearly two miles from the city . . . When the saint saw the column of smoke and flame wafted by the winds above the city walls, he is said to have raised his eyes and hands to heaven saying with tears: 'Lord, see what evil Penda does!' No sooner had he spoken than the wind shifted away from the city, and drove back the flames on to those who had kindled them, so injuring some and unnerving all that they abandoned their assault on the city so clearly under God's protection. (Bede, *A History of the English Church and People*, Penguin Books, p. 167.)

Saxon fortifications are hardly mentioned again until the end of the eighth century, when the wild Welsh came plundering into Mercia, and King Offa decided to keep them out

16

once and for all by building an immense bank and ditch which ran for about 120 miles. Offa's Dyke is still there in places.

The next invaders were the Danes, launching surprise attacks from their sleek shallow-bottomed boats. King Alfred of Wessex managed to rally his men and stand up to their assaults. When he made peace with them in 879, he wisely turned his attention to fortifying his towns – surrounding them with stone walls or stout palisades. From now on, the history of fortification becomes clearer. Alfred's son and daughter – Edward the Elder and Ethelfleda, Lady of Mercia – carried on with the work and by 924 (the year of Edward's death) well over thirty towns were defended. Ethelfleda's main stronghold was at Tamworth in Staffordshire and, because some parts of the banks and one of the gates have been excavated, we can get some idea of the shape of her fortifications.

The Saxon thegns lived in timber halls alongside the jumble of village huts and hovels; some were thatched with reeds and straw, others roofed with oak tiles or turf. The whole community clustered round the church. Many stone-built churches have survived and, being more fireproof than the rest of the buildings, would have been used as places of refuge in times of danger.

Florence of Worcester, A.D. *914:* 'Ethelfleda, the lady of the Mercians, led her people to Tamworth, and by God's help rebuilt that town . . .'
Ethelfleda would have worn clothes like the woman in the drawing above. Below is a reconstruction of the timber west gate at Tamworth, from inside the town. Huge timber posts and beams held up the sides of the earth banks.

OUTER DITCH
SENTRY WALK

NTRY
ALK CARRIED
VER THE ENTRANCE
Y MEANS OF A
MBER BRIDGE

N

NORTH GATE
BANK
DITCH
WEST GATE
EAST GATE
MOUND OF LATER NORMAN CASTLE
SAXON WATER MILL

MUCH LATER ADDITIONS

Anglo-Saxon churches often look like copies of the wooden ones and this highly decorated tower at Earl's Barton, Northamptonshire, built at the beginning of the eleventh century, is one of the best examples; but most of them were more simple.

When the town of Oxford was fortified, the tower of St Michael was not only used as a belfry, but must also have been part of the defences of the north gate, as this map shows.

Saxon doorways are high and narrow, while the large window openings at the top of buildings often come in pairs with round or triangular tops, supported in the middle by a turned baluster shaft: a typical Anglo-Saxon feature. Small single windows were triangular-headed or round-headed. Some of these little round-headed windows look very similar to the later Norman ones.

The church tower at Earl's Barton (Northants) looks like a copy of an old timber tower. The pattern, suggesting posts and beams, would have been part of the structure of a wooden building but pure decoration on a stone one. The bells were hung behind baluster shafts – a common feature in Saxon churches. It is unusual to find so many in a row.

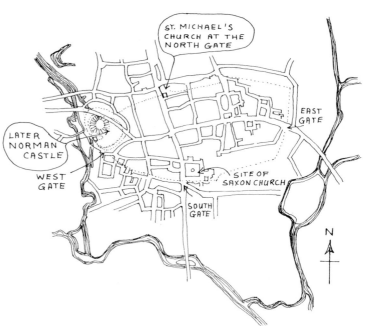

ST. MICHAEL'S CHURCH AT THE NORTH GATE

LATER NORMAN CASTLE

WEST GATE

EAST GATE

SOUTH GATE

SITE OF SAXON CHURCH

N

TYPICAL ANGLO-SAXON WINDOWS

Oxford was protected by rivers and marshland: the only solid ground from which an attack could be launched was to the north. St Michael's church tower, left, was also the watch-tower for the north gate.

Oxford was fortified by Edward the Elder in 912. If his defences ran along the same lines as the later city wall, the Saxon town would have been laid out inside the dotted line on this modern map.

Saxon architecture flourished in England until Edward the Confessor came to the throne. Edward had been brought up at his uncle's court at Rouen and had watched Norman masons working on massive stone buildings in a completely different architectural style that was based on the buildings that the Romans had left behind: Romanesque. This is a general term describing buildings that were being put up all over Europe from about A.D. 475 to 1150. For example, there is French Romanesque and German Romanesque. When we talk about an English *Norman* church we mean that it was built in the Norman Romanesque style (see the chart at the end of the book).

When King Edward sailed from Normandy in 1042 he brought the Norman Romanesque style of architecture with him, and having a strictly religious turn of mind, he did not build himself a castle, as another man might have done, but set his masons to work on Westminster Abbey: the first Romanesque building in England. This is where *The Castle Story* begins.

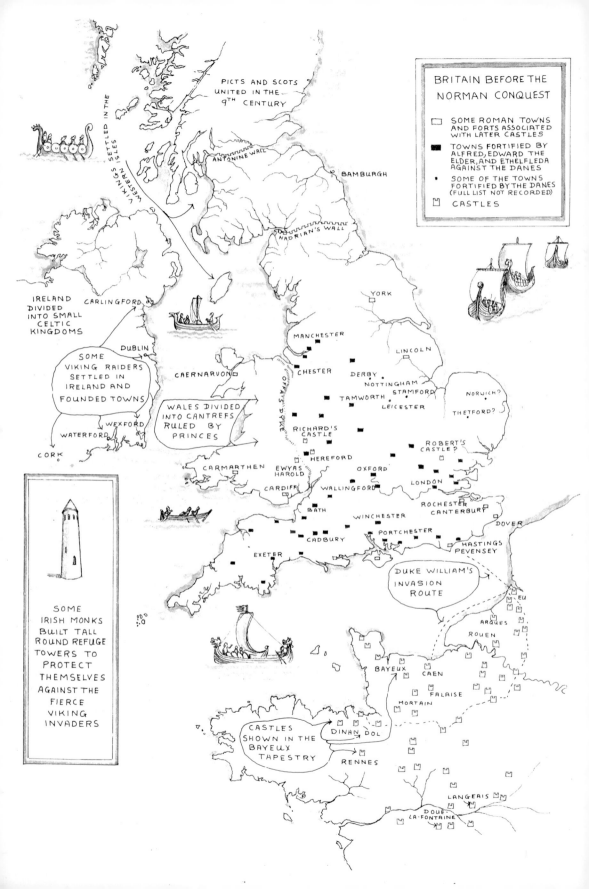

BRITAIN BEFORE THE NORMAN CONQUEST

☐ SOME ROMAN TOWNS AND FORTS ASSOCIATED WITH LATER CASTLES

■ TOWNS FORTIFIED BY ALFRED, EDWARD THE ELDER, AND ETHELFLEDA AGAINST THE DANES

• SOME OF THE TOWNS FORTIFIED BY THE DANES (FULL LIST NOT RECORDED)

⌂ CASTLES

PICTS AND SCOTS UNITED IN THE 9TH CENTURY

ANTONINE WALL

VIKINGS SETTLED IN THE WESTERN ISLES

BAMBURGH

HADRIAN'S WALL

YORK

IRELAND DIVIDED INTO SMALL CELTIC KINGDOMS

CARLINGFORD

DUBLIN

SOME VIKING RAIDERS SETTLED IN IRELAND AND FOUNDED TOWNS

WEXFORD

WATERFORD

CORK

MANCHESTER

LINCOLN

CAERNARVON

CHESTER

DERBY

NOTTINGHAM

STAMFORD

NORWICH?

TAMWORTH

LEICESTER

THETFORD?

WALES DIVIDED INTO CANTREFS RULED BY PRINCES

OFFA'S DYKE

RICHARD'S CASTLE

ROBERT'S CASTLE?

CARMARTHEN

EWYAS HAROLD

HEREFORD

OXFORD

LONDON

CARDIFF

WALLINGFORD

ROCHESTER

CANTERBURY

BATH

WINCHESTER

DOVER

PORTCHESTER

CADBURY

HASTINGS

PEVENSEY

EXETER

SOME IRISH MONKS BUILT TALL ROUND REFUGE TOWERS TO PROTECT THEMSELVES AGAINST THE FIERCE VIKING INVADERS

DUKE WILLIAM'S INVASION ROUTE

EU

ARQUES

ROUEN

BAYEUX

CAEN

FALAISE

MORTAIN

CASTLES SHOWN IN THE BAYEUX TAPESTRY

DINAN

DOL

RENNES

LANGEAIS

DOUÉ LA-FONTAINE

DIGGING IN
BEHIND EARTH AND
TIMBER DEFENCES

2

'THEN THE KING SENT FOR ALL HIS COUNCIL AND ordered them to come to Gloucester near the later Feast of St Mary. The foreigners then had built a castle at Hereford in Earl Sweyn's province, and had inflicted every possible injury and insult upon the king's men in those parts.' (*English Historical Documents*, Eyre & Spottiswoode, vol. II, p. 122.)

These lines, taken from *The Anglo-Saxon Chronicle* refer to the year 1051. The 'foreigners' were some of King Edward's Norman friends who had accompanied him to England and had been given lands next to the Welsh border. This was a dangerous district, because the king of North Wales, Gruffydd ap Llewelyn, was inclined to side with King Edward's enemies and come raiding over English territory. Added to which, the Anglo-Saxons disliked the high-handed newcomers, with their alien language and alien ways. Faced with this situation, the Normans built castles for themselves because they wanted to live behind the solid defences that they had been used to at home.

There are the remains of three pre-Conquest castles in the county of Hereford and Worcester: Ewayas Harold, Richard's Castle and Hereford. The Norman barons may have built castles in other parts of England, and there is mention of Robert's Castle which was probably the one at Clavering in Essex, but if there ever were any more of them, then they have vanished without a trace.

Hereford must have had defences of some kind ever since the days of Offa. By 913 it was protected by a stout bank, palisade and ditch on both sides of the river Wye; while a cathedral had been built on the north bank. It is almost certain that the castle banks overlooking the river in the corner of the Saxon town were made by Ralph the Timid, son of King Edward's sister and the Count of Vexin.

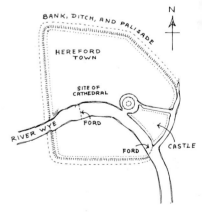

KITE SHAPED SHIELDS WERE SPECIALLY DESIGNED FOR HORSEMEN

Norman knights rode great stallions, trained to bite and kick in battle. The stirrup, introduced some time in the Dark Ages, had given riders more stability in the saddle: a tremendous advantage when wielding a sword or spear.

In order to find out what these early castles looked like, it is necessary to know something about the people who introduced them to England. The Normans were originally a group of Viking raiders who had settled on land at the mouth of the Seine in 911: their neighbours called them 'northmen'. They stopped using Danish laws, became devout Christians and adopted the customs and habits of the folk round about. The warriors copied the Frankish way of fighting on horseback instead of on foot, and discovered that this was a much better way of winning battles. (King Edward's nephew Ralph the Timid, who built the castle at Hereford, had tried to persuade the Anglo-Saxon thegns to fight on horseback when he was attacked by Gruffydd ap Llewelyn in 1055, but the thegns were not trained for this kind of warfare, and were utterly defeated.) The Norman barons honoured their new God by building huge stone churches in the Romanesque style – also copied from the Franks – and they built themselves castles to live in.

Great lords had been building castles in the northern parts of France since the end of the ninth century. As early as 864, Charles the Bald had laid down a law forbidding anyone to build a castle without his permission, which shows that castles existed at that time. More than a hundred years later, Fulk Nerra (the Black), Count of Anjou, built about thirteen castles in his territory. Castles were part and parcel of the *feudal system*, the way of life people had evolved out of the need to protect themselves against marauding Vikings and other enemies. The peasants and serfs tilled the land and did armed service for their local baron, and the baron undertook to give armed service to his king, duke, or count – whoever happened to be at the top of the hierarchy. In return, the king protected his barons and the baron protected his own people, often by sheltering them inside the walls of his castle in times of danger.

Although there must have been many different sorts of castles in the eleventh century, they can roughly be divided

22

One of the earliest keeps is at Langeais (Indre et Loire): a ruined hall with large windows on the upper floor and store-rooms underneath.

into two categories. There were those where the main defence was a keep, and those where the garrison had to rely on the strength of their outer walls or palisades. A *keep* was the strongest part of a castle, whether it was a tower, a hall or a gatehouse; it was the place that people ran to for shelter when they were being attacked, and if a baron was rich enough to pay for the transport of stone, or lived in a rocky district, then he could build a stone keep. For example, a tower was built at Rouen by Duke Richard I between 943 and 946 (there is nothing left of it now) and others are mentioned in the chronicles. When an ordinary ground-floor hall was burnt down at Doué-la-Fontaine, near Blois, it was rebuilt about 950 as a keep; all the lower openings were blocked and a new hall was placed at first-floor level, with the safety of the thick walls underneath. Fulk Nerra built a keep at Langeais, on the river Loire, sometime before 995, and this was also a first-floor hall, raised up on a basement. A keep had to be large enough to house all the baron's family, household, retainers and soldiers when they were under attack. It would be sited in a well-chosen position and surrounded by a stout wall to protect not only the keep itself, but any outbuildings and stables that clustered round its walls.

The vast majority of Norman barons, as well as King Edward's friends who had settled in England, built earth-and-timber castles; and these castles were like miniature forts. All the buildings a baron needed to shelter his household and dependants were protected by a stout wooden palisade standing on a high bank which was just inside the all-important **outer ditch**. This enclosure is called the *bailey*, and some of the early castles had nothing more than these simple defences – apart from a good gatehouse: they were baileys standing on their own.

Castles of this type were vulnerable because, if the enemy managed to burn down the outer palisade, the garrison had no second line of defence, and had to stand and fight it out. They needed a keep, and in a timber castle it had to be made of

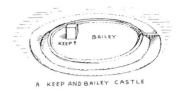

A KEEP AND BAILEY CASTLE

Little is known about very early castles. The strongest fortresses would have had a stone tower or first-floor hall surrounded by a stone wall or timber palisade and an outer ditch.

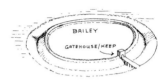

A CASTLE WHERE THE STRONGEST BUILDING IS THE GATEHOUSE

Some homesteads were simply defended by a palisade, bank and ditch: the stout timber gatehouse would probably be the strongest building in the castle.

Most 11th-century barons built motte-and-bailey castles. The earth mound was hard for enemies to climb and the timber keep commanded a wide view of the surrounding countryside.

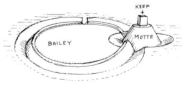

A MOTTE AND BAILEY CASTLE

THE NORMANS OFTEN SHAVED THE BACK OF THEIR HEADS

William of Malmesbury tells us the Normans took care how they dressed, ate and drank with moderation, and lived 'with economy in large houses'. They loved fighting, but resorted to cunning when force failed. 'They plunder their subjects though they protect them from others . . .' The English wore short clothes, had 'their beards shaved, their arms laden with gold bracelets, their skin adorned with punctured designs; they were wont to eat until they became surfeited and drink until they were sick . . .'

wood. No one knows who first thought up the idea of putting an artificial mound alongside the bailey, but certainly a keep perched on top of a rock or hill was in a far stronger position than one that was not. By the middle of the eleventh century, the castle builders had decided that, if a natural hill did not exist, they had better make one. *Motte* in Old French means 'clod of earth' and a castle motte was a huge, smooth-sided earth mound with a flat top for the keep to stand on.

Castles tended to make the barons dangerously powerful, and they had to be ruled with a firm hand. When Robert the Devil of Normandy, died in 1035, he left his dukedom to his illegitimate son, William, then a boy of eight; so the barons started to fend for themselves, strengthen their strongholds or build new ones, and make war on each other. Luckily, Duke William showed a firm character at an early age and managed to control his barons. By the time King Edward the Confessor was a frail old man, William, who said he had been promised the throne of England, had got such a grip on his country that he was ready to make good his claim.

Here is an extract from William of Jumièges's account of Duke William's invasion:

He therefore hastily built a fleet of three thousand ships. At length he brought this fleet to anchor at Saint-Valery in Ponthieu where he filled it with mighty horses and most valiant men, with hauberks and helmets. Then when a favourable wind began to blow, he set sail, and crossing the sea he landed at Pevensey where he immediately built a castle with a strong rampart. He left this in charge of some troops, and with others he hurried to Hastings where he erected another similar fortress. (*English Historical Documents*, vol. II, p. 216.)

Little is known about these two instant castles. There was a large oval Roman fort overlooking the port at Pevensey, East Sussex; William probably used the ancient ruins and strengthened them by digging a bank and ditch to defend the

24

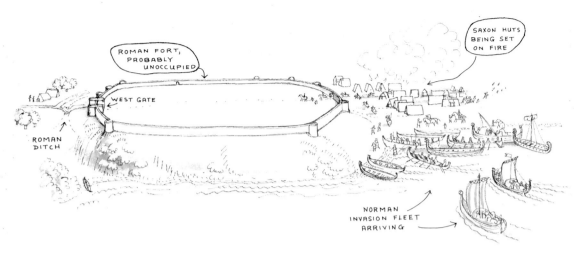

Labels in image:
- ROMAN FORT, PROBABLY UNOCCUPIED
- WEST GATE
- ROMAN DITCH
- SAXON HUTS BEING SET ON FIRE
- NORMAN INVASION FLEET ARRIVING

main gateway or, alternatively, he may have cut off part of the walled enclosure to make a smaller stronghold. There is no positive proof that the castle at Hastings, also in East Sussex, was on the same site as the later fortress, although a small sandy mound has been discovered; the Bayeux Tapestry shows soldiers digging an earth mound and putting a palisade on top.

On landing at Pevensey, William sheltered his army inside the ancient walls which he would have found slightly less ruined than they are today. The fort was almost surrounded by sea and marshland, and the only solid ground lay where the road led inland to the west, so the west gate was strongly defended by two bastions and a ditch. There are traces of a later ditch – probably the 'rampart' mentioned in the account of William's invasion. The East Gate is shown left.

ARCHERS WOULD HAVE STOOD ON GUARD WHILE SUPPLIES WERE CARRIED INTO THE FORT

Labels in plan:
- N
- EAST GATE
- POSTERN
- LATER CASTLE
- ROMAN DITCH
- NORMAN DITCH
- WEST GATE (WITH GUARD ROOMS)
- HARBOUR

25

After King Harold and the cream of the Anglo-Saxon army had been killed at the battle of Hastings, Duke William became king of England and was quick to consolidate his position. He knew that he had to keep a close watch on every Saxon town and village, so he encouraged his barons to build castles at strategic points all over the country. At the same time, although he got on well with them, he was careful not to give the men who had fought beside him at Hastings too much power. The Norman barons discovered that, instead of being given single large tracts of land where they could build massive central fortresses, they were granted widely scattered estates, and each estate needed its own small stronghold.

Oxford, Wallingford and Windsor were all castles on the river Thames. Oxford Castle was just outside the Saxon town (see page 27), while Wallingford Castle occupied about a quarter of the fortified Saxon settlement.

The Normans chose the sites for their castles carefully, and if a good vantage-point overlooking a town was occupied by Saxon huts, they were ruthlessly pulled down. At other times the castle was placed just outside the city boundaries, as at Oxford. Important road junctions and river crossings had to be guarded; supplies were carted along the muddy tracks and what was left of the straight Roman roads, but it was easier to transport goods by water. Rivers were the lifelines of the foreign invaders, who often returned to their estates in Normandy, so, wherever possible, castles were built on river banks.

Castles were built in a hurry because the Normans expected to be attacked at any time. The unfortunate conquered Saxons supplied the labour force, working in gangs day and night.

OXFORD MOTTE, TAKEN FROM ✳ ON MAP BELOW

ST GEORGE'S TOWER ↙

Remains of these motte-and-bailey castles are scattered all over England, often hidden in a bumpy field or surrounded by modern houses. Most of the later stone castles started off as small-scale earth-and-timber fortresses, built at the time of the Conquest.

The shape of these castles can usually be traced from their remaining earthworks but, because the timber parts have rotted away, it is impossible to tell what they actually looked like. However, using the evidence of the Bayeux Tapestry, old carvings, and a great deal of guesswork, it is worth trying to reconstruct the well-preserved earthworks at Berkhampstead in Hertfordshire.

This castle was built by King William's half-brother, Robert, Count of Mortain. There were three entrances to the bailey: the main gateway to the south, another to the north, and a postern to the east. The word *postern* is used for a small,

Oxford Castle, founded by Robert d'Oilgi in 1071, not only had a motte (of uncertain date) but also an exceptionally strong stone church tower, built in 1074, providing two places of refuge. The main entrance faced the town, but another gateway, between the motte and the tower and defended by them both, gave access to the river.

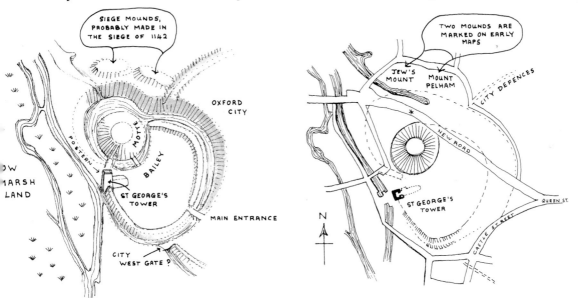

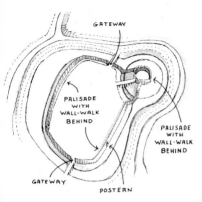

GATEWAY

PALISADE WITH WALL-WALK BEHIND

PALISADE WITH WALL-WALK BEHIND

GATEWAY

POSTERN

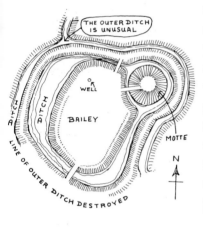

THE OUTER DITCH IS UNUSUAL

WELL

BAILEY

MOTTE

DITCH

LINE OF OUTER DITCH DESTROYED

N

single doorway that was let into an outer wall or palisade, and it was an important escape route. Most castles of this period had only one main gateway and, without a postern, a castle garrison could find themselves completely trapped, even by a relatively small besieging force, which would simply have to mount guard on the solitary exit. A postern gave a man the chance to slip away under cover of night; or a group of soldiers could use it to rush out and make a sudden sortie. (This is why it is also called a *sallyport*.)

Ditches surrounding motte-and-bailey castles were usually dry; but if the ground was low and marshy, as at Berkhampstead, then water would flow into them. The ditch was crossed at the main entrance by a timber bridge which had removable planks at the end of it. This *drawbridge* was either drawn back into the gatehouse passage, or lifted up by means of counterweighted beams, leaving a gap between the bridge and the gateway, with the ditch yawning below. A timber gatehouse must have been roughly similar to the surviving stone ones: a square wooden tower, with the passage running through the middle of it, and one or two rooms up above. Sometimes there would have been no gatehouse at all, but merely a flat platform over the gate for the defenders to stand on.

The sophisticated defences of the later castles evolved from the simple arrangements of these early motte-and-bailey strongholds. These sketches are based on Berkhampstead Castle. Nothing is known of the position of the first hall, chapel and other buildings of the bailey, which were rebuilt later; while a stone wall replaced the old palisade surrounding the bailey.

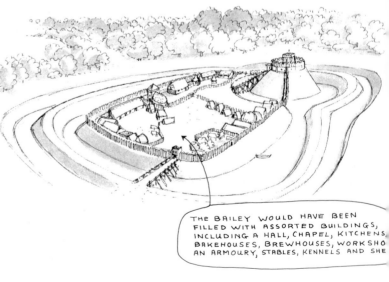

THE BAILEY WOULD HAVE BEEN FILLED WITH ASSORTED BUILDINGS, INCLUDING A HALL, CHAPEL, KITCHENS, BAKEHOUSES, BREWHOUSES, WORKSHO AN ARMOURY, STABLES, KENNELS AND SHE

IN NORMAN TIMES THERE WAS WATER IN THE DITCH.

Count Robert was an important man, and his bailey at Berkhampstead would have been full of buildings: a hall for the general use of his household, servants and soldiers, where he would feast with them and deal out rough justice; then, alongside, perhaps under the same roof, there would be a private room for himself and his family. There would have been outside kitchens and open hearths; a brewery, bakehouse and numerous store-rooms. The smithy, armourer's shed and other workshops would have stood beside stables, kennels, barns and all the usual farmyard clutter. The castle had to be completely self-supporting to withstand a siege, and the most important item of all was the well.

Without a motte, the garrison, standing at the low level of the bailey, would have had difficulty in seeing what the besieging army was up to. The motte was made by digging a circular ditch, piling the earth in the centre, firming it down with layers of stone or timber, and making the sides smooth with clay. A well was sunk at the bottom of the motte and the earth heaped up round the stone shaft as work progressed.

Ditches round motte-and-bailey castles were usually dry unless the land was low-lying and marshy or water could be supplied from a near-by stream or river. There are two ditches round Berkhampstead Castle, which is unusual. They held water until recently when the neighbouring land was drained.

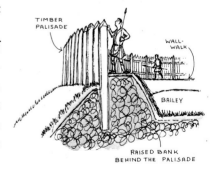

TIMBER PALISADE
WALL-WALK
BAILEY
RAISED BANK BEHIND THE PALISADE

29

The easiest way of getting into a timber castle was to burn down the gatehouse doors and the palisades. Fire was used a great deal throughout the medieval period.

Where a natural hillock was roughly the right size and shape, it could be turned into a motte by cutting out rocks or anything else that might afford a foothold to an enemy. A ditch would then be dug round it.

A steep timber stair led over the ditch to the top of the motte which was defended by a high palisade with a wall-walk behind. There might have been a square timber tower in the middle or, in a few cases, a hall, or perhaps a high watch-tower built up on stilts, allowing the soldiers to rush under it from one side of the motte to the other when they were being attacked. Sometimes there would be no tower at all, just the outer palisade. A supply of arms would be stored at the motte top, so that the defenders could shoot arrows, hurl javelins, and throw down the huge stones piled up in readiness. The water from the well was used not only for drinking, but for putting out the fires lit by the enemy at the base of the highly inflammable timbers.

The usual plan, as at Berkhampstead, was to have the motte just outside a kidney-shaped bailey, but there were no definite rules. Sometimes, as at Windsor, a second bailey was added, while at Lewes and Lincoln a new motte was built in a better position; so these castles have two.

Stone was a better material to use than wood, because the obvious way to destroy a wooden building was to set it on fire. Bonfires would be lit against the palisades, or the timbers would be touched off with blazing pine-brands or cressets – small iron baskets on the end of poles. A terrifying substance called *Greek fire* had been used for some time in the eastern Mediterranean (probably made of naphtha, quicklime and sulphur): once lit, it was almost impossible to put out and burnt quite happily on water. Earthenware pots of this stuff could be loaded on war machines, lit, and flung at the enemy. A greasy rag, bound round an arrow and fired into a palisade could soon set it smouldering.

Because castles were so easily burnt down, it was better to build a stone wall round the motte top, but this could only be

done where the motte had been shaped from a natural hillock and the earth was hard enough to take the weight of stone. This *shell wall* was many-sided, oval or circular, depending on the shape of the motte, with a simple arch or tower over the entrance passage. Stone or timber buildings would lean against the inside of the shell wall and the whole structure – being the strongest part of the castle – is called a *shell keep*.

The largest existing motte is at Thetford, and it must have been an immense labour for the miserably oppressed Saxon work force who made it. The site was originally an Iron Age fort, which may explain the double line of banks and ditches. Little is known of the layout of the castle and the imaginary defences on the motte top are based on the castle of Rennes in the Bayeux Tapestry.

There must have been many exceptions to the standard motte-and-bailey pattern of castle. For example, a strong hall could stand in a bailey without a motte to protect it, in which case the hall served as the keep, as at Chepstow (see page 38). The practical Normans also took advantage of existing Roman fortifications. In 1067 a castle was built inside the walled city of Exeter, Devon, the result of a revolt which is described by *The Anglo-Saxon Chronicle*:

> And Edric Cild [a mistake for Edric 'the Wild'] and the Welsh became hostile, and fought against the garrison of the castle at Hereford, and inflicted many injuries upon them. And the king imposed a heavy tax on the wretched people, and nevertheless caused all that he overran to be ravaged. And then he went to Devonshire and besieged the city of Exeter for eighteen days, and there a large part of his army perished. But he made fair promises to them, and fulfilled them badly; and they gave up the city to him because the thegns had betrayed them. (*English Historical Documents*, vol. II, p. 147.)

Exeter Castle gatehouse looks different today. The entrance passage was blocked at an early date and another gateway replaced the high bank and ditch that once stood to the right. There are three triangular-headed Anglo-Saxon windows in the tower: two in the front and one at the back.

After the city was taken, a castle was built on the high rocky area in the north-east angle of the Roman walls, so that

REAR WINDOW

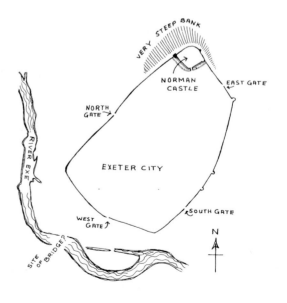

VERY STEEP BANK

NORMAN CASTLE

EAST GATE

NORTH GATE

RIVER EXE

EXETER CITY

SOUTH GATE

WEST GATE

SITE OF BRIDGE?

N

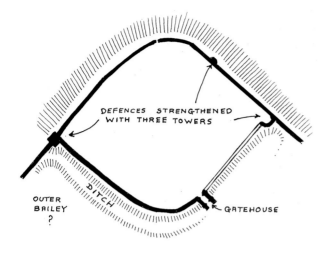

DEFENCES STRENGTHENED
WITH THREE TOWERS

OUTER
BAILEY
?

DITCH

GATEHOUSE

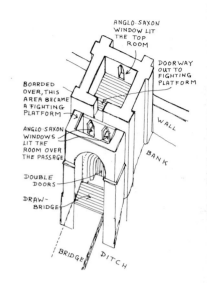

ANGLO-SAXON
WINDOW LIT
THE TOP
ROOM

DOORWAY
OUT TO
FIGHTING
PLATFORM

BOARDED
OVER, THIS
AREA BECAME
A FIGHTING
PLATFORM

ANGLO-SAXON
WINDOWS
LIT THE
ROOM OVER
THE PASSAGE

WALL

BANK

DOUBLE
DOORS

DRAW-
BRIDGE

BRIDGE

DITCH

a bank and ditch on the other two sides formed a square bailey. The gatehouse must be the oldest castle building left standing in England and, because there was no motte, it was probably used as the keep. The tower was built in the old traditional Anglo-Saxon way and the defeated people must have hated working on it. Two walls, joined by an arch, jut forward in front of the main entrance and would have had the drawbridge between them and a flat platform above, from which the defenders could hurl down rocks, spears and other missiles. The front of this kind of tower is occasionally called a barbican, although the word usually refers to a small walled enclosure – rather like a miniature bailey -- standing in front of the main gate, to protect it (see page 96). A *barbican* means an outwork of any kind, built to defend an entrance.

An enormous number of castles were built at the time of the Conquest and almost all were of timber. Some may have been really magnificent structures, with their huge posts carved, painted and gilded; but timber rots, and there is nothing left to photograph now – apart from the grassy banks. It is all that can be expected from wooden buildings that were pegged together more than nine hundred years ago.

The gatehouse had two sections. The inner part of the passage, closed by two pairs of doors, had two rooms above; while the front formed a kind of porch. If anyone tried to burn down the main door, missiles and water could be thrown from the fighting platform above.

NOT KNOWN
IF IT WAS A STONE
OR A TIMBER BRIDGE

33

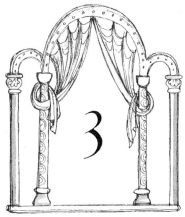

3

A QUIET LIFE
IN HALL
AND CHAMBER

Almost all early buildings were made of wood. Saxon England was covered with magnificent forests. Oak was most commonly used and the height and width of the building depended on the length of the timbers available. This is a close-up of the wooden wall at Greenstead-Juxta-Ongar (see page 37).

The very early halls were not expected to last long because the huge posts were driven into the damp earth and soon rotted. Later halls were built on stone foundations with the posts set on stone bases.

THE HALL WAS THE HEART OF THE CASTLE. EVERYTHING happened there.

The great majority of Norman barons and Saxon thegns lived in timber halls, which must have looked rather like farmyard barns. Some of them were quite small, but if the floor area of the hall needed to be wider than available timbers allowed, then the roof was supported by great posts and side aisles were added, like a church. These posts holding up the roof beams above, divide a building into regular sections which are called *bays*. A bay can vary from about 4·5 m to 6 m.

Originally, the entire household lived, slept and ate in the one hall, which was often shared by animals as well; the cows chewing the cud and the chickens scratching about must have given comfortable background noises to everyday life.

By the time the Normans had conquered England most of the animals had been pushed into the bailey and the baron had taken to eating his meals on a paved area, a step or two up from the earth floor. This platform is called a *dais*.

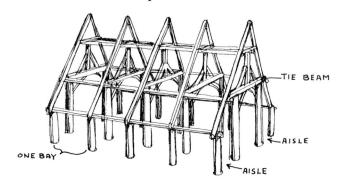

THE MAIN SUPPORTS OF A
FOUR BAY AISLED HALL

The general arrangement was for the baron's dais to be at the farthest end of the hall from the entrance door, which often had to stand slightly open if the fire was to burn properly. Because of the wind whistling in, it was usual in later halls to have a screen at the side of the door and another, if there was a back door, opposite. This area ultimately became known as the *screens passage*.

There were usually two store-rooms at the other side of the screens passage. The old French word for *buttery* was 'bouteillerie', meaning the store-room for casks and bottles; so this was where they kept the drink. *Pantry*, originally 'paneterie', was the bread-room (the French word for bread is still 'pain'). A supply of stale rounds of bread would be kept piled up in the pantry as these 'bread trenchers' were commonly used instead of plates. The timber kitchen was always placed well away from the hall, because the cooking was done over a blazing fire and so the whole structure could easily catch alight and go up in smoke. Large carcasses would be roasted in the open air. Again, in the later halls, the passage leading to the kitchen was usually placed between the buttery and the pantry, but if there was no kitchen passage the scullions had to come and go through one of the main doors.

Sometimes a hall would have a low loft over the little store-rooms, with a ladder leading up to it, and this was a private sleeping-place for the baron and his wife.

Wooden buildings were always a fire-risk, and the best arrangement was to have the roaring log fire in the centre of the floor, away from the walls. On a cold winter's day there must have been plenty of smoke curling round the rafters before it escaped through a hole in the roof or, in smaller

THE SPACE BETWEEN TWO MAIN POSTS IS CALLED A BAY

The 13th-century tithe barn at Great Coxwell (Oxon.) shows how roofs were supported by pairs of posts held together by tie beams. *The space between the posts and the outer walls are called* aisles. *Many early timber halls were* aisled halls. *No early aisled halls have survived: we can only guess the appearance of the 11th-century halls from the remains of the later ones. Aisled halls were built until about the end of the 14th century when new roofing methods were devised.*

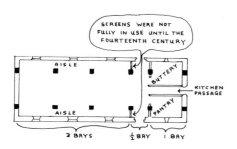

SCREENS WERE NOT FULLY IN USE UNTIL THE FOURTEENTH CENTURY

AISLE

BUTTERY

KITCHEN PASSAGE

AISLE

PANTRY

3 BAYS   ½ BAY   1 BAY

PLAN AND PERSPECTIVE DRAWING OF AN IMAGINARY 14TH CENTURY AISLED HALL

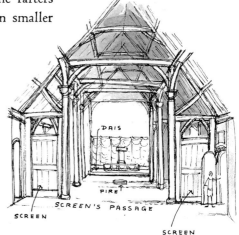

DAIS

FIRE

SCREEN'S PASSAGE

SCREEN

SCREEN

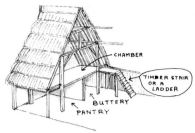

CHAMBER

TIMBER STAIR OR A LADDER

BUTTERY PANTRY

The great chamber *was often placed over the buttery and pantry. Gables are the triangular shapes at the top of the end walls of buildings. In early halls, smoke from the central hearth either curled through a hole in the roof or through a space left in the top of a gable, as with this (14th-century?) house (below left) in the Open Air Museum at Singleton (West Sussex): bottom is their reconstruction of a 13th-century thatched cottage.*

THIS TRIANGULAR AREA IS CALLED A GABLE

SMOKE HOLE

WATTLE AND DAUB

TIMBER FRAME

THATCH

halls, at the gable end. A hole in the roof would have let in the sleet and rain unless it was covered by a little hut-like structure called a *louver*, which had openings at the sides. Smoke hanging in the air probably accounts for the general lofty height of most halls.

All the members of the baron's household ate their meals in the hall, sitting at trestle tables: great thick boards resting on wooden frames. These tables could easily be dismantled and were stacked away at night, when straw mattresses were flung on the rushes and people settled down to sleep beside the dying embers of the fire.

The baron, no longer mixing freely with his men on equal terms, as in Viking days, needed a room of his own where he could sleep, talk privately with his family, and live away from the noise and bustle of the servants. This delightful retreat, where a man could forget his worries and imagine himself back in Normandy again, was called the *great chamber*. A great chamber was almost always on an upper floor and the idea probably started with the loft over the store-rooms.

Halls were either made of solid wood or they were *timber framed*, where the main supports of the building were of wood but the spaces were filled in with *wattle and daub*, a kind of basketwork of stakes and willow wands, daubed with clay and animal hair, finished with a layer of plaster. The roof above could be covered with a thatch of reeds or straw, turf, or little oak tiles called *shingles*.

The hall floor would be of trodden earth or clay, while the dais might be paved with stone. Rushes thrown on the floor and strewn with sweet-smelling herbs could keep the air fresh and mask the whiffs from rotting food that had fallen from the tables. The rushes would be swept away after the household had left, because each baron owned several castles and the great lords were constantly moving from one place to the next.

Even the walls of timber buildings could be plastered on the inside and they were probably decorated with paintings as well. The walls of the church at Greenstead-Juxta-Ongar in

The earliest timber wall in England, dating back to 1013, is at Greenstead-Juxta-Ongar church (Essex). The logs were originally driven straight into the ground, but the wood rotted and the foundations were eventually replaced by a brick wall. The oak was hacked away with an adze inside, and the surface left rough so that plaster would stick to it. The insides of buildings were often plastered.

Essex have survived since the beginning of the eleventh century; they were made of oak logs cut in half and driven into the ground with the flat surface facing inwards. This surface was deliberately hacked with an adze and left rough so that plaster would stick to it.

These were the usual sort of timber halls built in motte-and-bailey castles, but there must have been many variations, especially if the hall was put on the motte top, where space was restricted, in which case the building was more likely to have been shaped like a tower. It is impossible to give any clear descriptions because there is not enough evidence to work on.

Halls were not always built at ground level, in fact the barons would have felt more secure if the wide windows, necessary to let daylight into the hall, were higher up. A first-floor hall could be protected by the stout walls of a store-room underneath and, because store-rooms did not need much light, their walls could be pierced with slits that were too narrow for an enemy to squeeze through. A few stone first-floor halls have survived and (although it is more exactly a second-floor hall) the earliest one stands on a magnificent site overlooking the river Wye at Chepstow, Gwent. It was built by King William's most trusted friend, William Fitz Osbern, some time before he was killed in battle in 1071.

Chepstow is not a motte-and-bailey castle because the hall, following the pattern of the very early keeps at Doué-la-Fontaine and Langeais, was so strongly built that it was ob-viously intended to be used as the keep, and so a motte with its tower was unnecessary. The hall was raised up over a low, sloping, unlit store-room and a first-floor room which would have been used by the garrison. The main entrance was at the end of this first-floor room, an unusual position, and then a straight stair led from the side of the doorway, through the thick wall, and up to the hall above.

Chepstow Castle was enlarged and altered from 1190 onwards. These photographs and the plan below show how it looked at the end of the 13th century, when an extra storey had been added to the tower and the rest of the castle was built. The great tower originally stood between two small baileys, with stone walls defending the easily accessible southern side, and a timber palisade probably ran along the cliff edge, overlooking the river.

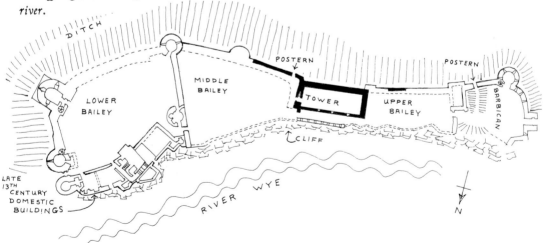

13TH CENTURY
UPPER FLOOR

HALL

GARRISON'S
QUARTERS

LATER
ADDITION

STORE
ROOM

Above: A fully armed Norman knight wore a knee-length mail hauberk (shirt of tiny interlaced metal rings) and a conical helmet which sometimes had a strip of iron to cover the nose. Patterns on flags and shields had no particular meaning and heraldry was not introduced until later.

Right: Norman doorways are nearly always round-headed; but this one has a flat lintel, or horizontal stone slab, making it square; the area above was filled in and decorated.

39

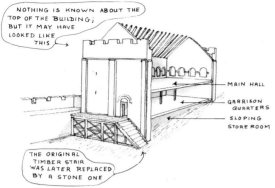

NOTHING IS KNOWN ABOUT THE TOP OF THE BUILDING; BUT IT MAY HAVE LOOKED LIKE THIS

MAIN HALL
GARRISON QUARTERS
SLOPING STORE ROOM

THE ORIGINAL TIMBER STAIR WAS LATER REPLACED BY A STONE ONE

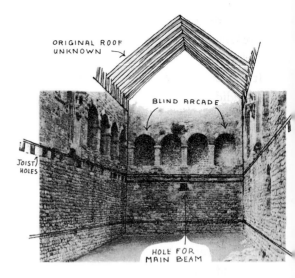

ORIGINAL ROOF UNKNOWN

BLIND ARCADE

JOIST HOLES

HOLE FOR MAIN BEAM

A plan shows the general shape of a building: the position of the stairs, doors and windows. The north wall of Chepstow tower is thinner than the others, because no one was expected to lead an assault up the sheer cliff from the river. A timber stair led up to the main doorway where, built into the thick wall and lit by two tiny slits, a flight of stone steps rose to the hall above. This type of stairway is often called a mural stair.

Joist-holes show that the timber floor of the hall rested on beams running across the room, and these, in their turn, were supported by a massive central beam propped up by a line of posts running down the middle of the floor below. It is a vivid link with the past to remember that the austere Norman *blind arcade*, or series of shallow round-headed recesses, was built only five years or so after the battle of Hastings.

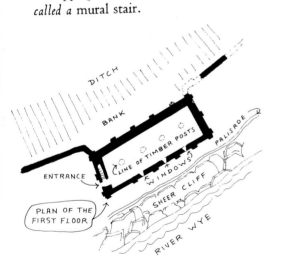

DITCH
BANK
ENTRANCE
LINE OF TIMBER POSTS
PALISADE
WINDOWS
SHEER CLIFF
RIVER WYE
PLAN OF THE FIRST FLOOR

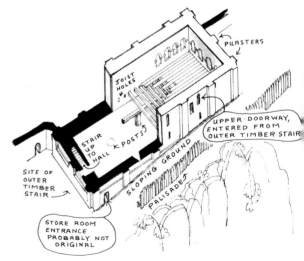

PILASTERS
JOIST HOLES
STAIR UP TO HALL
POSTS
SITE OF OUTER TIMBER STAIR
UPPER DOORWAY, ENTERED FROM OUTER TIMBER STAIR
SLOPING GROUND
PALISADE
STORE ROOM ENTRANCE PROBABLY NOT ORIGINAL

40

Another early first-floor hall stands at Richmond, North Yorkshire. This is easier to understand, because Richmond is a rocky district and the stone-built castle is far more complete. It was built by Alan of Brittany sometime after 1071 on a splendid site overlooking the river Swale. A masonry wall enclosing a bailey is called a curtain wall, and the towers bestriding this wall are called mural towers. At Richmond, the triangular bailey was enclosed by a stone curtain wall, defended by four square mural towers, and entered through a massive gatehouse which would have been used as the keep. Most gatehouses were smaller: about the same size and shape as the one at Exeter. The hall at Richmond was built right into a corner of the bailey wall, where the steep rocky bank dropped down to the swirling waters of the river below.

The first-floor hall was reached from an outside staircase and there were two store-rooms below, each entered from a separate door and lit by narrow windows on the river side. A line of beam-holes show that a *timber hoarding*, or wooden gallery, was fixed outside these windows so that defenders could stand on the hoarding and shoot down at an enemy

Richmond Castle was first built with an unusually large stone gatehouse, but during the second half of the 12th century further storeys were added, the doorways were blocked, and the building was turned into a massive keep. The inner archway has been opened up again and this is the original entrance to the gatehouse passage. The sketch below shows the position of the hall, towers, walls and gatehouse.

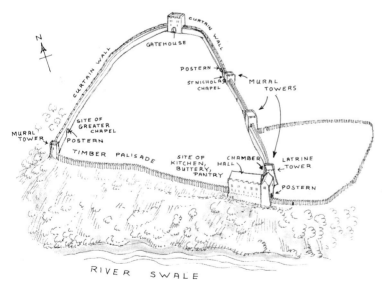

41

LATER BUILDINGS

HALL

CHAMBER

STORE ROOMS

BEAM HOLES F
TIMBER HOARDI

clambering up the rocks below. The gallery was probably reached from some other part of the castle wall, because the window slits were too narrow for a man to squeeze through. A passage ran from the ground-floor store-rooms to an outer postern: a convenient back door down to the river.

Great chambers were almost always built over store-rooms, and when they were attached to a first-floor hall the two rooms were at the same level. At this early date, the normal position for the great chamber was over the buttery and pantry at the screens end of the hall; but at Richmond it was at the dais end, directly above the postern passage. A *latrine* tower, or lavatory, stood next to the great chamber and this was divided into two shafts which went down to a deep pit, so large apparently, that it never had to be cleaned out.

The Normans never doubted the existence of God, and the laws of the Roman Catholic Church were rigidly obeyed. Mass had to be heard each day and castles were always equipped with one or two chapels. At Richmond, the vanished 'greater chapel' stood against the west wall of the bailey, and

Richmond Castle had a first-floor hall built over store-rooms. The great chamber was directly above the postern passage. The windows overlooking the river still have central pillars like the one above, and they would have been closed inside by wooden shutters.

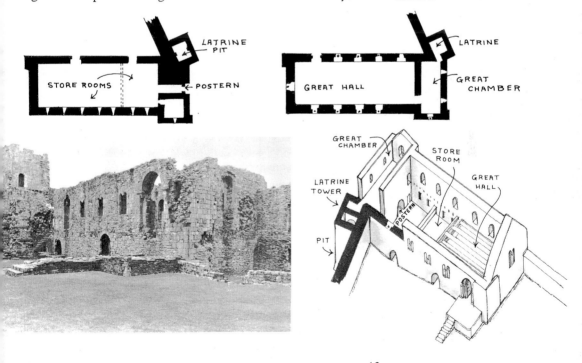

ALTAR

BLIND ARCADE
(SHAFTS MISSING)

This is the east window, set between two round holes, in the tiny chapel of St Nicholas, built into the north-east tower at ground level. Below is the entire castle with its late 12th-century keep.

the tiny chapel of St Nicholas is built into the base of one of the square mural towers. Nowadays, it is just an ordinary, damp, square cell, with a dim light coming through the small east window, flanked by two round holes; but it was once a sacred place and the walls are lined with a blind arcade of arches where the Norman barons once sat at prayer.

Few castles were as strongly fortified as Richmond and Chepstow; although there is another fine example at Ludlow, Salop (see page 74). Here, men could lock themselves into secure stone buildings. Most barons had to be content with less. The network of strongholds that kept such a tight grip on the people of England in the years immediately following the Conquest were almost entirely made up of motte-and-bailey castles. The majority of these were defended by their stout timber towers and palisades; but occasionally there was one which could boast a shell keep, if the motte had been carved out of a natural hillock and stone was easy to come by.

This almost sums up the situation; but not quite. Before William I died in 1087, men had been hard at work for some time on two majestic buildings that were neither fortified halls nor extra-strong gatehouses: they were mighty stone keeps.

GREAT SQUARE TOWERS AND HOW TO TAKE THEM

4

AFTER 1066 WILLIAM I HAD QUICKLY ESTABLISHED several earth-and-timber castles in London 'against the fickleness of the vast and fierce populace'. One of them was built right into the south-east corner of the city, making good use of the old Roman wall, which had been repaired by King Alfred in 885 and was still standing. The river ran to the south and it needed only a bank and ditch on the other two sides to make a strong rectangular bailey, not far from the important bridge over the Thames.

In 1078 William decided to turn this ordinary timber castle into a far stronger fortress: one which would strike awe into the hearts of the conquered people and serve as a place of refuge for himself in case they rose up against him. He probably wanted to have something in London similar to the tower in his ducal palace at Rouen. When the new keep was built, it dominated all the other defences, and the entire castle became known as the Tower of London; while the keep on its own is often referred to as the White Tower, because it was regularly given a coat of whitewash. The citizens of London would have watched the huge walls going up, with amazement, because, apart from Westminster Abbey, they would never have set eyes on a building of this size before. The White Tower and the great keep at Colchester, Essex, which was standing before 1086, were the first two stone towers of their kind in England.

Dressed as a bishop, Gundulf would have worn vestments like the ones shown above.

Between 1066 and the early 12th century it is recorded that the Normans built four castles in London: Baynard's, Montfichet, Ravenger's 'little castle', and the Tower of London. This is a plan of the Roman walls and the Tower of London set in the south-east corner of the city.

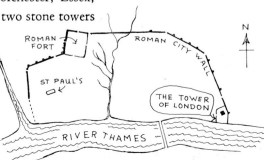

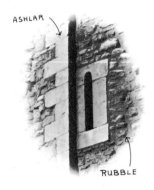

Almost all the Norman windows in the White Tower have been replaced; but four two-light openings at the top left-hand side of the south face are original.

ASHLAR

RUBBLE

QUOINS

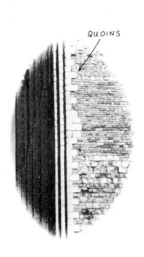

The man who supervised the building of the keeps at London and Colchester was Gundulf, the 'monk of Godly reputation' who had just become Bishop of Rochester. They are *hall-keeps*. Instead of arranging the hall, great chamber, chapel, keep and store-rooms as separate buildings scattered about the bailey, they are cunningly packed together in one rectangular tower.

The walls of a keep had to be immensely thick, otherwise an enemy would try battering his way in with a ram: the walls of the White Tower measure about $4\frac{1}{2}$ metres at the base, tapering to about 3 metres at the top.

In Norman times the lower windows of the White Tower were narrow slits and the only large openings were up above, well out of reach of scaling-ladders: a general rule for all keeps. Unfortunately, these windows were enlarged in the seventeenth century by Sir Christopher Wren, but he left some windows which appear to be original at the top south-west corner. There were no professional architects in the eleventh century and Gundulf and his master mason would have worked out the details of the building together, chalking out the plans and elevations on wooden boards. They were not being particularly exact with their measurements when they laid out the foundations because none of the walls are the same length and only one of the corners is a right-angle.

The huge store-rooms were invariably at the bottom of the keeps and they had to be large enough to hold all the food and other provisions needed by the garrison in time of siege. Then there always had to be a well, because water was of prime importance. The well for the White Tower is in the west store-room.

People exploring these dark rooms often call them 'dungeons', imagining they were immense prisons. *Dungeon* is derived from the old French word 'donjon' which means a keep. Even now, a keep is sometimes referred to as the donjon. Because prisoners were often securely held behind the thick walls of the keep – and because, in later times, when castles

46

The keep is built of rough uncut stones which are called rubble; *the corners and main divisions of the building are picked out in* ashlar, *or stone that has been cut to a regular shape. Corner stones are called* quoins.

NORMAN PALISADE

ROMAN WALL AND BASTION

were no longer lived in by the great lords, many of the keeps were turned into local jails – the sense of the word gradually changed. When people were imprisoned in the White Tower, they were probably locked in the sub-crypt: a couple of floors below the chapel and at the same chill level as the store-rooms.

The main entrance to a keep was always at the top of an outside flight of steps, at first- or second-floor level, directly above the store-rooms. The entrance to the White Tower was on the side facing the river and may have been reached by a timber stair, which could be either easily destroyed or partly pulled back into the building, in the event of an attack.

There were no trees tall enough to span such a large building, so the roof beams were supported by a thick spine-wall running up the middle. All the floors of the keep are to the same plan: one large room running north–south; then a smaller room and the chapel shape on the other side of the dividing wall, which is pierced by numerous archways – presumably to lighten such a great weight of masonry, and to

When first built, the White Tower was defended by the Roman wall and a bank, ditch and palisade on the other two sides. There may have been a Roman wall along the river bank, but as yet no foundations have been discovered. The drawing above gives a rough idea of what the tower looked like.

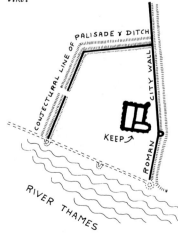

47

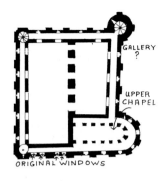

GALLERY
?

UPPER
CHAPEL

ORIGINAL WINDOWS

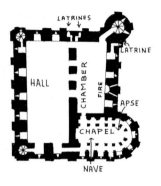

LATRINES

LATRINE

HALL

CHAMBER

FIRE

APSE

CHAPEL

NAVE

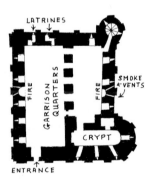

LATRINES

FIRE

GARRISON QUARTERS

FIRE

SMOKE VENTS

CRYPT

ENTRANCE

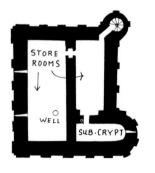

STORE ROOMS

WELL

SUB·CRYPT

allow people to pass from one side of the keep to the other. The archways could always be curtained off, if necessary, or blocked with wooden screens.

The chapel has a rectangular *nave* (the part of a church reserved for the congregation), and the *chancel* (the part reserved for the priest) has a rounded *apse*. English churches always face east and the reason for this is rather obscure, but it may be because the rays of the rising sun can shine through the window behind the altar, as the symbol of the resurrection. The Chapel of St John in the Tower of London is Gundulf's greatest achievement. The massive pillars are there to support a gallery which overlooks the chapel from the third-floor level and joins up with the passage which passes through all four outer walls of the keep. The chapel would have been darker before the windows were enlarged, the main source of light filtering down from openings placed opposite each other on either side of the passage. A series of openings or windows of this kind, built high on a wall in order to illuminate the area below, is called a *clerestory*.

The rooms on the entrance floor of a keep were generally used by the men of the garrison and the rooms above reserved for the king (if it was a royal castle), or the baron who owned it. Most of the time a castle was maintained by a relatively small skeleton staff: the castellan, his household and chaplain, a few soldiers, a watchman and a porter. The king and his barons were always moving from one place to the next, and the buildings of a castle would only be used to their full capacity in wartime or when the owner himself came riding over the bridge and into the bailey, followed by his retinue of friends, soldiers and servants.

A *castellan* was, quite simply, the man in charge of a castle. The word *constable* is often used as well. Constable comes from the Latin 'comes stabuli', meaning count of the stable. He became the man in charge of the king's military forces, and his duties varied from commanding a castle to organizing an army. It is a flexible word. A great baron might employ several constables: one for each of his castles.

48

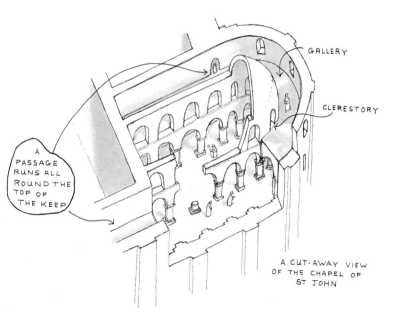

GALLERY

CLERESTORY

A PASSAGE RUNS ALL ROUND THE TOP OF THE KEEP

A CUT-AWAY VIEW OF THE CHAPEL OF ST JOHN

The main source of light for St John's Chapel came originally from paired openings on either side of the gallery on the storey above. A series of upper windows or openings of this kind is called a clerestory. Castle halls, like the chapels, often had a clerestory, and if the White Tower was first designed without an upper floor then the passage running round the top of the keep would have overlooked the hall and chamber below, the large arches forming a clerestory.

The White Tower must have been a cold place in winter. There are two fireplaces on the first floor while, on the second floor, there is a fireplace in the great chamber, but none in the hall, which was either left unheated or warmed by some kind of portable brazier. The fireplaces had no chimneys, and the smoke just curled through the thickness of the walls and came out of pairs of holes at the sides of the building. There is no kitchen in the keep; the cooking would have been done over open hearths and in a timber kitchen outside in the bailey.

Gundulf's great keep at Colchester was built to roughly the same plan as the White Tower, but on a grander scale. Unfortunately, the upper floors have been destroyed and all that is left is the squat shape containing the basement store-rooms and garrison-quarters above. Because Colchester was a Roman city and because there was no easy supply of local stone, many reused Roman tiles are built into the walls. On the inside of the keep some of these tiles are laid herringbone fashion. *Herringbone work* is where tiles or stones are set at a slant in alternating lines, giving a fishbone effect; it was used by Roman, Saxon, Norman and even later masons, but generally indicates a building of an early date. Norman walls were usually built of *rubble*, or uncut stones, laid in rough lines; with *ashlar*, or stone that has been cut and worked to a smooth regular shape, at the corners and round doors and windows. Corner stones are called *quoins*. Sometimes, in the better-quality buildings, the walls are laid with a double line of ashlar with a mixture of rubble and mortar thrown in the middle. Finally, as with the White Tower, medieval buildings were often finished off with a layer of plaster and paint.

William I did not live to see the Tower of London completed as he died near Rouen in 1087, and work was still going on ten years after William Rufus came to the throne. In 1097 the timber defences on the two sides of the castle facing the city were replaced by a stone wall: we know this because the writers of *The Anglo-Saxon Chronicle* complained bitterly about the way their people were compelled to do all the work: 'Also,

The south-east corner of the White Tower showing the curved shape of the chapel. The drawing below indicates the general plan of the building and the position of the three main floors. The top floor is not included as it was probably a later addition.

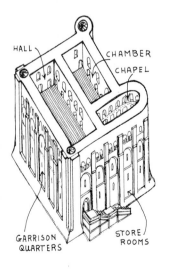

HALL

CHAMBER

CHAPEL

GARRISON QUARTERS

STORE ROOMS

50

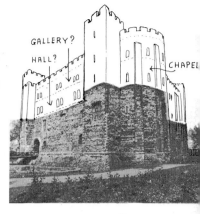

many shires whose labour was due at London were hard pressed because of the wall that they built about the Tower and because of the bridge that was nearly all carried away by a flood, and because of the work on the king's hall, that was being built at Westminster, and many a man was oppressed thereby.' (*English Historical Documents*, vol. II, p. 174.)

William Rufus did not stay in the White Tower when the court was in London but at Westminster, where he could watch the progress of this new hall: the largest in Europe. He used it for the first time at Whitsuntide in 1099. The next year he was dead. He had been a tyrannical king and the only man who had cause to be sorry about the fatal hunting accident in the New Forest was his chief minister, Ranulf Flambard, Bishop of Durham. Ranulf Flambard had been responsible for squeezing enough money out of the people to pay for his master's extravagances and he was intensely disliked for this reason. When William Rufus's younger brother, Henry I, took the throne, he laid hands on the bishop as a popular gesture and had him 'confined in fetters in the Tower of London'. Ranulf Flambard was the first person ever to have been held there, and the first to escape.

Ranulf Flambard was cunning. 'Indeed, he had great ability and fluency of speech, and although he was cruel and passionate, such was his generosity and constant good humour, that he rendered himself a general favourite.' He got on such good terms with his jailers that he not only appears to have been

Colchester keep may have looked like this but as only the first two floors remain, it has to be guesswork. The entrance doorway was replaced in Norman times, and all the large windows are very much later. The walls are built of layers of stone alternating with Roman brick, and this rough masonry was probably hidden under layers of plaster and whitewash.

Herringbone masonry (where stones are laid slantwise) was used by Roman, Saxon, and Norman masons, and even later; but it usually indicates a building of an early date. This photograph was taken inside Colchester keep.

51

Extravagantly long garments came into fashion when William Rufus was king; the length of men's hair scandalized members of the older generation, who recalled the austere days of William I. But long garments remained fashionable: Henry I would have worn clothes like the ones in this drawing.

Only the lower part of the keep at Canterbury remains and there is no clue to indicate exactly when it was built. But it was a three-storey tower with a forebuilding.

released from his fetters, but was soon giving extravagant dinners.

He fared sumptuously for a prisoner, and kept daily a splendid table for himself and his keepers. One day a cord was brought to the bishop in a flagon of wine, and, causing a plentiful banquet to be served, the guards having partaken of it in his company, washed it down with Falerian cups in the highest spirits. Having intoxicated them to such a degree that they slept soundly, the bishop secured the cord to a mullion in the centre of the tower window, and, catching up his pastoral staff, began to lower himself by means of a cord.

Unfortunately, the portly bishop had left his gloves behind and he cut his fingers to the bone as he clutched his crosier and slid down the rope: it was too short to reach the ground, and so he fell the rest of the way, landing with a bump, and 'being much bruised, groaned piteously'. His friends had been waiting below with a good supply of his treasure and some horses, which enabled them to gallop away, get to the coast, and then sail over the Channel to Normandy. This story is told by the English-born monk Ordericus Vitalis in his *Ecclesiastical History of England and Normandy*; and it is a pity that he does not go into even greater detail and tell us exactly where in the Tower of London the bishop was kept. One imagines that he started off being chained to the wall at the level of the store-rooms and then charmed his way up to the comfortable apartments with warm fireplaces (and wide windows) at the top of the keep.

Henry I started with a shaky seat on the throne because the barons favoured his elder brother, Robert of Normandy; Henry is said to have built castles in Sussex – none of which have survived – to forestall his brother's threatened invasion. It may have been about this time that the keep was built at Canterbury, Kent, but it is in such a ruined condition that it is extremely hard to date.

Although Robert actually landed at Portsmouth early in 1101, war was averted and a peace was patched up. However,

Robert ruled his duchy of Normandy badly and was in such a weak position that five years later Henry invaded the country and defeated his elder brother at the battle of Tinchebrai. Robert was shipped over the Channel to England and spent the rest of his life under lock and key in Cardiff Castle, South Glamorgan (a motte-and-bailey fortress, built inside a Roman fort). After that, Henry was more anxious to defend the possessions he had taken in Normandy than to protect his lands north of the Channel. He built few royal castles in England and, of these, not many have survived. The best example is the keep at Norwich, Norfolk; but only the inner parts of the walls are original because the outside was re-faced in Victorian times. Norwich is a rare example of a heavy stone keep being built on top of a motte (there is another keep in a similar position at Guildford). The initial motte-and-bailey castle had been thrown up at Norwich in 1067 – the year following the Conquest – and the great keep was probably put up between 1120 and 1130.

In square keeps of this period, the second floor is often a couple of storeys high, with a gallery running through the thick outer walls at the upper level, and with openings opposite each other in order to let daylight into the hall below: in fact, a clerestory. This was the case at Norwich. A gallery had several advantages: it made the hall look more impressive; it allowed a man to walk right round the keep and see what was happening in the surrounding countryside; then, if he turned round, he could watch what was going on in the hall below. Last, but by no means least, it must be remembered that large

LOOKING DOWN FROM THE GALLERY

A timber castle was built at Norwich in 1067, and the motte, originally cut from naturally high ground, must have been enlarged when the massive stone keep replaced the old wooden tower. The outside of the keep was re-faced in Victorian times. It is now a museum.

N

FOREBUILDING

FIRE HALL
LATRINES
WELL
CHAMBER CHAPEL

MOTTE

GALLERY

THIS AREA NOW COVERED BY MUSEUM CASES

LORD AND LADY CELEBRATING A FEAST DAY →

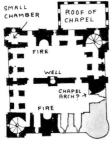

SMALL CHAMBER

ROOF OF CHAPEL

FIRE

WELL

CHAPEL ARCH ?

FIRE

3RD FLOOR

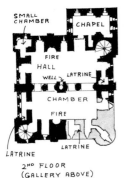

SMALL CHAMBER

CHAPEL

FIRE

HALL

WELL   LATRINE

CHAMBER

FIRE

LATRINE

LATRINE

2ND FLOOR
(GALLERY ABOVE)

ENTRANCE LOBBY

DRAWBRIDGE

TOWER

PORTCULLIS

SMALL CHAMBER

FIRE

POSTERN

WELL

LATRINE

FIRE

LATRINE   LATRINE

1ST FLOOR

PRISON?
WITH LATRINE

DRAWBRIDGE PIT

STORES

WELL

STORES

SHAFTS FROM LATRINES ABOVE

GROUND FLOOR

openings were always high up on the outer wall of a keep in case an enemy tried to use a ladder and climb in, they therefore allowed the daylight to filter down to the hall which, at floor level, was lit only by small slits.

Henry I kept rigid law and order. If one of his barons dared to make a castle too strong, the king, who technically owned all his subjects' castles, was likely to demand the keys and take it for himself.

Henry I had about twenty children, but the only son born in wedlock was drowned in 1120. He then had to make arrangements for his sole legitimate daughter, Matilda, to succeed him. Matilda had been married to the Holy Roman Emperor, Henry V, and when she returned to England after his death, she retained her title of Empress. In 1126 the barons swore fealty to the Empress Matilda, but they mistrusted the idea of a woman on the throne, sensed difficult times ahead, and speeded up their building activities: replacing the timbers of their motte-and-bailey castles with stone walls. Other types of castle were still rare, but towards the end of his life King Henry allowed some of his favourite barons and bishops to build themselves magnificent stone keeps, many of which were to be the cause of much trouble later on. The best example is at Rochester, Kent, built by the Archbishop of Canterbury, William de Corbeil, sometime after 1126.

Churchmen often built castles and a bishop would appoint a castellan to be in command of the garrison. Rochester had been yet another of Gundulf's castles, but it was quite a modest place compared to London or Colchester. He had cut off a corner of the Roman town, used the Roman walls (repaired and heightened) for two sides of the bailey, and erected a new wall, defended by an outer ditch, to the north and east. A few stretches of Gundulf's wall are still there. William de Corbeil built his keep inside the old bailey.

The differences between Rochester and the earlier keeps are that Rochester has an extra floor, is narrower, and has a *fore-building* (so had the keep at Norwich, built about the same

54

time). Forebuildings were designed to protect the entrance. Instead of walking right into the main building, visitors had to pass through a small lobby under the eye of a watchful porter. The base of a forebuilding often served as the prison: a horrible dank cell, lit by only a tiny shaft of light, and sometimes entered – or dropped into – from a trapdoor above. The upper floor of a forebuilding made a good position for a chapel, while the roof above became a fighting platform, commanding the area round the steps.

The keep at Rochester had formidable defences. The steps started at the north-west face, turned a corner and ran through a small turret that has now disappeared. There was a drawbridge at the top of the steps, defending the main door; and finally, to the right of the entrance lobby, a portcullis could be lowered in order to cut off the lobby from the main body of the keep. 'Portcullis' means a sliding gate or door and a *portcullis* was a timber grille with iron fittings, which ran up and down in a groove in the walls of the passage. Portcullises were generally hauled up by means of ropes wound round a winch; most of the time they would be kept suspended in the room above and only come crashing down when the entrance was threatened. At Rochester the portcullis was hung in the space between the two floors, so that the lower part of the grille covered the entrance arch, while the top bar lay flush with the floor of the chapel passage, held in place with ropes, pulleys and winches.

The plans of the keep are opposite.

PORTCULLIS

RECESS FOR A LAMP?

PORTCULLIS GROOVE

This drawing of Rochester keep is cut off at first-floor level to show the position of the portcullis and other defences. The entrance steps were under surveillance from the roof of the small tower, from the windows and roof of the forebuilding and from the top of the keep itself. There was only one way into the building but if this was blocked by an enemy, the garrison could escape through the postern.

PORTCULLIS SLOT

DRAWBRIDGE

← POSTERN
(A WOODEN BRIDGE SPANNED THE GAP TO THE CURTAIN WALL)

PORTCULLIS INSIDE

THIS TOWER WAS UNDERMINED IN 1215 AND REBUILT c 1223

VICTORIAN ARCH ON SITE OF WATER GATE

ROMAN CITY WALL REBUILT 1087-9 AND HEIGHTENED AGAIN LATER

William I commanded a castle to be built in the walled Roman city of Rochester sometime before 1086, and soon afterwards William Rufus ordered Gundulf, Bishop of Rochester, to replace it with a stronger fortress. Gundulf sited his new castle in the southwest angle of the old Roman wall, which was made higher, and built a wall and ditch to defend the other two sides. The rectangular stone keep was built inside Gundulf's bailey after 1126.

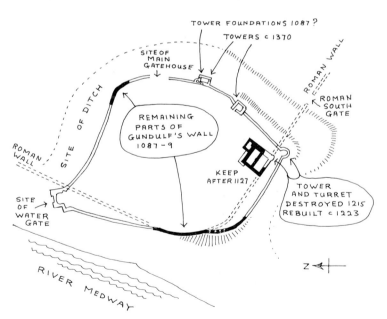

TOWER FOUNDATIONS 1087 ?

TOWERS c 1370

SITE OF MAIN GATEHOUSE

ROMAN WALL

ROMAN SOUTH GATE

ROMAN WALL

SITE OF DITCH

REMAINING PARTS OF GUNDULF'S WALL 1087-9

KEEP AFTER 1127

TOWER AND TURRET DESTROYED 1215 REBUILT c 1223

SITE OF WATER GATE

RIVER MEDWAY

56

GALLERY

JOIST HOLES
FOR TOP FLOOR

WELL

JOIST HOLES
FOR HALL
FLOOR

The keep was divided into equal halves by a thick spine-wall which had a well-shaft in the middle of it, so that water could be drawn up to each floor in a bucket: a splendid arrangement. As usual, the wall supported two low-pitched roofs, well hidden behind the parapet so that they could not be damaged by missiles flung from war machines. There was a double line of pigeon holes built into the wall just above the north roof. The Romans had used pigeons for carrying messages, so had the Saracens, and they may have been used for that purpose in England at this time; but their main use was for the table. There would always have been a good supply of pigeons fattening up on the peasants' cornlands and preening themselves on the sunny south slope of the roof. These birds would be an important source of food in time of siege.

Rochester keep is a tall narrow building compared to the White Tower. There were dimly lit store-rooms below the entrance floor and the great hall above occupies the space of two storeys, with a gallery running round the upper level, as at Norwich. The dividing wall is pierced with a superb arcade, decorated with the zigzag ornament that was so popular at that time. There were a couple of extra rooms right at the top of the keep, under the roof, and these were probably used as sleeping-quarters, although traces of a fine Romanesque arch suggest a second and larger chapel. After all, it was an ecclesiastical building, and two chapels may have been necessary.

The zigzag ornamentation round the arches of the arcade, fireplace and gallery openings is typical of this period. The gallery ran through all four outer walls of the keep at the level of the upper part of the hall and chamber, connecting with the two spiral stairways: a chilly place in winter, with the wind whistling through the inner and outer openings.

MEN AND WOMEN WORE
ONE GOWN OVER ANOTHER,
WITH A CLOAK OVER ALL
TO KEEP OUT THE COLD

MERLON

CRENEL

DOUBLE LINE OF
PIGEON HOLES

BEAM HOLE
FOR TIMBER HOARDING

The area of wall above the wall-walk is called a parapet, *and when it was built for defence, with* merlons *for men to shelter behind and* crenels *they could shoot through, it is called a* crenellated *(or embattled)* parapet.

Part of a fine archway on the top floor of the keep, blocked up at a later date. Upper rooms were often used as sleeping quarters, but these apartments may have been kept for the private use of the archbishop: a hall and then a chamber and chapel divided by a partition. The archway could be part of the chapel east window.

Looking at the keep from the outside, gaping holes can be seen running just below the *crenellated* parapet, in line with the wall-walk behind. A *crenel* is the gap for a man to shoot or throw stones through and a *merlon* is the solid part of the parapet, intended to give him shelter. At Rochester, the defenders would have stepped through the crenels on to the timber boards beyond, because the holes once held the beams for a timber hoarding, or gallery, which jutted out all round the top of the keep. A defender standing at the top of a tower could do little damage to a man standing close to the wall directly underneath, but if the defender could step out on to a hoarding it was another matter: he could drop stones or other missiles over the timber parapet or through gaps in the boards. Hoarding was used a great deal: round the tops of keeps, along the outside of curtain walls or other buildings (as with the hall at Richmond), and round gatehouses. If an enemy tried to burn down the heavy timber gatehouse doors, the bonfires could be put out by pouring water through the holes in the hoarding.

Some keeps have more fireplaces than others, and the Normans probably made use of small movable braziers which could stand in the middle of a room. At Rochester, as in the White Tower, the round-headed fireplaces had slanting smoke-vents which ended in holes in the outer walls. There was another way of dealing with the smoke, not so commonly used, which can clearly be seen in the keep at Portchester, Hamp-

58

BEAM HOLES FOR TIMBER HOARDING

MERLON

CRENEL

TOP FLOOR

GALLERY

HALL

CHAPEL

ENTRANCE LOBBY

TOWER

PROBABLE SHAPE OF WALL

PRISON?

LATER DOORWAY

EXISTING STONE-WORK

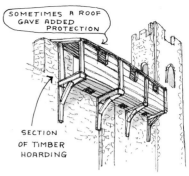

SOMETIMES A ROOF GAVE ADDED PROTECTION

SECTION OF TIMBER HOARDING

Hoardings *were timber galleries jutting out at the top of a wall to protect the area at the bottom. The defenders could step through the crenels, stand on the hoarding and shoot arrows through the gaps in the sides, or drop rocks and other missiles through holes in the wooden floor on to the enemy attacking below.*

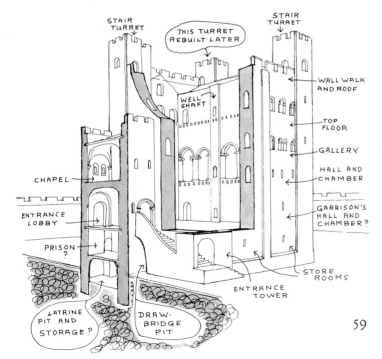

STAIR TURRET

THIS TURRET REBUILT LATER

STAIR TURRET

WALL WALK AND ROOF

WELL SHAFT

TOP FLOOR

GALLERY

HALL AND CHAMBER

CHAPEL

GARRISON'S HALL AND CHAMBER?

ENTRANCE LOBBY

PRISON?

STORE ROOMS

ENTRANCE TOWER

LATRINE PIT AND STORAGE?

DRAW-BRIDGE PIT

This cut-away drawing of the keep shows the position of the floors. The castellan and men of the garrison would have occupied the first floor, while the magnificent hall and chamber above were reserved for the archbishop, the king, or an important visitor. It is uncertain what the top floor was used for – see facing page.

59

The front of the fireplace has been destroyed; but this photograph shows the smoke cavity above the hearth with the three holes leading outside.

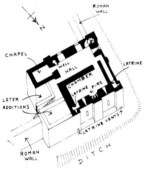

Portchester keep, built early in the 12th century and made higher later, was placed in a corner of the Roman fort (see page 13). The latrine vents are just above the ditch, allowing the rubbish to fall outside the castle. The triangular smoke holes are just visible in the central pilaster, and the building is dotted with tiny holes which took the ends of putlogs, or lengths of timber scaffolding, set up when the keep was being painted or repaired.

shire. Here, there is a yawning beehive-shaped cavity over the hearth where the smoke could collect before filtering out through three small holes.

Most keeps were amply supplied with *latrines*, otherwise known as privies or guarderobes. The latrine passage often led off from a window recess, turned a sharp bend, and ended in a stone or wooden seat. The drainage shaft went straight down through the thick wall and ended in a hole which could be cleared out at regular intervals; alternatively, the waste simply discharged into the ditch.

In general, there were two types of keeps. There were the stout squat hall keeps, with the hall and chamber alongside each other on the same level, as with the White Tower, Colchester and Norwich; then there were others, like Rochester, which were tall narrow buildings with an extra floor up above. These buildings which are higher than they are wide, are often called *tower keeps*. The room on the top floor may have been used for people to sleep in, or as the lord's private chamber, with his hall down below. At Portchester the keep started off as a hall keep and then it was turned into a tower keep when

two more floors were added at the end of the twelfth century.

Castle Hedingham, Essex, is a good example of a tower keep, similar to Rochester but built on a smaller scale and faced with smooth ashlar instead of rubble. Steps led up to the forebuilding (now vanished) and a portcullis hung over the entrance doorway. The great hall is spanned by a single sweeping arch and, as usual, a gallery runs round at the upper level. It looks as if the top floor was used for general sleeping accommodation and the lord and his lady would probably have preferred to put their bed in one of the tiny chambers, built into the thickness of the wall.

All these massive square stone keeps had one serious weakness: they could be undermined. This happened at Rochester, some eighty years after it was built, when King John laid siege to some of his rebel barons. The king's miners drove a tunnel right under the south-east corner of the building; then the passage was shored up with pit props, stuffed with straw and the fat of forty pigs, and set ablaze. The fire destroyed the foundations of the heavy corner turret, causing it to tear away from the rest of the building and come crashing down by the

The keep at Castle Hedingham is intact apart from the forebuilding and the rest of the parapet. The great hall was spanned by a single arch and there was a gallery running round at the upper level.

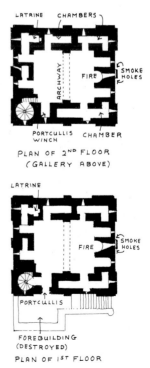

LATRINE   CHAMBERS

ARCHWAY   FIRE   SMOKE HOLES

PORTCULLIS WINCH   CHAMBER

PLAN OF 2ND FLOOR
(GALLERY ABOVE)

LATRINE

FIRE   SMOKE HOLES

PORTCULLIS

FOREBUILDING
(DESTROYED)
PLAN OF 1ST FLOOR

SLEEPING QUARTERS

GALLERY

GARRISON QUARTERS

HALL

FOREBUILDING   STORE ROOMS

force of its own weight. The king's men were able to rush through the breach and into the keep, while the defenders hurriedly barricaded themselves in behind the thick dividing wall. The well-openings were, luckily, on their side and they had water to drink; but they were so hungry that they were forced to eat the horses that they had brought into the keep with them. It was starvation that made them surrender in the end.

Undermining a corner of a keep was the standard way of taking it. The defenders would try to protect themselves by sinking counter-mines: tunnelling away underground in a desperate attempt to locate the enemy's passage and put a stop to the work before it was too late.

However, few barons dared to rebel against Henry I and there are no stories of keeps being undermined on English soil during his peaceful reign. This strong, clever, ruthless king died near Gisors in 1135, when both Rochester Castle and Castle Hedingham were brand new fortresses. The entry in *The Anglo-Saxon Chronicle* is full of foreboding: 'Then forthwith these lands grew dark, for everyone who could forthwith robbed another . . . He [Henry] was a good man, and people were in great awe of him. No one dared injure another in his time. He made peace for man and beast.' (*English Historical Documents*, vol. II, p. 199).

It was the end of an era.

The corner tower of Rochester keep was destroyed in the siege of 1215 and replaced by a round tower in the early years of the reign of Henry III, when the rest of the castle was repaired and set in order. Accounts say that the keep was given a coat of whitewash.

The knights of Henry I, riding to battle, would have looked much the same as the knights who fought at Hastings; but the hauberk and the garment beneath it were far longer than in the time of William I.

62

SIEGECRAFT, CHIVALRY AND SHEER BRUTE FORCE

5

WHEN KING HENRY'S NEPHEW, COUNT STEPHEN OF Blois, ignored Matilda's claim and put himself on the English throne in 1135, almost every important town and village he passed through on his royal progress was overlooked by a castle of one sort or another. The great majority were the ones that had been established by his grandfather at the time of the Conquest. William I had always laid down strict laws to make sure that none of these castles became too strong, but although Henry I had followed the same policy, all over the country rotting timbers were gradually being replaced by stone walls. The shell keeps crowning the mottes usually had a projecting square gateway at the top of the steep flight of steps, with timber buildings leaning against the inner face of the circular or many-sided wall.

Henry I had left a promising situation: law and order respected throughout the land and a heap of treasure in the storerooms at Winchester. Chivalrous and generous to a fault, Stephen was soon enjoying his riches and handing out lavish gifts; but there were difficulties ahead. He had been the first, after the king of Scotland, to swear loyalty to his cousin, the Empress Matilda, and now he had broken his oath and taken her crown. All the barons who secretly remained loyal to her – or who wanted to take advantage of his unstable situation – were able to garrison their castles, raise their drawbridges, fix thick bars behind their doors, and defy their king.

Few early shell keeps remain to their full height. Lewes Castle, Sussex, had two mottes and in the late 11th or early 12th century, a shell keep was built on the southern mound. There are foundations of a square entrance tower, and wooden buildings originally leant against the inside wall. The towers were added in the 13th century.

This is the view from the road leading up to Carisbrooke Castle from the north. Foot-soldiers, like this one guarding the approach, wore ordinary clothes, and fought with spears.

Baldwin de Redvers, for example, had inherited great estates and was a powerful baron. He surrounded himself with armed men and, after much swaggering and boasting, installed himself in the king's castle at Exeter; refusing to give it up.

The siege followed the standard pattern. Stephen immediately sent 200 horsemen with 'glittering arms and standards fluttering in the air', to cut off any supplies that might be on their way to the castle; then followed at his leisure with 'a glorious, or I should rather say a terrifying retinue of squadrons and companies'. These comments were made by the unknown writer of *The Deeds of Stephen (Gesta Stephani)* who was alive at the time. The King and his army then settled down to keep a watch on the castle walls and stare at the underside of the drawbridge, defiantly raised beneath the lofty arch.

At first, Baldwin hurled insults, and javelins and arrows flew from the battlements. Sudden sorties were made from the postern and the soldiers indulged in lively skirmishes. King Stephen retaliated:

> Sometimes he joined battle with them by means of armed men crawling up the mound [this must have been the steep bank outside the Roman wall, because there was no motte]; sometimes by aid of countless slingers, who had been hired from a distant region, he assailed them with an unendurable hail of stones; at other times he summoned those who have skill in mining under ground and ordered them to search into the bowels of the earth with a view to demolishing the wall; frequently too he devised engines of different sorts. (*Gesta Stephani*, Thomas Nelson & Sons, p. 22.)

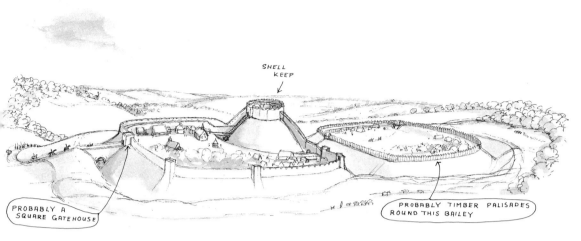

SHELL KEEP

PROBABLY A SQUARE GATEHOUSE

PROBABLY TIMBER PALISADES ROUND THIS BAILEY

Despite the miners, war machines, siege towers and scaling-ladders – to be used in a direct assault – the usual way of taking a castle was to cut off supplies and starve the garrison into submission. This took time. King Stephen spent most of his reign sitting outside one castle or another. It was nearly three months before Baldwin's forces showed any sign of running short of provisions. Then disaster struck: the weather was hot and the well went dry.

So, when the water failed, all had recourse to wine to satisfy their needs, but it did not last long, necessity driving them both to make loaves with wine instead of water and to use wine for any food that had to be boiled. The fire also and the torches, which the king's engineers were cleverly and skilfully flinging among them to burn their engines or consume their dwellings, they always met with wine to put them out, until they had no more a drop of wine left than a drop of water. (*Gesta Stephani*, p. 26.)

King Stephen was rash enough to allow Baldwin de Redvers his freedom after the siege of Exeter, so the baron, unrepentant as ever, immediately summoned fresh forces and garrisoned the castle he had recently rebuilt at Carisbrooke in the Isle of Wight.

Carisbrooke Castle has one of the finest shell keeps in Britain. Built sometime before 1136, it was even higher in Baldwin's time than it is now and would have been topped

Carisbrooke Castle originated as a rectangular Roman fort. The Normans built a castle with a motte and two baileys on the site before 1078, and some time before 1136, Baldwin de Redvers replaced the old wooden palisades with the present stone walls. This drawing shows how it might have looked then, and the plan of the shell keep is below.

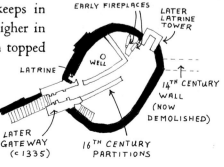

EARLY FIREPLACES

LATER LATRINE TOWER

WELL

LATRINE

14TH CENTURY WALL (NOW DEMOLISHED)

LATER GATEWAY (c 1335)

16TH CENTURY PARTITIONS

A castle was defended from the parapets of the keep, the gatehouse, the mural towers and the wall-walk. The garrison fought with spears, bows and arrows, or stones, either hurled by hand or flung from the same kind of slings the Celts had used. The Norman bow was drawn to the chest – not to the ear. This came in later with the Welsh longbow.

with a crenellated parapet. This keep was reserved for emergencies and Baldwin and his family would have lived in a stone hall down in the bailey. Once again, King Stephen hurried to besiege his rebellious subject, and Baldwin must have anxiously peered down both of his wells, muttering something about the same disaster never happening twice: but it did. The water-level dropped, the wells dried up, and he was forced to surrender for the second time.

Not all castles were as well built as Carisbrooke and the besiegers sometimes managed to breach the defences by using war machines of one sort or another. Modern machines are worked by electricity or explosions of some kind; but the ancient Greeks had perfected a way of flinging heavy objects by twisting animal sinews and other materials into a tight springy skein and then releasing it suddenly. In general, this energy was used to operate two sorts of machines: catapults and ballistas. Catapults flung the missiles upwards from the end of a long beam, and the ballistas worked on the same principle as a crossbow, the gigantic bolts or the stones being fired horizontally.

These Greek machines had been copied by the Romans, but many of the secrets were forgotten during the Dark Ages and they had lost some of their efficiency by the time they were

66

MEN HURLING STONES

ENTRANCE TOWER 14th CENTURY ADDITION

THE KEEP WAS ORIGINALLY HIGHER

'Wight is an island in the sea . . . Baldwin had a castle in it, very finely built of stone and very strongly fortified . . . when he fortified his castle in Wight firmly and impregnably against the king, he had made a careful calculation that, just as there was abundance of food in it, so there should be a supply of water adequate for the number of the garrison. But this too was brought about by the providence of God . . . that both the water should fail owing to a sudden drought and that he and his adherents would be smitten with despair of resistance to the king.' (Gesta Stephanie, p. 29.)

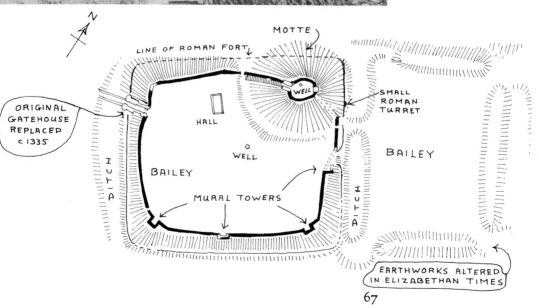

MOTTE

LINE OF ROMAN FORT

WELL

SMALL ROMAN TURRET

ORIGINAL GATEHOUSE REPLACED c 1335

HALL

WELL

BAILEY

BAILEY

DITCH

DITCH

MURAL TOWERS

EARTHWORKS ALTERED IN ELIZABETHAN TIMES

67

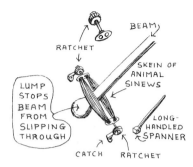

RATCHET

BEAM

LUMP STOPS BEAM FROM SLIPPING THROUGH

SKEIN OF ANIMAL SINEWS

LONG-HANDLED SPANNER

CATCH   RATCHET

THE SKEIN IS TWISTED UNTIL IT IS VERY TIGHT...

...AND THE TENSION HELD WITH THE CATCH

being made by medieval engineers. Because Norman walls were usually made of a double line of good-quality stonework with a rubble filling between, the outer surface could be cracked by a barrage of rocks flung from the war machines, allowing the enemy to tear away the facing stones and get to grips with the loose mixture of rubble and mortar in the middle.

Therefore, once the curtain wall had been softened up, the miners would descend into the ditch, climb the opposite bank and start hacking away with picks and shovels at the damaged stonework. The defenders would do their utmost to stop the work by leaning over the parapet, or timber hoarding if there was one, and dropping down anything they could lay hands on. The miners worked under a *penthouse*, or movable timber shelter, which could be draped with raw animal hides to prevent it from being set on fire. When the miners had hacked out a hole big enough for them to creep into, they were sheltered by the wall itself and could tunnel through to the other side, unhampered.

Twisted animal sinews and other materials provided power for medieval war machines. These drawings show the principle behind the way they worked, but reconstructions are only guesswork because none of the machines have survived. The catapult on the right flung the missiles upwards while the balista on the opposite page fired its giant arrows – or stones – horizontally, working to the same system as the crossbow.

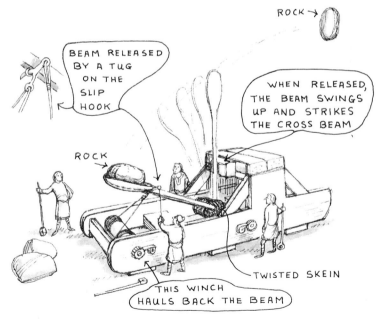

ROCK →

BEAM RELEASED BY A TUG ON THE SLIP HOOK

WHEN RELEASED, THE BEAM SWINGS UP AND STRIKES THE CROSS BEAM

ROCK →

TWISTED SKEIN

THIS WINCH HAULS BACK THE BEAM

68

King Stephen often ordered his men to build a *siege castle*. The diggers would pile up an earth mound, not far from the wall, but well out of range of enemy arrows; and then a timber tower was built on top. This allowed the besiegers to shoot down into the bailey and they could also see what the trapped garrison was up to. A couple of these siege mounds were built outside Oxford Castle, and their positions are clearly marked by the way the road curves round to avoid them (see page 18). They were probably put there when King Stephen besieged the Empress Matilda in 1142 (the two cousins had been warring against each other ever since the Empress had landed in England, three years earlier). At that time Oxford Castle had been standing for about seventy years and appears to have been in much the same state as when it was built. Here is the description from *The Deeds of Stephen*.

> Now Oxford is a city very securely protected, inaccessible because of the very deep water that washes it all round, most carefully encircled by the palisade of an outwork on one side, and on another finely and very strongly fortified by an impregnable castle and a tower of great height. (*Gesta Stephani*, p. 92.)

Few people managed to escape from a besieged castle, but the resourceful Empress Matilda snatched the opportunity when she saw it, making good use of the water and St George's tower.

The king besieged Oxford Castle for three months, by which time there was not a scrap of food left in the fortress and everyone was expecting the Empress to surrender. Winter had come and 'all the ground was white with an extremely

King Stephen besieging Farringdon Castle: 'And without delay, setting up engines most skillfully contrived around the castle, and posting an encircling ring of archers in very dense formation, he began to harass the besieged most grievously. On the one hand stones or other missiles launched from the engines were falling and battering them everywhere, on the other a most fearful hail of arrows, flying around before their eyes, was causing them extreme affliction.' (Gesta Stephani, p. 120.)

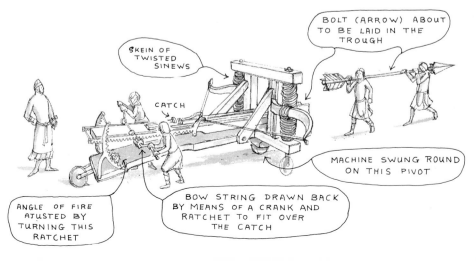

SKEIN OF TWISTED SINEWS

BOLT (ARROW) ABOUT TO BE LAID IN THE TROUGH

CATCH

MACHINE SWUNG ROUND ON THIS PIVOT

ANGLE OF FIRE ATJUSTED BY TURNING THIS RATCHET

BOW STRING DRAWN BACK BY MEANS OF A CRANK AND RATCHET TO FIT OVER THE CATCH

A team of men with an ordinary timber beam on their shoulders could make a basic battering-ram, but far more damage could be done if the beam was slung from a wooden framework. The defenders would try to set these contraptions on fire, and the raw animal hides protected both the wood and the men working underneath. The smell must have been dreadful!

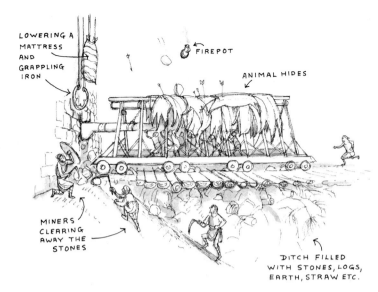

LOWERING A MATTRESS AND GRAPPLING IRON

FIREPOT

ANIMAL HIDES

MINERS CLEARING AWAY THE STONES

DITCH FILLED WITH STONES, LOGS, EARTH, STRAW ETC.

heavy fall of snow and there was a very thick crust of ice on the water'. The king's forces were anticipating their victory, 'breaking the silence of the night with the blaring of trumpets or the cries of men shouting loudly'. They were off their guard and failed to notice the Empress as, dressed in white to match the snow, she was lowered by ropes from the tower and then glided silently over the ice-covered water. Together with three of her knights, she struggled on foot through the deep snow as far as Abingdon, then took horse and galloped to the friendly castle of Wallingford (see map on page 26).

Most garrisons were imprisoned inside their castles, unable to escape, and had to suffer starvation and listen to the steady beat of the battering-ram breaking up their defences. A battering-ram was a simple device: a long pole with a lump of iron, sometimes shaped like a ram's head, fitted to the end. The pole was slung from the roof of an equally long shed-like structure that could be pushed to the castle ditch on wheels or rollers. The ditch first had to be filled with earth, logs, and stones until a ramp had been made for the ram to stand on and it was then firmly wedged into position. The defenders would fling down lumps of burning pitch, firepots and stones, which would bounce off the raw hides draped over the roof of the ram to protect it.

70

As the iron head battered away at the stone wall, the defenders would try to cushion the blows by lowering straw mattresses, or anything else they could find. Sometimes they tried to catch the ram's head with a hook, called a grappling-iron, or a chain: in fact they used every contrivance they could think of, to prevent the enemy from breaching the wall and rushing into their bailey.

Stephen's rebellious barons were not the only men to live in military surroundings. Bishop Roger of Salisbury, who had started his career as chaplain to Henry I and become the king's right-hand man, virtually ruling England when Henry was in Normandy, was a great castle builder. There were also his two nephews, the bishops of Lincoln and Ely, who:

> loved display . . . disregarding the holy and simple manner of life that befits a Christian priest they devoted themselves so utterly to warfare and the vanities of this world that whenever they attended court by appointment they too aroused general astonishment on account of the extraordinary concourse of knights by which they were surrounded on every side. (*Gesta Stephani*, pp. 48–9.)

All three bishops were much criticized by King Stephen's barons: 'They built castles of great renown, raised up towers and buildings of great strength, and not to put the king in possession of his kingdom, but to steal his royal majesty from him and plot against the majesty of his crown.'

Of the castles in question, only the foundations of Old Sarum, Wiltshire, the half-ruined walls of Sherborne, Dorset, and perhaps the core of the gatehouse at Newark, Nottinghamshire, still exist.

Henry I had allowed Bishop Alexander of Lincoln to fortify his manor at Newark and he turned it into 'a magnificent castle of very ornate construction'; but this was almost certainly a timber stronghold and if there was a stone hall or chapel in the bailey, there is little evidence to show it. Bishop Alexander may also have had a stone gatehouse; but if this was so, then his original stonework now lies buried under the

The stones in the centre of Newark gatehouse may have been laid before 1135, in the time of Bishop Alexander of Lincoln, but the tower was rebuilt towards the end of the 12th century, and altered yet again later.

THIS DRAWING IS TAKEN FROM BISHOP ROGER'S EFFIGY

OUTER
RAMPART

TOWN
RAMPART

CASTLE
RAMPART

Old Sarum was almost certainly an Iron Age hill-fort and the Saxons built their town inside the ancient ramparts. The Norman castle was surrounded by a huge bank and placed right in the middle of the town, with a bailey to the north. The cathedral and other ecclesiastical buildings occupied about a quarter of the remaining space.

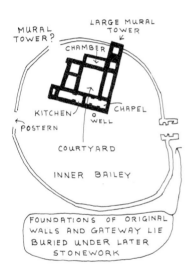

MURAL
TOWER?

LARGE MURAL
TOWER

CHAMBER

KITCHEN
POSTERN

CHAPEL

WELL

COURTYARD

INNER BAILEY

FOUNDATIONS OF ORIGINAL
WALLS AND GATEWAY LIE
BURIED UNDER LATER
STONEWORK

The buildings of the castle were arranged round a courtyard and this was filled with chalk up to first-floor level so as to give it extra light.

later work. The tower was enlarged and re-faced between 1173 and 1180.

Massive circular earthworks indicate that Old Sarum must have been an Iron Age hill-fort and the ancient defences were used again to enclose a flourishing, but windswept, Saxon town. As usual, the Normans built a castle soon after the Conquest to dominate the people, and they built a cathedral as well. Then, between 1107 and 1135, when Henry I was at the height of his power, the great Bishop Roger of Salisbury glorified God by extending the cathedral, then honoured himself by building palatial apartments inside the castle.

At that time Old Sarum (also called Old Salisbury) was the seat of the bishopric, and the castle and cathedral were both under the rule of Bishop Roger. The cathedral and other ecclesiastical buildings took up about a quarter of the Saxon town, while the castle had been built right in the centre: a huge circular bank and ditch formed the inner bailey and there are indications that there was an outer bailey to the north. Only foundations are left of Bishop Roger's buildings, which were grouped round a courtyard in much the same way as monastic buildings are grouped round a cloister. They must have been similar to the buildings in his castle at Sherborne, where far more stonework is standing.

Sherborne was also built during the reign of Henry I: a new castle on a new site. There were a couple of rectangular towers on the curtain wall and the bailey was entered through

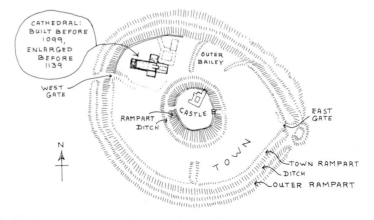

CATHEDRAL:
BUILT BEFORE
1099,
ENLARGED
BEFORE
1139

OUTER
BAILEY

WEST
GATE

EAST
GATE

RAMPART
DITCH

CASTLE

TOWN

TOWN RAMPART
DITCH
OUTER RAMPART

N

a choice of three gateways (unusual in a fortress of this period). In the middle of the bailey stood a large keep, guarding the hall, chamber, chapel and other apartments, which were raised up on store-rooms and grouped round a courtyard. It is not surprising that King Stephen resented the extravagance of his bishop, whose estates were thus 'glorified beyond measure by various adornments and buildings, without any sparing of expense'. Fragments of carved stonework which still grace the ruins show that the castle at Sherborne was equal to any royal castle, in the high standard of ornamentation and magnificence.

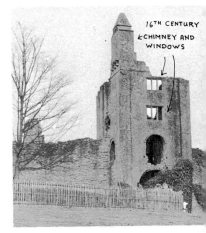

16TH CENTURY
CHIMNEY AND
WINDOWS

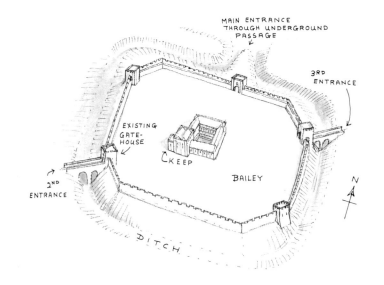

MAIN ENTRANCE
THROUGH UNDERGROUND
PASSAGE

3RD
ENTRANCE

EXISTING
GATE-
HOUSE

KEEP

BAILEY

N

2ND
ENTRANCE

DITCH

The main buildings at Sherborne were also grouped round a courtyard, with a strong rectangular keep at one of the corners. The castle is ruined, but fragments of carving show a high standard of craftsmanship. There were three gatehouses to the curtain wall and the one above still survives. The upper floors were rebuilt in the 16th century.

DING

MAIN BODY
OF KEEP

COURTYARD

FINE CARVING

At this time Ludlow Castle had a stone-built inner bailey defended by square towers and a huge gateway with carved arcades on either side of the passage, above and right. Later the passage was walled up, the gatehouse made higher, and turned into a keep. The plan is below.

Although it must be remembered that most castles were still basically earth and timber, some of the barons had got their hands on extremely solid, stone fortresses. Ludlow Castle had been seized by Gervase Paganel right at the start of Stephen's reign, and the king wanted to take it back and return it to its rightful owner. It had been built about 1090 and, as at Richmond, the strongest part of the castle was the gatehouse, which served as the keep, while the bailey wall was defended by small square towers projecting out into the ditch.

Stephen camped outside the walls as usual, flung stones with his war machines and built a couple of siege towers near by. As it happened, Henry of Huntingdon, son of King David I of Scotland, was with the besieging army and, being

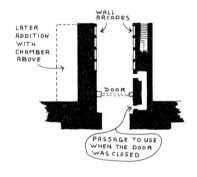

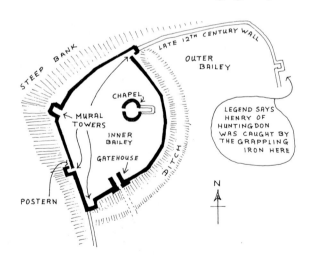

young and wanting to prove his valour, he rode his horse in a foolhardy way too close to one of the square mural towers. He was caught by a grappling-iron that was being dangled from one of the windows, and dragged out of the saddle. Renowned for his gallantry, King Stephen flung himself into the fray and managed to untangle the victim before he was hauled up the wall and into the castle.

The pride of Ludlow Castle is the chapel, which was built early in the reign of Henry I. It is a rare example of a circular nave, though the long chancel, where the priest officiated, is missing.

The gatehouse at Ludlow was unusually massive. A blind arcade decorated both sides of the passage and when the two-leaved doors were barred at night, late-comers could pass through a short passage arranged in the thickness of the wall. The room over the wide entrance passage probably served as the hall, while a narrow chamber and latrine were slightly later additions.

It was probably soon after the siege of Ludlow that the passage through the old gatehouse was walled up, extra floors were added, and the whole building was turned into a more conventional keep. A similar alteration was to be made to the gatehouse at Richmond.

The castle chapel has a round nave (like the Temple Church, London), and the chancel once stood to the east. Inside, there is a beautifully decorated blind arcade, where the barons used to sit. The chapel was altered when an upper floor was put in, supported by carved heads: the walls were raised and the crenellated parapet added. The chapel might originally have had a conical roof.

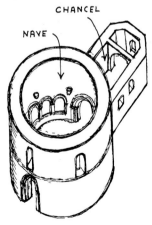

CHANCEL

NAVE

PORTCULLIS →

PORTCULLIS
GROOVE

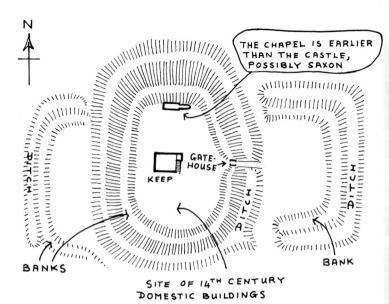

N

THE CHAPEL IS EARLIER
THAN THE CASTLE,
POSSIBLY SAXON

GATE-
HOUSE →

KEEP

DITCH

IULIA

IULIA

BANKS

BANK

SITE OF 14TH CENTURY
DOMESTIC BUILDINGS

Castle Rising keep is defended by a huge oval bank and ditch with additional earthworks of uncertain date. The semi-ruined square gatehouse, set between high flanking banks, has the remains of a stairway, evidence of an upper floor; a portcullis would have hung in the room over the passage.

PORT-
CULLIS
↓

IMAGINARY
UPPER
FLOOR

EXISTING
STONEWORK

Few gatehouses were as large as these. Where a castle had the security of a good strong keep – either on the motte top or in the form of a tower – the gatehouse could be quite small, as at Sherborne, with just a single room over the passage for the portcullis to hang in, or perhaps another room above that. There could be a tiny guard-room at ground-floor level as well. There are the ruins of a typical small gatehouse, fitted with a portcullis, at Castle Rising in Norfolk.

Castle Rising seems remote from the fury of Stephen's wars. It was built about 1150 for the widow of Henry I, Adelize, the Fair Maid of Brabent, and her second husband, William d'Aubigny. The keep is a fine example of late Norman architecture and was designed for comfort as well as defence.

It is a hall keep, with store-rooms below and the hall and chamber alongside each other at first-floor level. There were further rooms above that, but the building was never as tall as the tower keeps of Rochester and Hedingham. The steps leading up to the forebuilding are enclosed by a richly decorated wall and there was a postern passage, starting from a doorway next to the chapel and crossing over the stairway at right angles. The chapel, like the rest of the building, is carefully decorated. A passage running alongside the hall led to a

PASSAGE TO KITCHEN

The keep is built on lines similar to Norwich, with a fore-building running along the side of the building, defended by pairs of doors at the bottom, in the middle, and at the top. A murder-hole in the floor of the postern passage not only allowed missiles to be dropped on enemy heads; but let water be poured through if enemies attempted to set the centre door on fire. These photographs show the high quality of the carvings.

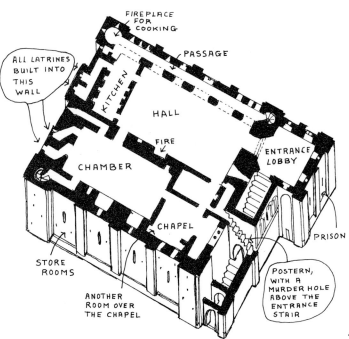

FIREPLACE FOR COOKING

PASSAGE

ALL LATRINES BUILT INTO THIS WALL

KITCHEN

HALL

FIRE

CHAMBER

ENTRANCE LOBBY

CHAPEL

PRISON

STORE ROOMS

ANOTHER ROOM OVER THE CHAPEL

POSTERN, WITH A MURDER HOLE ABOVE THE ENTRANCE STAIR

77

POSTERN

THIS PART REBUILT

tiny kitchen where cooking would have been done on a small scale; but the bulk of the roasting would have taken place in a kitchen outside in the bailey. The latrine shafts were placed together in the end wall and the whole keep was well planned and compact.

King Stephen's reign went from bad to worse and civil war brought with it a state of anarchy. He never had time to build castles for himself, whereas his barons had been hurriedly throwing up timber motte-and-bailey strongholds without asking royal permission. This kind of unauthorized fortress is called an *adulterine castle*. The *Anglo-Saxon Chronicle* had something to say about the general situation:

> For every powerful man built his castles and held them against him and they filled the country full of castles. They oppressed the wretched people of the country severely with castle building. When the castles were built, they filled them with devils and wicked men. Then, both by night and day they took those people that they thought had any goods – men and women – and put them in prison and tortured them with indescribable torture to extort gold and silver – for no martyrs were ever so tortured as they were. (*English Historical Documents*, vol. II, p. 199.)

This woman is descending the long flight of steps from the entrance lobby at Castle Rising. Crusaders returned from the eastern Mediterranean with silks and muslins for their wives and daughters. Light floating draperies were the fashion, held in place with long knotted girdles.

CHANGING TIMES

6

KING STEPHEN DIED IN 1154 AND WHEN MATILDA'S son, the young and energetic Henry II, took up the reins of government, he took a long hard look at all the castles scattered over England. William of Newburgh shows how he dealt with the situation:

> First he issued an edict against the mercenaries who under King Stephen had streamed into England from foreign parts, as much for the sake of booty as for the profession of arms ... These he ordered to return to their own country and appointed a day after which to prolong their stay in England would be attended with certain danger. ... Next he ordered the newly erected castles, which had not been standing in the days of his grandfather, to be razed to the ground, with the exception of a few sited in advantageous places, which he desired either to retain for himself or to be maintained in the hands of peaceful men for the defence of the realm. (*English Historical Documents*, vol. II, p. 323.)

Timber castles were easy enough to destroy: stone ones were not quite so simple. For example, the powerful Bishop of Winchester, Henry of Blois (who was also Stephen's brother), had built himself five castles and a palace, living in near-regal splendour. One of these castles was half-way along the

Henry II was efficient, hard working and always in a hurry: garments that were easy to wear tended to return to fashion. He was nicknamed 'curtmantle' because he wore a short cloak and his seal shows no long skirts fluttering from beneath his hauberk.

The Bishop of Winchester's castle at Farnham had a motte and square stone tower. The inner bailey was placed inside the large outer bailey. A ditch cut off the level ground to the north, while the southern rampart was protected by the steep hill dropping down to the town below.

road from Winchester to London, at Farnham in Surrey. The walls of the tower were about 6 metres thick and had been laid at ground level with a motte heaped up round them. The king's workmen managed to demolish the tower as far as the motte top; but the lower part is still buried inside the mound.

When the king ordered the castles to be razed to the ground, he was ordering them to be *slighted*, or levelled. Sometimes this was too great a task for the demolition gang, and they would only tear down part of the walls, leaving the castle in such a ruined state that it could no longer be properly defended.

So much for castles that were being wiped from the map; the king was also strengthening existing royal strongholds and occasionally building new ones, but not always in the same old way. There had been changes since the time of Henry I. New ideas had been blowing across Europe from Outremer, as the Holy Land was called, and from other parts of the eastern Mediterranean. People travelled. Ever since the First Crusade, in the time of William Rufus, returning warriors had been giving glowing descriptions of the palaces, strongholds, and city defences they had encountered on the way. The most impressive barrier of all was the Land Wall outside Constantinople (now called Istanbul), which had been standing ever since A.D. 413. This was a triple defence, allowing three tiers

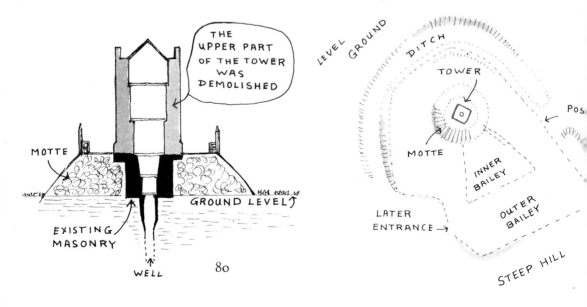

THE UPPER PART OF THE TOWER WAS DEMOLISHED

MOTTE

GROUND LEVEL

EXISTING MASONRY

WELL

LEVEL GROUND

DITCH

TOWER

MOTTE

INNER BAILEY

OUTER BAILEY

LATER ENTRANCE →

POS

STEEP HILL

80

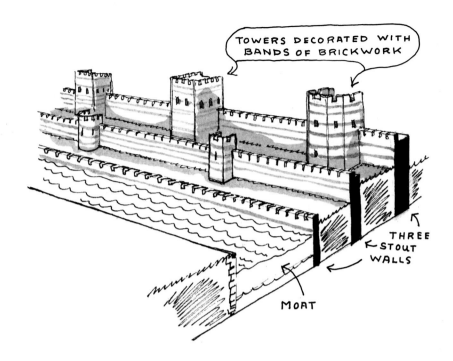

TOWERS DECORATED WITH BANDS OF BRICKWORK

THREE STOUT WALLS

MOAT

of archers to shoot over each other's heads – four in some places, where the wall was pierced with arrow-slits. There was first a high inner wall which had massive projecting towers at close regular intervals; then a space; then a slightly lower wall, also with towers; then another space; and finally a low wall overlooking the ditch. These two systems – one high wall being defended by another lower wall; and the mural towers being placed close together – were to be used in later European castles.

No one seems to know which country was responsible for the introduction of the pointed arch. In Romanesque buildings, doors and windows were built with semicircular arches above the openings, and passages were covered with tunnel-like *barrel-vaults* or *groined vaults*, which are like two tunnels crossing each other at right angles. This semicircular shape meant that the height had to depend on the width to be covered. A pointed arch, on the other hand, could be high or low, as the designer wished. It was far more flexible. The new

The Land Wall outside Constantinople was built between A.D. 413 and 447 to defend the city against the Ostrogoths and the Huns. It was a formidable barrier and the walls were designed in such a way that archers could fire their arrows from three levels and had full command of the areas between the towers.

81

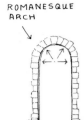

ROMANESQUE ARCH

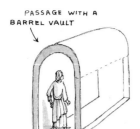

PASSAGE WITH A BARREL VAULT

PASSAGE WITH GROINED VAULTS

GROIN

A ROUND ARCH HAD TO BE THE SAME HEIGHT AS THE WIDTH IT COVERED

PASSAGES WERE OFTEN COVERED WITH SIMPLE BARREL VAULTS LIKE TUNNELS

····OTHERWISE GROINED VAULTS WERE USED. GROINS ARE THE SHARP ANGLES

SMALL CHAMBERS WERE OFTEN COVERED WITH GROINED VAULTS

These diagrams show the differences between the commonest forms of Romanesque and Gothic vaulting. Groined vaults, like two tunnels crossing each other, are usual in castles, and in the Gothic period the groins were covered with stone ribs. Rib and panel vaults were more suitable for churches, which did not need thick walls.

shape fitted into the new vaulting system. The masons had discovered that they could build a lighter roof if stone ribs were arched across from one support to the next, forming a framework which could hold thin panels. This discovery of rib-vaulting was more useful for churches, which demanded impressively high roofs and large windows, than for castles, which needed thick walls and narrow openings for defence. The new building technique was first used in Durham Cathedral, well before 1133; but we usually think of the *Transitional style* – when round Romanesque arches and pointed *Gothic* arches are mixed up together in the same building – as being from 1150 to 1200. Like *Romanesque*, the word *Gothic* is a general term, and refers to any building set up in western Europe which used the principle of the pointed arch in its design (see the chart at the end of the book).

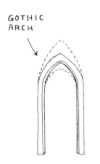

GOTHIC ARCH

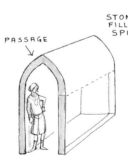

PASSAGE

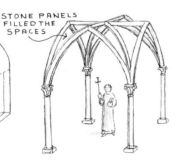

STONE PANELS FILLED THE SPACES

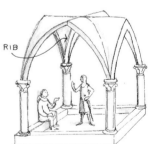

RIB

A POINTED ARCH COULD BE HIGH OR LOW REGARDLESS OF THE SPACE UNDERNEATH

AFTER THE 12TH CENTURY PASSAGES WERE OFTEN COVERED WITH POINTED VAULTS

AREAS COULD BE SPANNED BY A FRAMEWORK OF RIBS SUPPORTING STONE PANELS····

···BUT POINTED FORMS OF GROINED VAULTING WERE USUAL IN CASTLES, WITH STONE RIBS COVERING THE GROINS

82

In castles, other new ideas were afoot. The old square keeps had proved unsatisfactory for two important reasons: bitter experience had shown that the corners could be undermined, and the defenders could only see straight ahead as they peered through the narrow window slits – there was always a blind spot at the angle of the building where an enemy could lurk unseen. For some time, the master masons in various countries had been experimenting with circular or many-sided keeps, trying to find a better shape. Henry II was not the man to ignore new ideas and when he built a royal castle to defend the east coast of England, and incidentally to keep the quarrelsome neighbouring barons in order, he too tried out a revolutionary design. Work began on a site overlooking Orford harbour, Suffolk, in 1165.

JOGGLED ARCH WITH STONES CUT IN STEPS

Orford keep belongs to the Transitional Period. *The windows are round-headed, although rectangular on the inside. From the inside of the keep you can see that the pairs of windows are placed under a single pointed arch (see next page): a definite mixture of styles. The entrance doorway has an unusual joggled arch made up of specially shaped stones that fit into and support each other.*

IGHTS
ILL WORE
EIR
RADITIONAL
RMAN
RMOUR

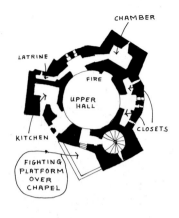

CHAMBER

LATRINE

FIRE

UPPER
HALL

KITCHEN

CLOSETS

FIGHTING
PLATFORM
OVER
CHAPEL

The keep at Orford is basically a tall round tower; but only the inside is a pure circle, the outside being built in straight sections. It is supported by three square turrets with a fore-building tacked on to one of them. As in most keeps, the store-room and well were at the bottom, and each of the two main floors contained a suite of rooms: a round hall, adjoining sleeping-chambers in the turrets, and the added luxury of a small kitchen where joints could be roasted, food kept hot and sauces made. But the main bulk of the cooking would still have been done in a timber kitchen outside in the bailey.

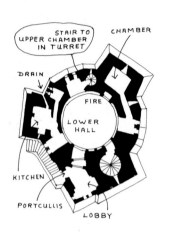

STAIR TO
UPPER CHAMBER
IN TURRET

CHAMBER

DRAIN

FIRE

LOWER
HALL

KITCHEN

PORTCULLIS

LOBBY

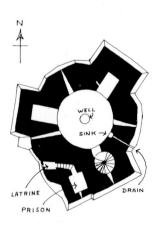

N

WELL

SINK →

LATRINE

DRAIN

PRISON

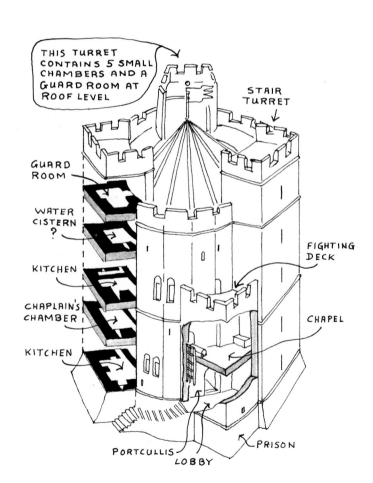

THIS TURRET
CONTAINS 5 SMALL
CHAMBERS AND A
GUARD ROOM AT
ROOF LEVEL

STAIR
TURRET

GUARD
ROOM

WATER
CISTERN
?

KITCHEN

CHAPLAIN'S
CHAMBER

KITCHEN

FIGHTING
DECK

CHAPEL

PORTCULLIS

LOBBY

PRISON

84

The castellan in this picture must have been an important baron because he is entertaining his guests in the upper hall: a more humble official would have dined with his men in the hall below.

When the keep was finished, the castellan must have enjoyed feasting his guests and pointing out the 'new look' of the hall. At that time painted wooden beams sprang from the *corbels*, or carved stones built to jut out from the wall, and went soaring up to a high pointed roof, giving a feeling of extra space and exciting new elegance. When the walls were plastered and painted, the general effect would have been delightfully cheerful.

The sea has receded, but Orford was a flourishing port at the time when the castle was built and its outer walls would have overlooked the harbour. Unfortunately, only the keep

85

HUGH BIGOD DRAWN FROM IMAGINATION

has survived, but an early drawing shows plenty of tall square towers projecting boldly out from the curtain wall and, luckily, a similar wall exists only a few miles away at Roger Bigod's castle of Framlingham, also in Suffolk.

The Bigods came over with William I, and Roger's father, Hugh Bigod, was one of the most untrustworthy villains in history: aiding and abetting King Stephen when he came to the throne and then deserting whenever it suited him. A born rebel, he supported young Henry when he fought against Stephen, and then almost immediately turned against him after he had been crowned king. One of the reasons for the building of Orford Castle was that King Henry wished to keep an eye on his treacherous subject. Framlingham had originally been a motte-and-bailey castle; but the motte had been levelled at some time, making a lower and wider area on which, about 1160, Hugh Bigod had built a stone hall and other buildings, though the outer defences were still timber. Hugh rebelled again, without success, against King Henry in 1173, and the king ordered the castle to be slighted. The palisades were destroyed but the stone hall was left standing. When old Hugh died in 1177, his son, Roger Bigod, inherited the castle and was granted permission to build the curtain wall and towers which are still standing today. They were almost certainly copied from the king's castle at Orford.

Hugh Bigod's castle, c. 1160, consisted of a stone hall and chapel on top of an old motte, which had been considerably lowered and levelled, and was probably surrounded by a palisade. The valley was dammed to form a shallow lake and protect the western side.

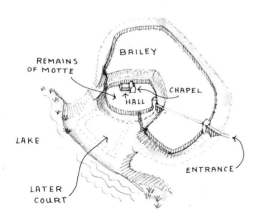

REMAINS OF MOTTE

BAILEY

CHAPEL

HALL

LAKE

LATER COURT

ENTRANCE

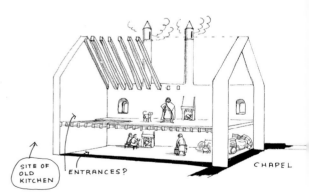

SITE OF OLD KITCHEN

ENTRANCES?

CHAPEL

WER
ND
ALL
1190
LATER
CHIMNEY
TOPS
SMOKE
VENT
RREL-
LTED
AMBERS
c1190
ORIGINAL
WINDOW
c1160
FIRE-
PLACES
JOIST
HOLES
ORIGINAL
WINDOW
c1160

Roger Bigod's curtain wall, c. 1190, was built against the side of Hugh's old stone hall: the chimneys and windows (the left-hand one was later converted to a doorway) were left enclosed in the newer masonry. The ground was originally lower, and the beam holes indicate a first-floor hall with a store-room below; but both rooms had fireplaces, and it may have been a ground-floor hall with Hugh's chamber above.

Medieval chimneys were often covered at the top and the smoke came out of holes at the sides. This is the smoke vent of the right-hand chimney.

Both castles show that lessons had been learnt since the start of the century. There had been no towers at all on the curtain walls of some early castles (Eynsford Castle, Kent, is one example), and only a few widely spaced ones at Ludlow and Richmond; but Framlingham Castle has thirteen towers to defend the inner bailey. Most of the towers are three-sided and open at the back; but the wall-walk was carried across the towers on wooden floors, and from this level upwards they had a timber backing. Because the towers were placed close together, archers could stand on top of a couple of them and shoot down an enemy who was in easy range as he approached the area in the middle. This sort of system made a curtain wall almost impregnable.

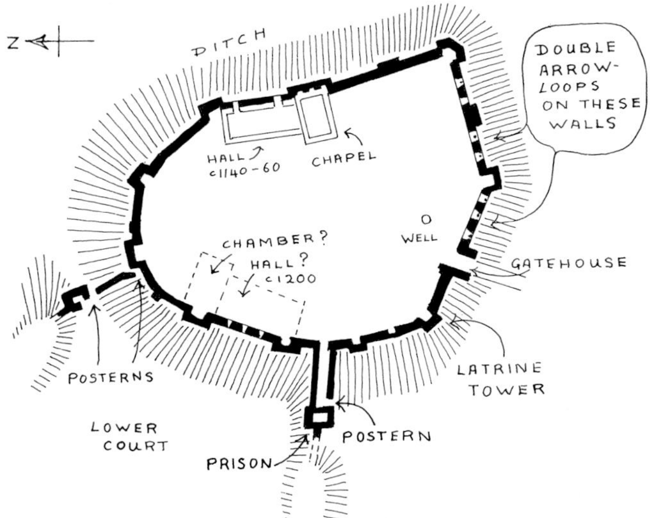
DITCH
DOUBLE
ARROW-
LOOPS
ON THESE
WALLS
HALL
c1140-60
CHAPEL
WELL
CHAMBER?
HALL?
c1200
GATEHOUSE
POSTERNS
LATRINE
TOWER
LOWER
COURT
POSTERN
PRISON

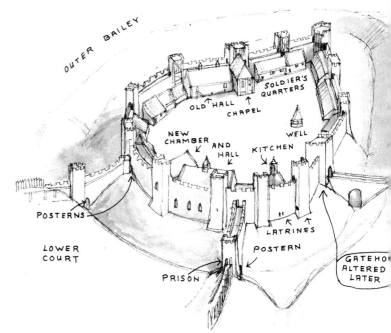

Roger Bigod's curtain wall, with its thirteen square towers, replaced his father's wooden palisade. The old hall was kept as an extra lodging house and about 1200 a new hall was built on the other side of the bailey with kitchen quarters alongside. All these buildings have now disappeared and an 18th-century house stands on the site of the later hall and chamber.

OUTER BAILEY

OLD HALL

CHAPEL

SOLDIER'S QUARTERS

NEW CHAMBER AND HALL

KITCHEN

WELL

POSTERNS

LOWER COURT

LATRINES

POSTERN

PRISON

GATEHO ALTERED LATER

THIS AREA FILLED IN WITH TIMBER

FLOORS DIVIDED THIS AREA INTO ROOMS

88

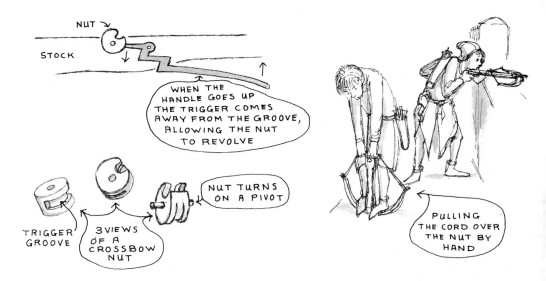

When the handle goes up the trigger comes away from the groove, allowing the nut to revolve

Nut turns on a pivot

Trigger groove

3 views of a crossbow nut

Nut

Stock

Pulling the cord over the nut by hand

Up to this time, curtain walls had been made of solid masonry up to the level of the wall-walk, where the archers stood and shot their arrows through the crenels or stepped out on to the timber hoarding. Now, as in the Land Wall outside Constantinople, *arrow-loops* were introduced below the wall-walk. There are pairs of arrow-loops in the south curtain wall at Framlingham, joined together by a single arch on the inside, making a recess which allowed enough space for a couple of crossbowmen to hitch up the cords of their weapons before releasing another bolt. Crossbows were being increasingly used, despite the complaints of the clergy who said they were inhuman devices, only to be used against devils and infidels.

Early crossbowmen used the muscles of their arms (above) and the more powerful leg muscles (below) to pull the cord over the nut and bend the bow. (An alternative method, winching the cord back with a cranequin was introduced later.)

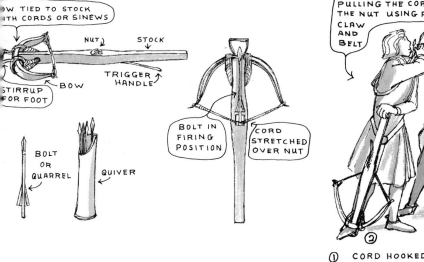

...w tied to stock ...ith cords or sinews

Nut

Stock

Trigger handle

Bow

Stirrup for foot

Bolt or quarrel

Quiver

Bolt in firing position

Cord stretched over nut

Pulling the cord over the nut using a claw and belt

① Cord hooked over claw, foot in stirrup

② Standing up and straightening leg pulls cord over nut

③ Bolt ready to fire

Trebuchets were giant slings, like the ancient hand slings that were still in use. The stone was put in a net, swung round and released as the tail of the net slipped off the beam end. Because the stones were so big the trebuchet needed a counter-weight. A small trebuchet could be hand operated; but a winch had to be used to haul down the beam of a giant trebuchet and raise the heavy counterweight. A stone was laid in the net on a tray of sand: when the beam was released, the counterweight fell, the beam swung up, and the stone was flung out with considerable force.

STONE

NE

GIANT TREBUCHET
IN ACTION

PULLEY

WOODEN TUB
FILLED WITH
LEAD, STONES, ETC
MADE A
COUNTERWEIGHT

POSITION
OF TREBUC
WHEN NO
IN USE

SMALL
TREBUCHET

HAND
SLING

STONE
IN
SLING

PULLEY

WINC

NORMAN
SHORT-BOW
STILL IN USE

MAN ABOUT TO
KNOCK OUT THE
PIN HOLDING THE
BEAM DOWN

MEN
BRINGING
STONES

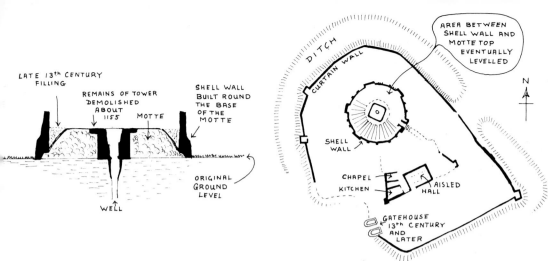

LATE 13ᵗʰ CENTURY FILLING

REMAINS OF TOWER DEMOLISHED ABOUT 1155

MOTTE

SHELL WALL BUILT ROUND THE BASE OF THE MOTTE

ORIGINAL GROUND LEVEL

WELL

DITCH

CURTAIN WALL

AREA BETWEEN SHELL WALL AND MOTTE TOP EVENTUALLY LEVELLED

N

SHELL WALL

CHAPEL

KITCHEN

AISLED HALL

GATEHOUSE 13ᵗʰ CENTURY AND LATER

A new stone-throwing machine had been invented: the *trebuchet*. Whereas existing machines had been powered by the combination of twisted skeins and springy lengths of wood, these new contraptions worked on the principle of the counterweight. They came in all sizes and were immensely popular. Small trebuchets could be worked by one man, whereas it took a gang of about twenty men to operate the giant trebuchet, which could have an arm up to fifty feet long.

War machines were used by both sides when a castle was under attack. A castle usually had one turret on the curtain wall that was made of solid masonry for a war machine to stand on. The attackers either made their machines on the spot, chopping down near-by trees and using the green wood,

At Farnham in the late 12th century, after Bishop Henry's tower had been torn down, a shell wall was built at ground level, enclosing the motte (see page 80). The towers were like the ones at Framlingham, but they were solid up to the level of the motte top. The upper parts of the towers have been demolished.

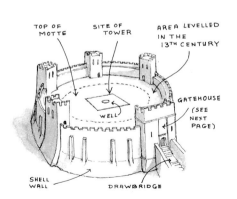

TOP OF MOTTE

SITE OF TOWER

AREA LEVELLED IN THE 13ᵗʰ CENTURY

GATEHOUSE (SEE NEXT PAGE)

WELL

SHELL WALL

DRAWBRIDGE

MURDER HOLE

PORTCULLIS GROOVE

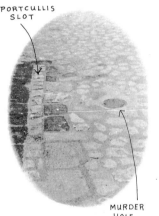

PORTCULLIS SLOT

MURDER HOLE

The top and bottom photographs are of Farnham gatehouse looking up the entrance passage. The middle photograph shows the floor of the guard-room over the passage, with the murder-hole and portcullis slot, which has been filled in.

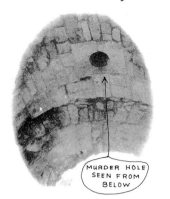

MURDER HOLE SEEN FROM BELOW

or they dismantled the machines, mounted them on slow-moving ox waggons, and carted them along the muddy tracks from one place to the next.

The exact date is not known, but it must have been about this time, late in the reign of Henry II, that the castle was refortified at Farnham. As mentioned before, the castle had been slighted and left with the chopped-off tower buried inside the motte. They now built a high shell wall with four turrets and a gatehouse, starting at ground level round the outside of the motte. The gap inside, between the shell wall and the motte, was not filled in until some time at the end of the thirteenth century. Three flights of steps were built against the inner-bailey wall and led over a drawbridge and into the gatehouse where there is a bar-hole, where a bar was slotted across the back of the door, and a portcullis groove. The blocked gap in the floor of the room over the passage shows where the portcullis was suspended and there is a circular murder-hole – sometimes called a *meurtrière* – through which the defenders could pour water to put out any fires that had been lit, or poke their weapons and drop missiles on the heads of any of the enemy who had got as far as entering the passage below.

Although Henry II's master masons were experimenting with new shapes like the keep at Orford and an octagonal keep built about 1171 at Chilham in Kent, his barons were conservative and the vast majority of keeps built during his reign were of the traditional square pattern. However, the standard of workmanship was higher than before: walls tended to be faced with ashlar instead of rubble, and the decorations round doors and windows were more delicately carved. Increasing numbers of small private chambers were being built into the thick outer walls. Massive keeps such as Kenilworth, Warwickshire (see pages 124–5), and Scarborough, North Yorkshire, belong to this period. Old buildings were altered and improved. But the largest and most spectacular square keep of them all was perched on top of the chalk cliff at Dover.

This important site, guarding the entrance to England, had been used ever since Iron Age men dug the first banks and ditches. Then the Romans put a couple of lighthouses on each side of the harbour: one inside the Iron Age fort and the other on the opposite cliff. Anglo-Saxon huts were built inside the banks of the fort, forming a small town and clustering round their church and the remains of the lighthouse, which can both still be seen. King Harold either strengthened the town defences, or meant to do so, and, after Harold's death at Hastings, the victorious William I spent eight days at Dover, improving whatever banks and ditches he found there. And so matters rested until Henry II set his masons to work in 1168.

The keep, which was a hall keep, was built first, divided as usual by a cross-wall into hall and chamber, while the thick outer walls gave plenty of space for snug private rooms and deep window recesses. Unfortunately, the building was altered and spoilt when a solid artillery platform was built on the roof in the eighteenth century.

ROMAN LIGHTHOUSE

SAXON CHURCH

DITCHES ROUND IRON AGE FORT

LEVEL GROUND

SAXON CHURCH

ROMAN LIGHTHOUSE

STEEP HILLSIDE

BEACH

ENGLISH CHANNEL

FOREBUILDING

LATRINES IN THIS BUTTRESS

ROOF 1800

15TH CENTURY WINDOWS

LATRINE VENT

This is a photograph of the back of Dover keep, which was altered several times. The windows are mostly late 15th century. In 1800 the roof was made into a gun platform by putting brick vaulting over the hall and chamber.

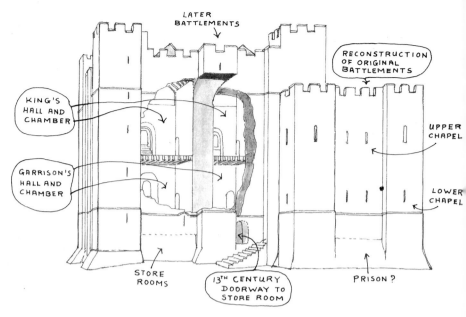

LATER BATTLEMENTS

RECONSTRUCTION OF ORIGINAL BATTLEMENTS

KING'S HALL AND CHAMBER

UPPER CHAPEL

GARRISON'S HALL AND CHAMBER

LOWER CHAPEL

STORE ROOMS

13TH CENTURY DOORWAY TO STORE ROOM

PRISON?

The forebuilding occupies the whole of the east face of Dover keep. The steps originally ran straight up the south side, turned inside the entrance door, crossed a drawbridge, and continued up to the second floor. The immensely thick walls gave ample space for small sleeping chambers. The latrines were grouped in the north wall with the main drain in the middle: the arch of the drain can be seen from outside.

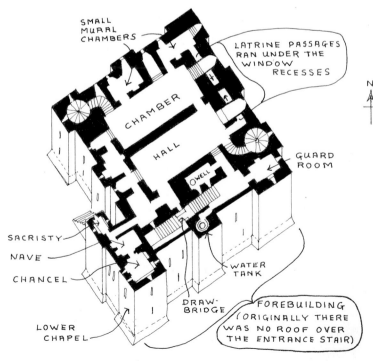

SMALL MURAL CHAMBERS

LATRINE PASSAGES RAN UNDER THE WINDOW RECESSES

N

CHAMBER

HALL

GUARD ROOM

WELL

SACRISTY

NAVE

CHANCEL

WATER TANK

LOWER CHAPEL

DRAW-BRIDGE

FOREBUILDING (ORIGINALLY THERE WAS NO ROOF OVER THE ENTRANCE STAIR)

The two chapels, with their highly decorated round-headed windows, show off the work of talented masons, and the columns are more delicately carved than the ones belonging to the earlier part of the century. The mixture of round and pointed arches in the graceful upper chapel clearly shows that the building belongs to the Transitional period.

Plumbing was excellent at Dover. The well came right up to the state apartments on the second floor and traces of lead piping show the water was partially laid on, a water cistern being fitted into the middle turret. Latrines were grouped together in the north wall and there is a cunning arrangement of latrine passages on the second floor, passing under the steps leading up to the high level of the window.

Although the keep was square and traditional, there was something new about the castle as a whole. The usual plan, as at Ludlow, for example, had been to have the inner and outer bailey alongside each other; but at Dover the inner bailey was placed right inside the outer bailey, which protected it right round the circuit of the walls. (The reason for this is explained later, on page 125.)

As at Framlingham, the inner curtain at Dover was defended every few yards by tall square projecting towers; but there was yet another improvement. The gatehouses to the north and south of the inner bailey at Dover consist of two towers placed close together, with the passage running between them – the first twin gatehouses in England. Both gatehouses were defended by substantial barbicans (as mentioned before, a

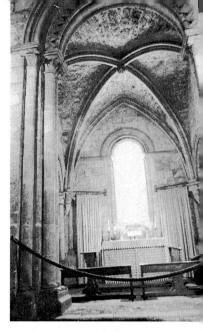

In the upper chapel clusters of slender pillars sprout stiff-leafed capitals and support round arches with the usual zigzag ornament. The chapel is covered with pointed groined vaulting – the groins (edges) covered with stone ribs. The lower chapel is very small, but equally beautiful. The window lit the altar from the right. Both chapels show the mixture of pointed and rounded shapes of the Transitional Period.

South Gate

Site of Barbican

Dover Castle was built inside the ramparts of the Iron Age fort. There are no traces of King Harold's defences, and the church and Roman lighthouse, which was used as the bell tower, are all that remain of the Saxon town. The keep was begun in 1181. The inner curtain wall was built round it in 1185, with twin-towered gatehouses defended by barbicans. The outer curtain was started in the time of Henry II but he died before it was finished. All the towers were square apart from the five-sided Avranches Tower with three arrow-loops on each face at two levels.

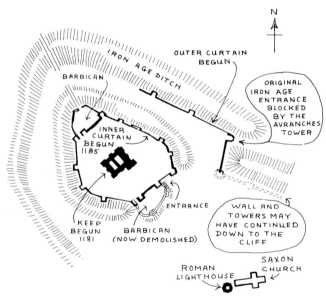

N

IRON AGE DITCH

BARBICAN

OUTER CURTAIN BEGUN

ORIGINAL IRON AGE ENTRANCE BLOCKED BY THE AVRANCHES TOWER

INNER CURTAIN BEGUN 1185

ENTRANCE

WALL AND TOWERS MAY HAVE CONTINUED DOWN TO THE CLIFF

KEEP BEGUN 1181

BARBICAN (NOW DEMOLISHED)

ROMAN LIGHTHOUSE

SAXON CHURCH

ALL THE TOWERS WERE ORIGINALLY TALLER

NORTH GATE

BARBICAN

barbican is an outwork of any kind, built to defend an entrance), and the north barbican is still standing. This is a
small walled enclosure and it was built in such a way that the
enemy host, rushing through the first gate, was forced to turn
and present a wider target as they ran past the archers sta-
tioned on the walls and towers, before storming the main gate.

By now, a castle's defences had become so efficient that it
was almost impossible to take it, except by starving the garrison into submission, threatening to hang an important hostage, or refusing to feed him if the keys were not handed over.
Blackmail was as good a weapon as any.

Castles built in England were likely to be copied to a greater
or lesser extent in Scotland and Wales; but it was only late in
the reign of Henry II that Ireland came directly under the
influence of the Normans.

Throughout the Dark Ages, Ireland had been split into
many kingdoms which fought against each other and against
the Viking invaders. Then, in 1166, the Irish king, Dermot
of Leinster, ran off with another king's wife and, in the quarrel that followed, invited a Norman baron, Richard de Clare,
nicknamed Strongbow, to help him. Strongbow arrived in
Ireland in 1170, married King Dermot's daughter and brought
with him the Norman system of castle building. Henry II
himself came to Ireland in 1172, in order to see what his vassal
Strongbow was up to. He intended to take the country over
and make it part of England and many Norman barons followed in his wake. The Irish warriors, who scorned wearing

*The huge keep at Trim,
County Meath, was built sometime between 1190 and 1220.
It is of the traditional square
pattern; but without any mural
chambers – as at Dover – and
extra rooms were added by
tacking them on to each face in
projecting blocks. The photograph
shows the entrance doorway in
the east block and the north
side of the keep where the
block has been destroyed.*

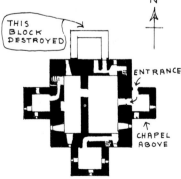

This couple wandering round the ruins of Hamelin's hall and chamber are in late 12th-century dress and look very much alike with their fur-lined cloaks, short embroidered gowns and long flowing undergarments.

3RD FLOOR

2ND FLOOR

armour and fought in linen shirts, were no match for the mailed knights, and the princes submitted to King Henry.

The Irish kings lived in timber buildings and the king is said to have held court in a hall made rather like wicker-work, of 'peeled osiers', in the manner of the country. When the Normans settled in Ireland, they guarded their new estates with motte-and-bailey castles, rebuilding them in stone as time went by. Soon massive rectangular keeps like Trim, Meath, built between 1190 and 1200, and Carrickfergus,

Antrim, built between 1180 and 1205, were dominating the landscape. Ireland was being subdued by means of the mighty castles in the same way that England had been subdued in the time of William I.

Ireland was behind the times, but experimental, up-to-date keeps were still being built in England. The most outstanding one of these was put up at Conisbrough, South Yorkshire, between 1180 and 1190 by Hamelin Plantagenet, half-brother to Henry II. It must have been the envy of every baron in the north. The tower is cylindrical, and enemy missiles would have shied off the smooth round surface more easily than from angled stonework. Six large buttresses rise from a steeply sloping *plinth*, and this plinth was so solid that no enemy could hack his way through. At the same time, the angle of the slope meant that if the defenders dropped stones from above, the stones would bounce away into the ranks of the enemy.

Instead of having the usual stair twisting up inside one of the turrets, the stair follows the gentle curve through the thick wall of the tower itself. The two upper rooms had fire-places of a new design: with pillars supporting straight *lintels* and large hoods to take away the smoke – a style that was to become almost universal in the next century. The rooms were fitted with another luxury: wash-basins. Small basins, called *piscina*, were usual in churches for the priests to use for rinsing out the sacred vessels, and they are found in castle chapels; but they were not common elsewhere in a keep. Water was carried through lead pipes from cisterns which were built into two of the buttresses right up at the level of the battlements. Of the other buttresses, two were solid, one held an oven and the other a pigeon loft.

The top photograph shows the wash-basin in the chamber. Water was supplied from the two cisterns built into the buttresses at the top of the keep. The smaller fireplace is in the chamber while the larger one is in the hall: both are covered with a jogged lintel.

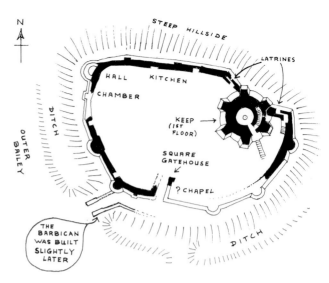

The tall round towers defending the inner bailey were solid up to the wall-walk and could not easily be undermined. Enemy missiles would ricochet off their curved surfaces while stones dropped by the defenders would bounce away from the sloping plinth into the ranks of the hostile force climbing up from the ditch.

By now, a keep was more likely to be used as an emergency stronghold than as a place to live in. Hamelin Plantagenet and his wife would have occupied the hall and chamber down in the bailey. The castle was strongly defended with a long narrow barbican (of a slightly later date) leading up to the gatehouse, and the towers on the curtain wall were solid up to the wall-walk, and round instead of square – a successful new development. There were to be many round-fronted, or *D-shaped* mural towers in the century to come.

7 THE RISE OF THE GATEHOUSE AND DECLINE OF THE KEEP

KING HENRY DIED AT CHINON IN 1189, HIS HEART broken by the behaviour of his rebellious sons. He had ordered a decoration to be painted in his chamber at Winchester Castle showing an eagle being attacked by its fledgelings, because that was how he felt about his own offspring. His third son, the warlike Richard I, inherited the throne; but he came to England only to raise money for his Crusade and concentrated his building energies on planning his masterpiece, Chateau Gaillard, on the frontier of Normandy. While he was away the regent, Longchamps, the unpopular Bishop of Ely, built a new wall round the Tower of London; of this, part of the south wall and the tower overlooking the river at the southwest angle, now called the Bell Tower, still stand.

While King Richard and his knights were battling against Saladin under the hot desert sun, English masons were chip-

THE BELL TOWER HAS AN OCTAGONAL BASE

Richard's seal shows him wearing a new type of helmet which covered his face and had a crest on top to show who he was. Later his shield was decorated with three gold lions on a red ground, which became the arms of England.

101

ROOF
ORNAMENT

CARVED
CAPITAL

ping away at stones for less-royal buildings About 1190 a hall was built in the bailey of an old motte-and-bailey castle at Oakham in Leicestershire. The motte was abandoned, leaving the castle defended by a timber palisade or perhaps a stone wall. It is not much of a castle, but the hall is one of the finest Transitional buildings in England.

The majority of halls at this time were still timber; some thatched with reeds or straw, and others covered with oak shingles. Oakham being in a stony district, the hall is built of stone and was roofed with stone tiles. The little figures at the gable-ends echo the carvings which must have sprouted from the roof of many an old vanished timber hall.

Inside, Oakham Hall is divided into four bays by magnificent pillars, and the side aisles make it look like a church. The entrance doorway has been moved from its original position at the screens end and the three doorways leading to the pantry, kitchen and buttery are – as always – in the end wall. An upper doorway shows where wooden steps probably led to the great chamber above these rooms. Foundations of the pantry, buttery and the kitchen passage between them have been discovered; but there is not enough evidence to show how the vanished chamber-block was built.

Oakham Castle hall belongs to the Transitional Period. The entrance doorway has a round Romanesque arch, but the windows are pointed Gothic shapes: a true mixture of styles. Ever since Norman times it has been the custom for noblemen passing through Oakham to donate horseshoes to the castle in honour of the original builder: Henry de Ferrers. (His name means a worker in iron.) This accounts for the huge horseshoes hanging on the walls.

TO THE
BUTTERY FOR
MORE WINE

TO THE KITCHEN
FOR MORE MEAT

TO THE
PANTRY FOR
MORE BREAD

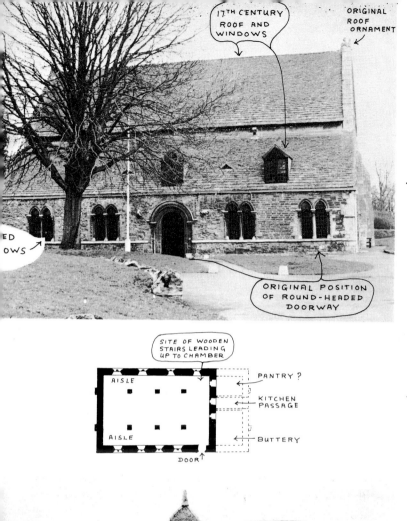

17TH CENTURY ROOF AND WINDOWS

ORIGINAL ROOF ORNAMENT

...ED OWS

ORIGINAL POSITION OF ROUND-HEADED DOORWAY

A description of 1340 says: 'The castle is walled . . . within a hall, four chambers, a chapel, a kitchen, two stables, a grange for hay, a house for a prison, a chamber for the gamekeeper and a drawbridge with iron chains.' Apart from the hall, all these buildings have now disappeared. There are traces of the rooms built against the end of the hall, but there is not enough information for me to be able to draw the chamber block. Although the bailey had a wall round it by the 14th century, it may originally have had a palisade.

SITE OF WOODEN STAIRS LEADING UP TO CHAMBER

AISLE

AISLE

PANTRY ?

KITCHEN PASSAGE

BUTTERY

DOOR

THE CHAMBER WAS OVER THE BUTTERY AND PANTRY

THIS WINDOW WAS ORIGINALLY CIRCULAR

LATER WINDOW

BLOCKED UPPER AND LOWER DOORWAYS

BUTTERY?   KITCHEN PASSAGE?   PANTRY?

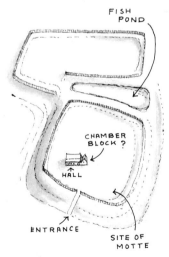

FISH POND

CHAMBER BLOCK ?

HALL

ENTRANCE

SITE OF MOTTE

KING JOHN USED ODIHAM CASTLE AS A HUNTING LODGE

Odiham Castle was built on low-lying land by a river between 1207 and 1212. The only part still standing is the keep – an octagonal tower with a store-room at ground-floor level and two rooms above. In 1216, when King John was at war with his barons, a tiny force of thirteen men defended the castle against Louis of France for eight days.

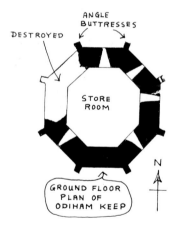

ANGLE BUTTRESSES

DESTROYED

STORE ROOM

N

GROUND FLOOR PLAN OF ODIHAM KEEP

King Richard was killed by a chance crossbow bolt outside Châlus Castle on the borders of Aquitaine, and his brother, John, elbowed his nephew Arthur aside to take the English throne. John was not liked and his highly suspicious nature never allowed him to trust anyone, not even his most loyal servants, so he needed the protection of strong castles. In fact, he managed to spend even more money on castle building than his father, Henry II – quite a record. Unfortunately, there is little left to show for it. The king had about ninety-five castles to keep in repair and most of the money went on maintenance: strengthening curtain walls and adding round or many-sided towers. John built himself four new castles, but only the wreck of Odiham in Hampshire survives, which gives little idea of what the original building looked like.

By 1204 John's possessions in Normandy had fallen to the French king, Philip Augustus, and he had to make do with his lands in England. One of his favourite residences was the high, windy stronghold of Corfe Castle, Dorset, where he kept his regalia, treasure and state prisoners. A stretch of wall, built with herringbone work and pierced with three round-headed window recesses, shows where an early hall once stood, built sometime before 1100; while the inner-bailey wall, enclosing the top of the hill, also belongs to this period. The huge keep, with a blind arcade decorating the upper part of the outer walls, was built before 1139. King John added a stout eight-sided tower – on the same lines as the Bell Tower in the Tower of London – and two D-shaped

KEEP

JOHN'S
HALL

JOHN'S
DITCH

LATRINES

MIDDLE
GATE
c1244

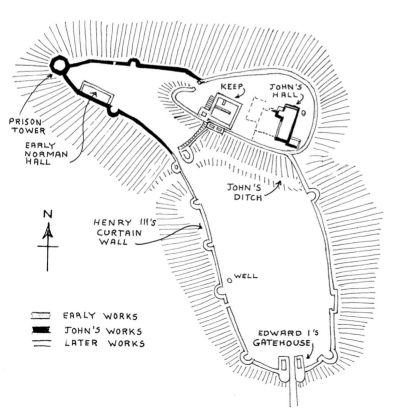

KEEP

JOHN'S
HALL

PRISON
TOWER

EARLY
NORMAN
HALL

N

HENRY III'S
CURTAIN
WALL

JOHN'S
DITCH

WELL

EDWARD I'S
GATEHOUSE

EARLY WORKS
JOHN'S WORKS
LATER WORKS

A Norman hall was built on the site of Corfe Castle sometime before 1100. The square keep was standing by 1139 and when John became king in 1199 the stone defences merely enclosed the top of the hill. He built a strong tower at the corner of the west bailey and added two D-shaped towers before starting work on the royal apartments of the inner bailey. These included several chambers, a hall, chapel, constable's lodging, wine cellar, kitchen and bakery (only the hall can be identified now). After John's death, his son and grandson completed the outer defences.

John's hall at Corfe was at first-floor level, with store-rooms below. It had two entrance doors placed side by side. The half-arch on the left may have led into his chapel. The drawing of King John, below, is taken from his effigy in Worcester cathedral.

towers to the western defences, and constructed what must have been a first-rate hall, and other domestic buildings, in the inner bailey. The castle was so thoroughly blown up with gunpowder by Oliver Cromwell in 1646 that less than half of the keep is left standing and the rest of the walls lie about as great chunks of masonry. John's hall is in ruins, but the tall pointed arches over the doors and windows show that by now the Gothic shape was well and truly established.

Castles continued to be built on the same lines as before, although new gatehouses tended to be larger and the outer ditches wider and deeper. If they could be flooded with water by altering the course of a near-by stream, so much the better: a wet boggy ditch was an excellent barrier. New castles, like Odiham, would be sited on low ground by a river.

The barons would always have preferred to live in a hall out in the bailey, rather than to be boxed up inside a keep. At Dover, for example, King John built himself a hall – now vanished – which was probably situated between the inner and outer curtain wall, instead of lodging at the top of his father's great keep.

When new castles were built, the masons lavished their attentions on the outer defences and the hall and chamber, while keeps dwindled to austere round towers, built as places of refuge, not for day-to-day living. These usually had an entrance over the store-room at first-floor level, with one or two floors above that, making the building tall enough to overlook the land on the far side of the curtain wall.

The best example of this type of keep is at Pembroke, Dyfed, built about 1200 by William Marshal, one of the most experienced soldiers of his age. He is lucky to have lived long enough to become a soldier at all. When he was about seven years old his father, John the Marshal, had arranged a truce with King Stephen and handed over his young son William as a hostage to guarantee his good behaviour. John the Marshal immediately broke the truce, declaring he could always have another son and, according to the rules of warfare, young William should have been hanged forthwith. On his way to the nearest tree, William admired a javelin which was being twirled in the air and asked if he could play with it. Watching the boy's spirited behaviour, King Stephen simply had not the heart to carry out the execution and, although the barons wanted to load William on to a war machine and toss him over the wall of Newbury Castle, his life was spared. All this happened in 1152. When he grew to be a man, William Marshal became a staunch servant to Henry II, spent a couple of years fighting in Syria, acted, with his brother, as marshal at Richard's coronation. and then joined John's household before John became king. William Marshal continued to prop up the tottering throne after John's death, holding it steady for the young Henry III.

When this admirable man married the heiress to the Earl of Pembroke, he took over the title and castle, which, at that time, was hardly more than a timber stronghold perched at the end of a rocky spur jutting out into the river. William Marshal built a stone curtain wall, a hall and a keep. The keep is a tall cylindrical tower, with immensely thick walls, pierced by occasional slits at the bottom to let in light and air, and with two good windows on the upper floors. There are fireplaces but no latrines: clearly not a structure to live in, but a stronghold to defend when cornered. The marshal and his family when they stayed at Pembroke would have used the first-floor hall alongside, which must have been connected to the keep by a wall-walk because there is a doorway high up

William Marshal's effigy in the Temple Church, London, shows him wearing a cloth surcoat over his mail hauberk. Surcoats had occasionally been worn from about 1160 onwards, but they were not in general use until the beginning of the 13th century. The diagram below shows a section through William Marshal's keep at Pembroke.

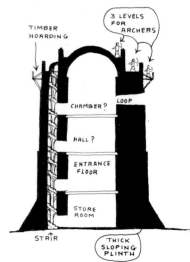

Most of the walls of Pembroke
Castle are of a later date, but
William Marshal's hall and
the keep were built about 1200
and still stand in the inner
bailey. It was roughly at this
time that knights' helmets were
fitted with face guards, with
slits to see through. Like
Richard I, some knights added a
crest to the top of their helmet
to show who they were.

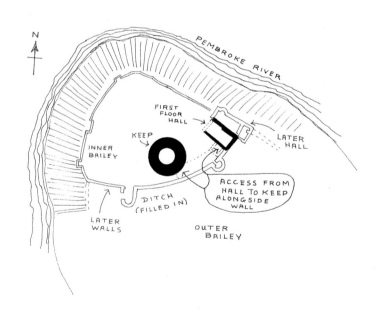

N

PEMBROKE RIVER

FIRST
FLOOR
HALL

LATER
HALL

KEEP

INNER
BAILEY

ACCESS FROM
HALL TO KEEP
ALONGSIDE
WALL

DITCH
(FILLED IN)

LATER
WALLS

OUTER
BAILEY

on the second floor. There is a stone dome to the top of the keep, with a fighting platform right up at the summit; another at the level of the battlements; and beam holes show where timber hoarding once jutted outside the keep – three fighting platforms in all, where archers could run round the circuit and shoot over each other's heads.

As keeps became smaller, so the outer defences had to be strengthened. The men of the garrison wanted to be able to shelter behind thick walls and at the same time harry the enemy, so the round, D-shaped, or many-sided towers were built to jut right out from the curtain wall. Some of these were almost as tall and solid as a keep.

King John often stayed at Kenilworth, where he built an outer curtain wall which ended in two massive towers at the vulnerable north corners. The square Swan Tower has crumbled away, but Lunn's Tower shows how impressive these mural towers could be. The ground-level guard-room is fitted with the very long arrow-loops which are typical of this time. There are two fair-sized living-rooms above, which are both equipped with fireplaces and latrines. A good enough lodging for a constable or a visiting nobleman.

John's rule ended in revolt and bloody civil war. The barons invited Prince Louis of France to come to their aid and help to edge the unpopular king off the throne. It was at this time, in 1216, that Dover Castle was to prove its defences.

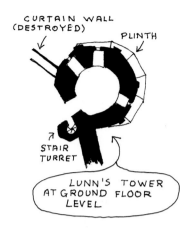

CURTAIN WALL
(DESTROYED)

PLINTH

STAIR
TURRET

LUNN'S TOWER
AT GROUND FLOOR
LEVEL

King John rebuilt the outer walls at Kenilworth with two stout towers (see page 111). Lunn's Tower had two chambers over the guard-room, which was fitted with long cross-shaped arrow-loops specially designed for crossbows. They allowed a sweeping range from left to right as well as a downward line of fire into the ditch.

STAIR
TURRET

LONG
CROSS-SHAPED
ARROW LOOP

UPPER
CHAMBER

FIREPLACE

LOWER
CHAMBER

GUARD
ROOM

STAIR
TURRET

MOST OF THE D-SHAPED TOWERS WERE CUT DOWN LATER AND USED AS GUN PLATFORMS

When Dover Castle was rebuilt after the siege of 1216, it was virtually impossible for an enemy to get into it. But two posterns were added to the north and east which had underground passages and gave the garrison the chance of making surprise sorties. The north passage ran through the first-floor room of the St John tower, standing at the ditch bottom.

ST JOHN TOWER ↓

The English coast had become the front line after the loss of Normandy, and King John had taken the precaution of completing the outer curtain at Dover, which his father had left half built. John's section of wall was defended by D-shaped towers, which had now become the standard shape. The gatehouse defending the north entrance was probably built as a pair of large D-shaped towers on either side of the passage. Louis of France brought up his army, laid siege to Dover Castle, and gave the outer walls a terrific battering with his war machines. After that, he undermined one of the towers of John's new north gatehouse and brought it crashing to the ground. Hubert de Burgh, in charge of the garrison, heroically held the breach, blocking up the gap with beams and urging his men to carry on the defence with sword and spear. The castle never surrendered; but it had been a near thing.

King John died suddenly at Newark Castle, and between them, William Marshal, Hubert de Burgh and others managed to drive out the French invaders and defend the crown until such time as the nine-year-old Henry III, John's son, was old enough to wear it. When Hubert de Burgh became regent after the death of William Marshal, he decided that the defences at Dover should never be cracked again. The wrecked gateway was completely blocked with three solid towers and a new gateway was inserted in the west curtain wall. The Constable's Tower, built between 1221 and 1227, is one of the most massive gateways in England. Guard-rooms stood on either side of the passage at ground level and the constable's suite of rooms was directly above. These apartments were sealed off from the rest of the building, and for a good reason. In those treacherous times, when foreign mercenaries were often employed and even a baron's own knights and men-at-arms could turn against him, it was well for a constable to take precautions against revolt from within as well as from without.

There were still timber castles about, even at the start of the thirteenth century. Hubert de Burgh came into possession

110

ALSO LATER ADDITION

TOP FLOOR WAS ADDED LATER

ENTRANCE

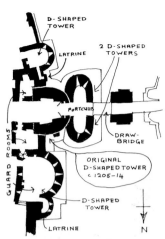

D-SHAPED TOWER

LATRINE

2 D-SHAPED TOWERS

PORTCULLIS

GUARD ROOMS

DRAW-BRIDGE

ORIGINAL D-SHAPED TOWER c 1205-14

D-SHAPED TOWER

LATRINE

N

One of King John's D-shaped towers, with the passage driven through the middle of it, is at the core of the Constable's Gate. Two similar towers, placed back-to-back, were added in front of the entrance doorway, and two more were tacked on at the north and south sides, making five D-shaped towers in all.

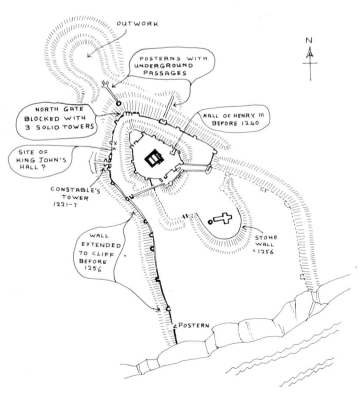

OUTWORK

POSTERNS WITH UNDERGROUND PASSAGES

N

NORTH GATE BLOCKED WITH 3 SOLID TOWERS

HALL OF HENRY III BEFORE 1240

SITE OF KING JOHN'S HALL?

CONSTABLE'S TOWER 1221-7

WALL EXTENDED TO CLIFF BEFORE 1256

STONE WALL c 1256

POSTERN

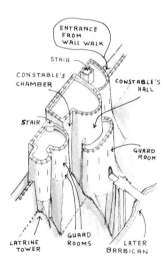

ENTRANCE FROM WALL WALK

STAIR

CONSTABLE'S CHAMBER

CONSTABLE'S HALL

STAIR

GUARD ROOM

LATRINE TOWER

GUARD ROOMS

LATER BARBICAN

At Skenfrith the curtain wall with its four round corner-towers, was built on level ground beside the little river Monnow. Soil from the ditch was carted inside the walls, making the bailey higher than the surrounding land. When the keep was built inside the bailey, more soil was heaped round its foundations, making it seem to stand on a mound. (The keep had to be considerably taller than the curtain wall.) Finally, the castle was white-washed and timber hoardings were fixed along the outer walls.

of a timber castle at Skenfrith, Gwent, and, sometime before his fall from favour in 1232 – and being one of the richest men in the land – he decided to rebuild it in stone. The keep is smaller than the one at Pembroke and consists of two floors and a basement; entered, as usual, at first-floor level. The lower parts of the hall and other domestic buildings are still standing, as well as the high curtain wall, with its round corner-towers. The entire castle was finished off with a layer of plaster and whitewash, as was the neighbouring White Castle, also in Gwent (sometimes called by the earlier name of Llantilio).

All in all, the first half of the thirteenth century found castle design at a low ebb: wide ditches; round keeps; round, D-shaped, or many-sided mural towers, with long arrow-loops; being the distinctive features. Shell keeps had only just gone out of fashion, and the new round keeps are occasionally found

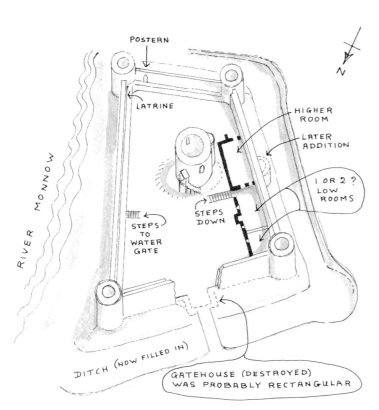

POSTERN

LATRINE

RIVER MONNOW

HIGHER ROOM

LATER ADDITION

1 OR 2? LOW ROOMS

STEPS TO WATER GATE

STEPS DOWN

N

DITCH (NOW FILLED IN)

GATEHOUSE (DESTROYED) WAS PROBABLY RECTANGULAR

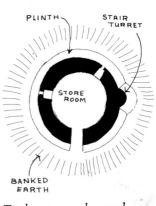

PLINTH

STAIR TURRET

STORE ROOM

BANKED EARTH

Timber steps and a porch once led to the first-floor doorway into the keep. The ground-floor entrance to the store-room is unusual, weakening the defences. As for the buildings alongside the west wall, the hall and chamber must have been on the first floor; while the existing damp rooms at the original ground level would have been used for stores.

2ND FLOOR WINDOW

LIVING QUARTERS BUILT UP AGAINST WEST WALL

BEAM HOLES FOR WOODEN PORCH

STAIR TURRET

1ST FLOOR DOORWAY

STORE ROOM DOORWAY

LATER WALL?

Tretower was a motte-and-bailey castle and by the mid 12th century a shell wall had been built round the low motte, with a first-floor hall and chamber, and a ground-floor kitchen within. About 1230 the domestic buildings were torn down to make room for the tall round tower, and the old shell wall was used as an extra defence.

on top of the early mottes which, by now, had been given plenty of time to harden. At Launceston, Cornwall, for example, the round tower is placed inside the old shell wall: one circle enclosed by another. An alternative, rather makeshift, arrangement was at Tretower Castle, Powys, where a twelfth-century hall and chamber had been built across the top of the motte, defended by a high wall and entered through a square gatehouse. Some of the buildings were partly torn down to make room for a tall round tower which was erected in the middle of the enclosure.

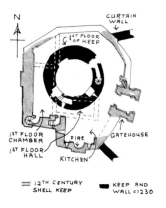

So much for the defences of early-thirteenth-century castles, but what about the people who lived in them? The descendants of the rough-and-ready warriors who came over with William I were becoming highly civilized. They enjoyed living with their wives and families in well-designed houses and loved above all things to listen to a good story. Here is an excerpt from a typical French romance, *The Lay of the Reflection*, which gives a good description of the clothes that people wore at that time. A handsome knight and his company are paying a visit to a beautiful (and married) lady.

114

With their horses under bit and spur they cantered to the fortress, passing through a new outer bailey enclosed with palisades and ditches. The knight had thrown back his cloak off his chest, as also his rich surcoat of scarlet silk trimmed with ermine and squirrel. They all had similar garments, and were wearing white pleated shirts besides, and chaplets of periwinkles and other flowers, and red-gold spurs to boot. I do not know how they could have been more elegantly dressed for a summer's day. They never drew rein until they came to the mounting block before the hall. The squires, well trained, jumped down one to each stirrup. The steward of the house saw them dismount in the courtyard: he ran from the gallery where he was standing to inform his mistress that the man she knew so well from hearsay was coming to call on her. The lady certainly did not redden with annoyance, she was, however, greatly amazed. She had been having her hair plaited, seated on a bright red cushion, and now this beautiful creature rose to her feet. Her maidens threw a silk cloak round her shoulders, enhancing the wondrous beauty that Nature, according to report, had already endowed her with. Although she wanted to go to meet them, they, for their part, made such haste towards her that they had already entered the chamber before she had time to leave it. It appeared from her manner in greeting them that their coming pleased her: as for them, they were more than happy that she had come even so short a distance to meet them. This gracious and estimable lady was wearing a filmy white gown which trailed behind her more than a yard's length on the fine rushes. (*Aucassin and Nicolette and Other Tales*, Penguin, p. 68.)

PLAITED HAIR
SQUIRREL CUFFS
PERIWINKLES
SHIRT
CLOAK
SILK CLOAK
ERMINE-LINED SURCOAT
GOLD SPURS

Clothes were getting more sophisticated and difficult to move about in: cloaks were often carefully draped and tucked under the elbows. Married women either wore their hair hidden under a veil or covered by a wide band of white linen: young girls wore their hair loose. Everyone enjoyed wearing chaplets of flowers.

KNIGHTS ON ACTIVE SERVICE SWAPPING STORIES

GOTHIC ARCHES AND PAINTED CHAMBERS

HENRY III SHOULD HAVE BEEN AN ARCHITECT INSTEAD of a king: he had a passion for building and was never happy unless he was planning the details of one of his houses or churches. Castles did not interest him as much. The great achievement of his reign was the rebuilding of Westminster Abbey. He had a happy family life and was fastidious about the places he lived in, hating bad smells and slovenly habits. Streams of precise orders were sent to his agents, telling them what to do.

> Since the privy chamber of our wardrobe in London is situated in an undue and improper place, wherefore it smells badly, we command you on the faith and love by which you are bounden to us, that you in no wise omit to cause another privy chamber to be made in the same wardrobe in such more fitting and proper place that you may select there, even though it should cost a hundred pounds. (Close Roll 30 Henry III.)

A *wardrobe* was a convenient little room next to the great chamber and it usually had a latrine beyond. Wardrobes were changing-rooms and store-rooms for clothes, which were often hung over rods that were fixed to the walls like towel rails; rich silks and furs would lie carefully folded in great chests. Alternatively, a confidential clerk might be found in a wardrobe sitting at a desk, quill in hand, hard at work writing letters on parchment to his lord's dictation.

HENRY III TALKING TO HIS MASTER OF THE WORKS

LARGE COMPASS

HORSE LITTER

BECAUSE OF THE BAD ROADS MOST PEOPLE TRAVELLED ON HORSEBACK

WOMEN RODE ASTRIDE AND SIDESADDLE

The court was often at Winchester, Hampshire, the ancient capital of England. The city had two castles: one by the abbey for the bishop, the other up the hill for the king. The royal castle had been heavily battered by Louis of France and needed repairing. In 1222, when Henry was a lad of fifteen, the old hall was almost completely pulled down and rebuilt and, although the rest of this important castle has vanished, it still stands in splendid condition. It is a ground-floor aisled hall, with clustered pillars to support the roof and tall windows with the new *quatrefoil* heads: all entirely in the *Early English* style. As explained on page 82, *Gothic* is the general term used to describe the variety of buildings put up in western Europe between the twelfth and fifteenth centuries which used the pointed arch. Early English refers to the style of Gothic architecture which flourished in England from about 1200 to 1307 (see the chart at the end of the book).

Winchester hall was modernized in the reign of Richard II: the pitch of the roof was lowered, the little window gables were taken away, and the wall carried up to a straight parapet. The large doorway in the centre of the building is Victorian, the two original entrances were to the left. Everybody travelled on horseback (or on foot) and carriages and litters like these were used only by those who were ill or very old.

LITTLE GABLES OVER THE WINDOWS

THESE STONE CIRCLES ARE NOW BUILT INTO THE INSIDE WALLS

THE HALL WOULD HAVE LOOKED LIKE THIS

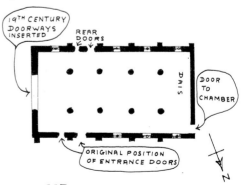

19TH CENTURY DOORWAYS INSERTED

REAR DOORS

DAIS

DOOR TO CHAMBER

ORIGINAL POSITION OF ENTRANCE DOORS

N

The pointed stone archways taking the weight of the roof were supported by these magnificent pillars of purbeck marble. The steeper line of the original roof can still be seen in the stonework of the east wall (not shown here) and the timber beams were carved and gilded.

Henry's busy clerks noted down every item bought and every penny spent in their careful accounts, and so we know how the hall was decorated. It was plastered, covered with whitewash, and *wainscoted*. Wainscot was a wooden boarding which covered the lower part of the wall and this was often decorated with paintings. A painted 'wheel of fortune' graced the area over the dais and a map of the world (wildly inaccurate to our eyes) was depicted on one of the other walls. Medieval people were fond of looking at pictures which had a strong moral slant or which illustrated parts of the Bible. Although glass was extremely expensive and usually reserved for churches, it was fitted to the windows; while the king's arms were painted on the wooden shutters.

Castles were crammed full of assorted buildings. At Winchester there was a bishop's chamber and a knight's chamber, the steward's chamber and a chamber for the king's chaplains. Then there needed to be accommodation for the host of scribbling clerks: the medieval civil service. These were housed in the king's *great wardrobe*, a place which had grown out of the little room next to his chamber, and was now under a separate roof. The king would have had another wardrobe where he could change his clothes and hang up his cloak. Henry III was a devout person and so there were numerous chapels. Then there was also a new kitchen and a buttery, and there must have been many smaller places which are not mentioned in the accounts. Perhaps the 'houses for the king's birds', built in the reign of Henry II, were still standing.

Buildings such as these were often linked together by a covered passage called a *pentice* or *penthouse*. 'Pent' means a slope, and so if the passage ran alongside a wall, the roof would slope up against it. A single-storey pentice could keep the rain off the food as it was carried from the kitchen to the passage leading into the hall, or a two-tiered pentice could be built from the queen's first-floor chamber to her secluded gallery in the chapel, so that she could walk to her devotions without having to go downstairs.

Winchester being a royal castle, it had to defend not only the king and his household, but his councillors, lawyers and clerks as well. It was the centre of the administration and also contained the deeds and records. When the king moved from one castle to the next, he carried this huge government staff with him. The castle of a great lord would have a similar function, but on a smaller scale. It was the seat of local government where courts were held, cases judged, and where the official documents were kept. The keep was used as a strong-room and contained the barrels of little silver pennies (some cut in half to make half-pennies) which had been taken from the king's tenants and were waiting to be picked up by the treasury officials on the king's next royal progress. Weapons would be stored inside the keep, and gold ornaments hoarded in chests, ready to be melted down and turned into ready cash if necessary. In time of war, fortunes could be made when important barons were captured and held prisoner – usually in a fair degree of comfort – until the huge ransoms were paid.

The hall is huge. The stone circle set high in the far wall is one of the ones that were placed in the gables over the windows. In the time of Henry III the floor was paved with earthenware tiles. This picture shows the kind of clothes people wore when attending the king's court. Musicians are playing at the head of the procession.

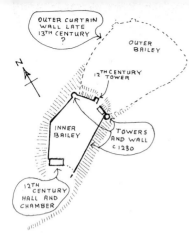

A castle was built at Manorbier in the 12th century, with a first-floor hall in the inner bailey and a small square tower defending the entrance. By 1230 the inner bailey was strengthened by a curtain wall, a stout round tower, and a small semicircular tower. It is thought that the outer bailey was walled in the late 13th century.

The early years of Henry's long reign were peaceful enough. He married Eleanor of Provence in 1236 and spent happy days watching the growth of Westminster Abbey and planning the details of a comfortable domestic range of buildings inside the Tower of London, just south of Gundulf's keep. There was even a private zoo which included an elephant – a present which was given to Henry by his brother-in-law, Louis IX – and the animals were housed on the south-west side of the castle. All these new buildings have been destroyed right down to the foundation stones; but the living-quarters in other, less important, castles have managed to survive better.

Manorbier Castle, Dyfed, tucked away in the south-west corner of Wales, gives a clear picture of the way people lived in the middle of the thirteenth century. A castle of this modest size was more likely to have a first-floor hall than a huge aisled hall like the one at Winchester. The hall at Manorbier had been built in the twelfth century; it was raised up over store-rooms and had a great chamber at a slightly higher level alongside, which gave space for a dark buttery to be sand-

GOODS WERE TRANSPORTED BY CART, PACKHORSE, MULE OR DONKEY

wiched between the chamber above and the store-room below.

As the thirteenth century got under way, so the domestic arrangements in the castle were gradually brought up to date. A chapel was built, in a haphazard way, at an odd angle to the curtain wall. Then, sometime after 1260, a new chamber block was squeezed into the space between the old hall and the chapel, so that the lord and his family could live further away from the noise, bustle, and smells of the kitchen quarters. Changing the position of the great chamber from the screens

The visitors arriving at Manorbier Castle, hawking on the way, are just about to enter the inner bailey, trotting over the drawbridge and under the portcullis. The gatehouse was not added until the end of the 13th century, and the constable would have lived in the room over the passage. The strong round tower to the left had replaced the old square tower as the main defence. The courtyard side of the first-floor hall and chamber is at left. (Plan overleaf.)

OLD 12TH CENTURY CHAMBER

BUTTERY

STAIR TURRET

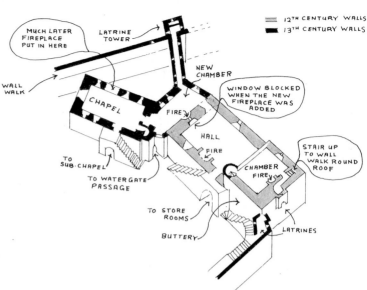

MUCH LATER FIREPLACE PUT IN HERE

LATRINE TOWER

12TH CENTURY WALLS
13TH CENTURY WALLS

NEW CHAMBER

WALL WALK

CHAPEL

WINDOW BLOCKED WHEN THE NEW FIREPLACE WAS ADDED

FIRE

HALL

FIRE

TO SUB-CHAPEL

TO WATER GATE PASSAGE

STAIR UP TO WALL WALK ROUND ROOF

CHAMBER FIRE

TO STORE ROOMS

BUTTERY

LATRINES

The dividing wall has gone, and the old chamber can now be seen from the hall. A spiral stair rising from the store-room to the hall and chamber was added in the 13th century. The new chamber block of two rooms over the passage was squeezed between the hall and the chapel.

WATCH TOWER

NEW CHAMBERS

CHAPEL

ENTRANCE TO SUB CHAPEL

STAIR TO CHAPEL

WATER GATE PASSAGE

WATER BEING CARRIED FROM THE WELL

end to the dais end of the hall became fashionable in the latter half of the thirteenth century: it was done over and over again.

Even this extra accommodation was not sufficient for the family at Manorbier and a third chamber was built directly over the new one, making three chambers in all. The original latrines being situated far away on the other side of the first great chamber, a long two-tier passage was built out from the new block to a latrine tower on the curtain wall.

Manorbier shows clearly that the trends of the times were towards greater privacy for the barons, who were no longer living in their crowded halls but withdrawing more and more into their own apartments. When new chambers were added there tended to be a complete lack of symmetry in the planning. Buildings were tacked on to the corners of other buildings, overlapping by the space of a doorway to allow people to pass from one room to the next, and no one seemed to worry if the angles were not square.

This castle on the coast of Wales was far away from the events that were happening in England. About the time when the new chamber was being planned at Manorbier, the

PHERD
Y
NDING
OCK

country was seething with discontent and King Henry had to lock himself and his family in the Tower of London for safety.

The rebellion that turned the king's happy daydream into a nightmare was led by his own brother-in-law, Simon de Montfort. Henry had been criticized for having been kept under the thumb of the Pope; for having favoured his own foreign relations at the expense of the other nobles; for having

The domestic buildings seen from the south, with the roofs hidden behind the high defensive wall. The women would have been kept busy spinning, weaving and sewing; but there must have been dull moments.

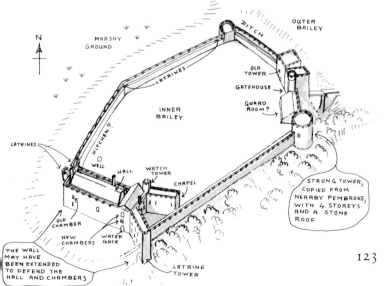

GIRL SITTING
IN THE NEW
CHAMBER OVER
THE PASSAGE

123

The upper floor of the water tower had a very pleasant chamber, sleeping-room and latrine; while the wall chamber alongside (a suitable lodging for a knight) had a chamber and latrine at ground-floor level. The doorway and windows are typical of the mid 13th century.

spent too much money on his building projects; and for neglecting the affairs of the country. After a bad harvest, widespread cattle disease, and the inevitable food shortage, the barons put forward their ideas of a reformed system of government in the Provisions of Oxford in 1258. The king reacted strongly against this and clung to his ancient rights. Louis IX of France, invited to arbitrate, upheld the king against the barons. Simon de Montfort became the champion of the rebels; he took up arms and defeated King Henry at the battle of Lewes in 1264.

When Simon had married Henry's sister, Eleanor, he had been given Kenilworth Castle as part of her dowry, and during the rebellion he used it as his headquarters.

Kenilworth probably started off early in the reign of Henry I as a motte-and-bailey castle, but there is no evidence to prove it. The property came into royal hands during the period 1155–60 when Henry II put a castellan in command, and the great square keep belongs to this period. It was greatly altered soon after, probably about 1200. As mentioned before, King John built the outer curtain wall with its two north towers. It was either in John's reign, or in the time of Simon de Montfort, that the water defences which John's engineers had found to be so effective were used on a grand scale. The castle had been built on the side of a valley which had a stream running through it; a long causeway was built right across the stream, damming it and flooding the valley with a sheet of water, while another pool was formed below. When the northeast walls were defended by a water-filled ditch, the castle virtually became an island.

So much water made the castle almost impregnable. The only vulnerable side was to the north, and this was guarded by John's pair of massive towers; no towers were needed on the stretch of wall bordering the lake, but a water tower – with a pleasant living-room on the upper floor, and another tiny chamber contrived in the thickness of the near-by wall – overlooked the lower pool.

124

Water defences, however, sometimes had their disadvantages. When Simon de Montfort's son carelessly camped outside the castle because he was too tired to complete the journey, he was suddenly attacked by Henry's son, Prince Edward (nicknamed Longshanks because of his great height). Most of the younger de Montfort's men were captured and he himself only managed to escape by swimming across the lake in his shirt.

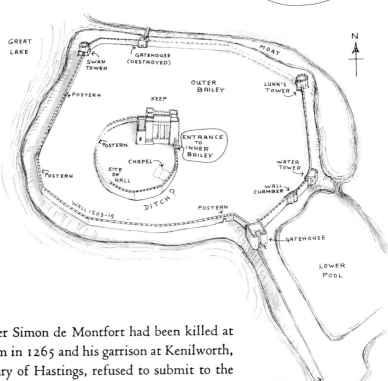

WATER TOWER
SEEN FROM THE
LOWER POOL

Throughout its long history, Kenilworth Castle was constantly strengthened and modernized; but the date when the long dam was built and the valley flooded is uncertain. The water tower, wall tower and the barbican were added in the mid 13th century.

GREAT LAKE

MOAT

N

SWAN TOWER

GATEHOUSE (DESTROYED)

POSTERN

OUTER BAILEY

LUNN'S TOWER

KEEP

POSTERN

ENTRANCE TO INNER BAILEY

CHAPEL

POSTERN

WATER TOWER

SITE OF HALL

WALL 1203-15

DITCH

WALL CHAMBER

POSTERN

GATEHOUSE

LOWER POOL

CAUSEWAY

BARBICAN DEFENDED BY A PALISADE

The test came after Simon de Montfort had been killed at the battle of Evesham in 1265 and his garrison at Kenilworth, commanded by Henry of Hastings, refused to submit to the king. The siege lasted from Easter to December, the defenders always hoping that Simon's son would manage to raise a force and come to their relief. Prince Edward collected a variety of war machines, as well as a siege tower called 'the bear', and barges were sent from Chester to be used on the lake. It was starvation that forced the garrison to surrender in the end: there was nothing wrong with the defences.

125

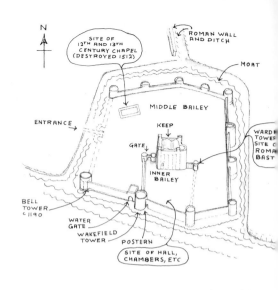

The Tower of London in the time of Henry III. The passage under the Bloody Tower was the water-gate, defended by doors and a portcullis. A portcullis still hangs in the room above, worked by a winch, ropes and pulleys. Part of the postern leading from Henry's private rooms to the river is beside the Wakefield Tower.

When the rebellion was over, Henry climbed back on his throne. Work continued on the Tower of London, which was growing into one of the strongest fortresses in the country. Early in his reign, as well as building the domestic range, Henry had improved the defences. He had built a large round tower – the Wakefield Tower – on the south wall, which was still washed by the water of the Thames, and this was to guard the water-gate alongside. Henry's visiting barons would step from their boats, climb the slippery steps and pass under the arch, which was protected by a heavy portcullis which hung from the wall of the chamber above. The ground floor of the Wakefield Tower was used as a guard-room, and the king had a pleasant chamber for his own use, up above. Part of a postern door still survives to show that there was a way up from the river to the king's private apartments and his hall beyond. A wall, pierced with many arrow-loops, was built from the Wakefield Tower to a twin-towered gatehouse joining the south-west corner of the keep, and this completed the inner bailey.

As in all Henry's buildings, everything was clean, neat and freshly painted. The hall and chamber were whitewashed inside and out, while the queen's chamber was decorated with false pointing (painted to look like well-dressed stone) and decorated with small formalized flowers. The wardrobe had a lead roof. In 1240 Gundulf's ancient keep, where the state records were kept, had been given a face-lift. The entire building was whitewashed – which must have required an army of painters – and the lead gutters were fitted with down spouts so that the white walls should not be streaked with the rain. Carpenters were called in to repair the timber hoardings round the top of the keep. Glass was fitted to the chapel windows: a new extravagance.

All this had been done before Simon's rebellion. Now, after 1265, the defences were strengthened yet again. The middle bailey was extended to the east of the Roman wall, which was half demolished, and the outer ditch was covered over. The inner bailey, containing all the vulnerable domestic buildings, was now protected on three sides by its wall, an area of land, and then another outer curtain wall. The river still defended the south side, but that too was about to be altered. The Tower of London was gradually being turned into a *concentric castle*, which is where one ring of defences encloses another. Prince Edward may have had a hand in these arrangements, and he certainly finished off the work his father had begun. During his reign a third curtain wall was built right round the new wall of Henry III, so that there was an outer bailey, a middle bailey and an inner bailey; one inside the other. New walls, wharfs and a second water-gate were built out into the Thames on the south side. It was Henry III and Edward I who jointly turned the Tower of London into the splendid fortress that we admire today.

Apart from a chamber in the Wakefield Tower, all Henry III's domestic buildings have been torn down: above is the ruined west side of his inner bailey. Edward I surrounded the castle with a new moat, sealed the old entrance with a tower (later used as a prison) and built a new entrance, with a barbican, to the south-west. A visitor had to pass through five gateways before reaching the king's hall in the inner bailey. Those who preferred to come by boat disembarked at the new water-gate. The wharf was used for unloading stores.

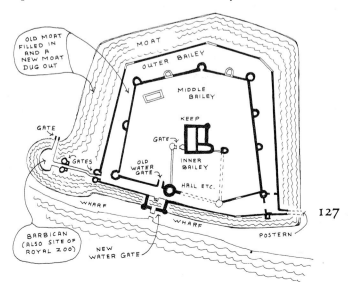

127

TROUBLE IN WALES AND OTHER MATTERS

9

WALES HAD BEEN A TROUBLE-SPOT EVER SINCE THE Romans pulled out of Britain. It was a difficult country to conquer, especially in the northern parts, because Welsh princes could always swoop down at the head of their spearmen, attack the invaders, and then hide away in their thickly wooded hills.

The various Welsh princes lived in small stone or timber fortresses, with square towers, perched high up on splendid rocky sites that were hard to get at and easy to defend. They clung to their ancient tribal way of life and obeyed their own laws – doling out rough justice to their subjects, who were mostly herdsmen and constantly on the move. The princes recognized the English kings as overlords, swearing fealty when a new one was crowned, but they strongly resented any meddling with their own internal administration. Wales, they protested, was a separate country, like Scotland, and capable of looking after its own affairs. They therefore claimed the right to build castles wherever they pleased in their own land, without first having to beg permission from the English king. This was a constant bone of contention because, in English eyes, so many castles made the Welsh people dangerously strong.

The Welsh princes warred against the English and each other until one of them, Llywelyn ab Iorwerth (Llywelyn the Great) persuaded the heads of the various states to pull to-

This map shows the extent of the Welsh territories in the early 13th century, and the three castles mentioned in the text. Other Welsh castles are marked on the map on page 153.

128

gether, and this put them into a much stronger position. Llywelyn had an illegitimate son, Gruffydd and, according to Welsh law, Gruffydd had as much right to succeed his father as the legitimate son, David. Because of this claim, when Llywelyn died in 1240 and David took the throne, he kept his half-brother locked away in his castles; finally, because Henry III did not consider Gruffydd to have any rights at all according to English law, the unfortunate man ended up as the king's prisoner in the Tower of London. He was killed when he tried to escape and the rope broke. Now that Gruffydd was safely dead and the king's support was no longer necessary, David rebelled and invaded the border country as far as Chester. In return, Henry raised an army and drove the Welsh right back to the west bank of the river Conway.

It was to maintain law and order in this dangerous territory that Henry built the only two castles of his reign: Dyserth, Clwyd, and Deganwy, Gwynedd. Dyserth was a new fortress, while Deganwy – originally a Norman castle with two mottes and one bailey – had been destroyed by David before he retreated over the river, and had to be almost completely rebuilt.

Wales was a poor country. The Welsh barons used local stone for their castles which were defended by rough rectangular towers (round towers in the 13th century) with little of the fine window tracery found in England. Llywelyn ab Iorwerth had a castle at Criccieth where his son Gruffydd was imprisoned in 1239. An inner ward, with a tall gatehouse, was added after it had fallen to the English (see page 153).

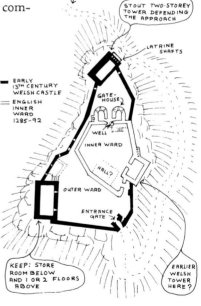

129

ENGLISH SOLDIERS
ON THE MARCH

MAIL
SHIRT

JACKET
REINFORCED
WITH
METAL
PLATES

By the middle of the 13th century, English soldiers were wearing all kinds of protective garments, while the Welsh soldiers fought in ordinary clothes. Llywelyn's forces in the north were mainly composed of spearmen; but archers from south-east Wales (the English sector) carried unusually long heavy bows made of elm.

WELSH
SOLDIERS
ON GUARD

WELSH
LONGBOW

David died childless in 1246; but Gruffydd had left three sons, one of whom was christened Llywelyn after his renowned grandfather, and it was Llywelyn ap Gruffydd who overruled his brothers and carried on with the Welsh war of independence. The details of the campaigns and truces would take up too much space to describe; but Llywelyn did so well that a council of Welsh lords voted him the first prince of all Wales in 1258. By 1263, he had extended his territories in all directions, starved the garrison of Deganwy into submission and captured the king's castle of Dyserth. These buildings had hardly been finished before Llywelyn ordered them both to be destroyed.

Henry III was raising an army in order to avenge these misdeeds when (as mentioned on page 123) he found that his own English barons were in revolt under the leadership of Simon de Montfort. The battle of Lewes, which brought victory to the rebels, was fought in 1264 and Simon de Montfort was finally slain at Evesham in 1265. All this time Llywelyn had been making the most of the situation, leading his warriors in a south-easterly direction, raiding the lands of the English lords. When peace was finally restored in England and Henry III was safely back on his throne, the king recognized Llywelyn's title of Prince of Wales; an act that was extremely unpopular with a young man called Gilbert de Clare. In his southern drive to extend Welsh territory, Llywelyn had got as far as the borders of Glamorgan, and this district was owned by the powerful de Clare family. Gilbert had just inherited his father's property, and, because he considered Llywelyn far too warlike a neighbour for the security of his own lands, he decided to protect himself. In 1266 Gilbert de Clare laid hands on his own Welsh vassal, Gruffydd ap Rhys, flung him into Cardiff Castle, and made plans for a new castle to be built on the land he had taken from his prisoner, at a place where the Romans had once built a fort: at Caerphilly, Mid-Glamorgan.

Few castles were built under such difficult circumstances. The masons, carpenters and diggers moved in on 11 April

130

1268. By September, Llywelyn had mustered an army at Brecon and then stepped over the border. At once Henry III anxiously sent councillors to try and obtain a peaceful settlement; but the talks took a couple of years and all this time the castle continued to grow. Llywelyn watched the progress until he could bear it no longer, and in 1270 he swooped down with his war bands and set fire to the whole thing.

After this disaster, Gilbert de Clare decided to build the sort of fortress that could not be destroyed so easily, and he started again on a fresh site alongside the charred ruin, where a low-lying length of pebbly ground stood between a near-by stream and a marshy area to the north. Water defences on the scale of Kenilworth were possible. Ditches were dug across the east front, and the stream was dammed, forming two sheets of water. Archers could be posted along the outer defensive wall running along the dam, in order to prevent an enemy from opening the sluices and emptying the lake. There was another barbican, in the form of an island, defending the west entrance.

The harassment continued; Gilbert's soldiers protected his workmen while Llywelyn's warriors laid siege to the entire building site. Henry III again sent his councillors to argue the rights and wrongs of the affair, and finally ordered Gilbert to remove his labourers altogether, installing a couple of bishops

These massive walls, backed by platforms of earth dug from the outer ditch, dammed the streams to the north and south and created two huge lakes as big as those at Kenilworth. A strong gatehouse guarded the entrance at the centre of the dam and there were two well-defended posterns at either end. The large semicircular bastion was for a war machine to stand on.

In place of the old square Norman keep, the entire inner ward had become the stronghold of the castle: defended by two massive gatehouses, four round corner-towers, and the narrow outer ward with its own low encircling wall. In addition there were the two platforms to the east, with their central gatehouse, and a hornwork to the west. A bastion is a solid platform or tower capable of supporting a war machine: hornwork is a barbican fronted by two half-round bastions, allowing the entrance to be defended by two war machines.

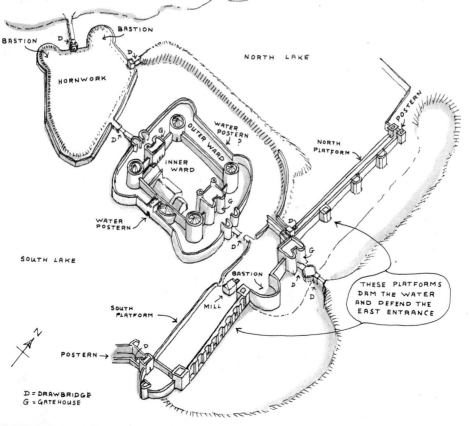

in the unfinished castle to keep the peace. After this, Gilbert's servants resorted to trickery: three of his knights presented themselves at the gate and told the porter that they had come to inspect the stores. As soon as the gate was open, they summoned forty men-at-arms, reoccupied the castle and pushed the bishops' forces out. Llywelyn protested, Henry III protested, and Gilbert said he was not to blame because he had been ignorant of the plan – but he must have been delighted. Finally, after Henry died in 1272, Gilbert was strongly supported by other lords who held lands on the Welsh border, and was able to finish his castle unmolested.

All in all, Caerphilly Castle was a tremendous achievement, and of a design that was well in advance of its time. It was the first true *concentric castle* to be built in the British Isles because, as explained on page 126, the Tower of London only became a concentric castle rather later.

The word *ward* means a defended area, like a courtyard or bailey. In a concentric castle the inner ward, which takes the place of the keep as being the strongest part of the fortress, is completely surrounded by the outer ward, which is usually a narrow space with walls on either side, like a passage. An enemy could be trapped in such a restricted area, becoming

ENTRANCE GATEHOUSE

The gatehouse, above, stands between the two platforms in the centre of the dam: when raised, the drawbridge fitted into the recess over the entrance arch, when lowered it rested on the six-sided pier in the middle of the ditch. The east gatehouse, on the left, guarded the entrance to the inner ward and was of three storeys, with the constable's suite of rooms on the upper floor. There were only two storeys to the west gatehouse.

INNER WARD TOWER BLOWN UP BY GUNPOWDER

EAST GATEHOUSE

WEST GATEHOUSE

HIGH INNER WARD WALL AND LOW OUTER WARD WALL

MODERN BRIDGE

EARLY 14TH CENTURY HALL

CHAMBERS

WEST GATEHOUSE

SOLDIERS UNLOADING BAGGAGE

EAST GATEHOUSE

Gilbert de Clare would have occupied the hall (replaced in the early 14th century), and chambers standing against the inner-ward wall. The constable would have used the suite of rooms on the second floor of the east gatehouse, while a less important official lodged in the room over the west gatehouse passage. Other knights would have found accommodation in the round towers.

a target to be pelted with missiles, with no space to manoeuvre, erect war machines, or operate a battering-ram.

The early castles had been defended by one main gatehouse and a postern or two. All the enemy had to do was sit and watch these exits and wait until the garrison, locked inside its own stronghold, was starved into submission. Now the emphasis was on attack. Caerphilly had a couple of large gatehouses with their immensely strong outer defences and numerous posterns: it would have required a huge army to watch every doorway.

All the domestic buildings were placed inside the secure inner ward. Knights and important officials, travelling as they did from place to place, expected comfortable lodgings at the journey's end. Suites of rooms with large fireplaces and convenient latrines were slotted into walls and towers, like modern flats. The castellan would have lived in the large room on the second floor of the main gateway and there was another, less spacious, chamber over the west gateway for a secondary official. When Gilbert de Clare arrived with his noisy retinue, he would have used the hall (which was replaced in the fourteenth century), chambers and chapel ranged against the inner curtain wall.

The domestic buildings in castles were not as stoutly built as the thick outer walls and so were often the first to be demolished: few halls and chambers have survived. Before moving on to the magnificent castles of Edward I, where his private apartments are often in ruins, it is important to get a clear idea of the way people lived at the very end of the thirteenth century.

'On Sunday next after St Martin's feast day, come to us, as you love us . . . at one o'clock to dine with us on good fat and fresh venison, and an equally fat crane . . .' (*English Historical Documents*, vol. III, p. 823.)

This invitation was sent by Godfrey, Bishop of Worcester, but it could easily have come from the master of Stokesay Castle, Salop. This charming place has nothing to do with the affairs of kings and princes, and is really little more than a fortified hall, owned by a rich wool merchant called Lawrence de Ludlow. The buildings have hardly been altered since the year they were set up.

Above: one of the fine windows in the constable's chamber. The little window below is at the level of the portcullis room, directly over the passage, and the shoot allowed water to be poured down if an enemy tried to set fire to the wooden doors.

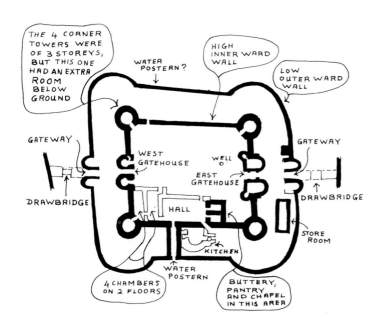

135

TRACES OF THE ROOF COVERING THE OUTSIDE STAIR

CHAMBER

17TH CENTURY CHIMNEY

HALL

LATE 13TH CENTURY CHIMNEY

THIS WINDOW HAS BEEN BLOCKED UP

OLD TOWER

DRAWBRIDGE PIT

STORE ROOM DOORWAY

Above: the east side of Stokesay hall seen from the courtyard. Below: the inside of the hall, looking towards the store-room at the base of the old tower, and the original timber staircase leading to the two rooms above it.

GOODS BEING CARRIED TO THE STORE ROOM

When Lawrence bought the property in 1281, it probably consisted of an old, aisled, timber hall, with the great chamber in the tower at the screens end and a wood-and-plaster kitchen and buttery out in the yard. Lawrence tore down the old hall and built the one that stands today. It is a ground-floor hall, with a high-pitched roof, and walls that were carried up to the same kind of little gables over the windows as were originally seen at Winchester. The old stone tower was retained; but a new chamber block was built at the dais end of the hall: the fashionable thing to do.

The new chamber was reached by leaving the hall, going into the yard and up some steps that were protected from the rain by a pent roof. The best barrels of wine, rare spices, and treasure chests would be kept in the ground-floor store-rooms. Lawrence could sit and chat with his friends in the chamber and also keep a sharp eye on the servants setting up the tables in the hall below, through a couple of squints inserted in the wall. *Squints* were tiny peep holes: look-out places from one room to the next.

The largest piece of furniture in a great chamber was usually the bed; but, as there was another small chamber next door, Lawrence and his wife may have slept in there. Several

136

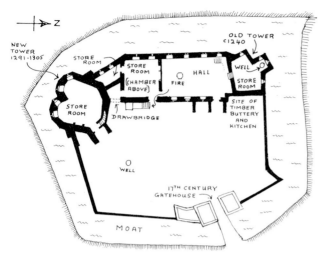

Stokesay Castle when the buildings were complete: only the gatehouse belongs to a later date. The old tower was originally defended by a timber hoarding which formed the basic support for the pleasant chamber, built about 1300, that juts out at the top. Lawrence de Ludlow would have used the other chamber at the far side of the hall, and his bed may have stood in a little room (re-built 1650) next door.

people might sleep in the chamber at once; not only the lord and his lady, but honoured guests and trusted servants as well. A servant would curl up on a straw mattress with a shaped log of wood for a pillow, while a guest might lie on a low truckle bed that could be stored under the great bed when not in use. People shared beds, even if they were strangers. A picture of an inn shows two or three in a bed, sleeping in nothing but their nightcaps. Curtains hanging round the beds gave privacy, and were tucked up in the daytime when the bed became something to sit on. In a royal castle the bed would become a throne for the king when he gave audience. However, Lawrence was only a merchant: he would never have presumed to own too smart a bed. A wooden box and a mattress stuffed with the best wool would be good enough for him.

SQUINT

SETTING UP THE HIGH TABLE

LAYING THE CLOTH

SETTING UP A SIDE TABLE

STREWING HERBS

Trestle tables were used. The long heavy boards rested on ordinary trestles like those used by carpenters today; or on great solid trestles, as shown on the right. When the meal was over, the boards were stacked against the wall, and the trestles put in a corner. Another of the hall windows is shown below. When the hall was first built, the upper parts of the windows were fitted with glass and only the lower parts had shutters.

BEAMS ORIGINALLY RESTED ON THESE CORBELS

Thirteenth-century domestic buildings often had fine long windows, and the thick walls allowed space for window seats where women could sit and embroider in a good light. Otherwise people sat on chests or benches or on cushions on the floor.

The buildings at Stokesay are almost exactly as they used to be. Plaster still clings to the walls and there are traces of wall paintings in the north tower. The rickety staircase gives a good idea of the way the carpenters worked and the timber roof has suffered only minor repairs. Herbs would be strewn among the rushes on the floor, and smoke would curl up from the central hearth, hang about the roof beams and filter through the round holes over the windows: there is no sign of a louver.

Long trestle tables were set up round the walls of a hall and the household sat on benches facing the centre of the room, while the food was served from the inner side. Clean white cloths were often draped over the table on the dais, a thick bread trencher or wooden platter served as a plate, and lumps of meat were picked out of the dishes with the fingers. Forks

138

CART CARRYING
SACKS OF
WOOL

CHAMBER

PRESENT
SLEEPING
CHAMBER
1650

LANCET
WINDOW

LATRINE

ARROW
SLIT

REMAINS
OF
CURTAIN
WALL

THESE
WINDOWS
MAY BE
SLIGHTLY
LATER

were introduced early in the fourteenth century.

Times being treacherous on the Welsh border, *licence to crenellate*, or fortify, the hall at Stokesay, turning it into a castle, was granted in 1292. These licences had been handed out since about 1195 and show how important it was for the crown to keep an eye on the strength of private strongholds. The moat was probably deepened at this time and flooded with water. A high curtain wall was built round the courtyard, which would have been cluttered with the usual outhouses, and a strong defensive tower was built at the south end. This tower was built like a small keep, with the store-room below, and the entrance at first-floor level, defended by a miniature drawbridge. Windows were reduced to narrow *lancets* and the stair was planned to run through the wall on the courtyard side to avoid weakening the outer face. The battlements at the top of the tower have slits in the merlons: a new improvement. Crossbowmen could shelter behind the merlons and shoot through the centres. The curtain wall would have been topped by a similar parapet.

There were no doorways between the new tower and the other buildings: it could be shut and defended like a miniature keep. The courtyard wall would have had the same kind of parapet as the tower, with arrow-slits inside the merlons. The lancet windows are typical of the 13th century.

139

Castle walls look grey and dismal now; but a well-kept castle would have looked rather different in medieval times, with all the trimmings of painted timber-hoardings, doors and shutters, and roof pinnacles picked out with touches of gilt. The masons believed that whitewash protected the stone and many walls shone white against the green countryside.

The interiors of buildings were painted and decorated as well, and we are lucky to be able to see one painted chamber which has survived intact. Defensive towers like the one at Stokesay were often attached to otherwise unfortified halls, and this was the case with Longthorpe Tower, Cambridgeshire, built about 1300. The walls were painted sometime early in the fourteenth century, and since then the paintings were lost under layer upon layer of whitewash. Now that the whitewash has been carefully removed we get a clear view of the background to courtly medieval life. The decorations completely transform an otherwise dull square room. The artist chose good moral subjects and even Henry III would have approved of them. There is the nativity, the seven ages of man, the wheel of the five senses, and a basket-weaver talking to a hermit; they are all depicted in glowing colours, and there would have been the sparkle of gold paint as well. If the owner of Longthorpe Tower could afford paintings of this quality, then the chambers of royal castles must have looked like something out of a fairy story.

All these paintings have meanings. The picture on the right, shows a nativity scene over the window, with pairs of apostles on either side, and marsh birds by the floor. The window behind the chess players was replaced in Tudor times; a 14th-century window is drawn in. The picture on the left shows the labours of the month at the top (partly destroyed), a basket-weaver talking to a hermit in the upper half of the recess, and – possibly – two philosophers disputing.

BOY PLAYING A PSALTERY

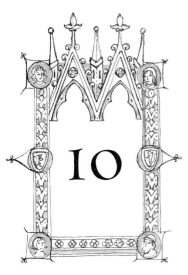

THE HEYDAY OF ENGLISH MILITARY ARCHITECTURE

10

KING HENRY III DIED IN 1272 AND THE PEOPLE OF England waited for his son, Edward I, to return from his crusade. Taking his time, Edward landed at Dover in August 1274. All the barons swore fealty to the new king except for Llywelyn ap Gruffydd, Prince of Wales, who had been busily extending his frontiers in Edward's absence and who felt he was now in a strong bargaining position. Llywelyn also complained about the way his brother, David, who had plotted to kill him, was being sheltered by the English at Shrewsbury. After the Welsh prince had been summoned for the third time and still failed to appear, King Edward became angry and mustered his army at Worcester. In 1277 Llywelyn found himself at war with one of the most skilled warriors of the day.

As a young man, Edward had been humiliated by Llywelyn's destruction of the two castles Dyserth and Deganwy, which were part of his earldom of Chester; so he decided to settle the question of Welsh rebellion once and for all. Previous campaigns had failed because the Welsh forces could hide away in the hills, wait until the English army had marched some way into their territory, and then attack from the rear and cut off supplies. Edward decided to build castles all along the coast so that the vital supplies could be carried by sea. Passing through France on his way home from the crusade, Edward had seen towns and castles designed as one unit – the town

This drawing, taken from the seal of Edward I, shows the crown on the king's helm and the leopards of England, gold on a red ground, displayed on his shield and the cloth housing covering his horse. These quilted housings had been in use from about 1230 onwards.

NORTH EAST
CORNER TOWER

3
LIVING
ROOMS

CIRCULAR
ROOM,
ENTERED
FROM A
TRAP
DOOR

MARSH
AND
SEA

The outer bailey of Flint Castle is almost entirely destroyed, but parts of the walls and towers of the inner bailey are still standing. The large round tower was the keep. It was surrounded by its own ditch and jutted out from the corner of the inner-bailey wall, dominating the entrance which, otherwise, was only defended by a small gatehouse.

forming an extra bailey tacked on to the side of the castle – and he planned to copy these. The new towns, strongly defended by the castles, could be filled with English traders and settlers who would feed and support the armies. The constable of the castle could also act as mayor of the town.

Edward was a splendid organizer. He not only summoned his household knights with their men-at-arms, his feudal levies and his hired mercenary soldiers; but he also sent clerks to scour the country for an army of masons, carpenters, smiths, carters and diggers (some of these last from the fenlands of East Anglia because they were used to the job of channelling water). Building tools were stored alongside the piles of arms and armour at Chester. The building workers were treated like soldiers: a knight in command of each gang.

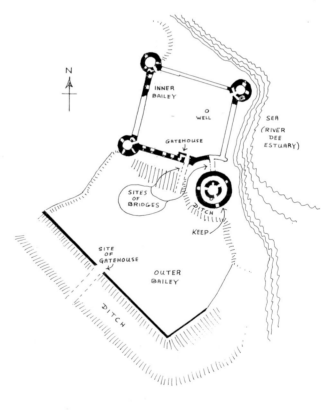

N

INNER
BAILEY

WELL

SEA
(RIVER
DEE
ESTUARY)

GATEHOUSE

SITES
OF
BRIDGES

DITCH

KEEP

SITE
OF
GATEHOUSE

OUTER
BAILEY

DITCH

1ST FLOOR WINDOW

DITCH

ARROW SLIT
AT STORE ROOM
LEVEL

The circular store-room, surrounded by a passage, and the floor above, are all that remain of the great tower at Flint. It was probably a three-storey building like the Tower of Constance, below, built by St Louis at Aigues Mortes, Gard, and it may have had a similar central shaft to light the interior. At Flint, the hall was in the middle, with several chambers, including a chapel, radiating from it.

Not far from this main supply-base, on the marshy low-lying coast, there was a spur of sandstone rock jutting into the sea, locally known as 'The Flynt'. It was here that Edward told his diggers to lay out the banks and ditches of his first castle-and-town complex.

Flint Castle, Clwyd, was straightforward and simple in plan and, although it was started in July 1277 and not finished until about 1280, it was hurriedly built to protect a large number of people. When completed, it had an outer bailey and a square inner bailey, with drum towers at three corners, and a great round tower – originally much higher than it is now – surrounded by its own ditch, attached to the fourth. This tower looks like a throwback to the start of the century; but Edward might have been thinking of St Louis's Tower of Constance, which he had seen in 1270 as he passed through Aigues Mortes, a port on the south coast of France, on his way to the crusade. The castle and town at Flint were defended by a double line of ditches with the banks topped by timber palisades.

Acting according to his plan, Edward left the building site at Flint and pressed on slightly south of the coast until he came to Rhuddlan, also in Clwyd, where he found a castle and settlement already there, overlooking the important ford across the river Clwyd. Originally a stronghold of the ancient

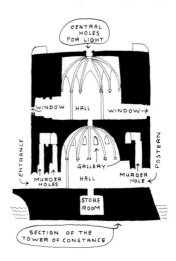

CENTRAL HOLES FOR LIGHT

WINDOW   HALL   WINDOW→

ENTRANCE   GALLERY   POSTERN
↓ MURDER HOLES   HALL   MURDER HOLE ←

STORE ROOM

SECTION OF THE TOWER OF CONSTANCE

143

Rhuddlan is a concentric castle: the high-walled inner ward is surrounded by a low-walled outer ward. The town was defended by a bank, ditch and palisade. The main entrance to the castle faced the town. A second gate to the south-east was closed soon after being built. Originally water came right up to the water-gate and ships could unload their goods at the dock-gate, where part of the ditch was flooded.

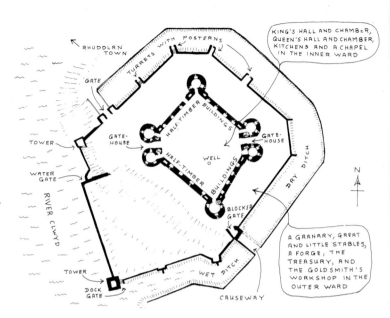

Welsh princes, the place had been captured at the time of the Conquest by a Norman baron who had built a motte-and-bailey castle. The fortress had been a bone of contention, changing hands on and off ever since. In September 1277 Edward ordered his men to start digging the trenches for a new castle and town to the north-west of the old Norman timber fortress. By now a talented master mason, Master James of St George, whom the king had encountered on his homeward journey through Savoy, had arrived to supervise the works. (He may have landed in England slightly earlier.)

The inner ward of Rhuddlan Castle was planned in a shape like a squashed square; with two gatehouses opposite each other and single towers at the other two corners. The outer ward completely enclosed the inner ward, so this is a concentric castle. Rhuddlan being some way inland, the hardest work of all must have been digging the two miles of canal, which had to be deep enough to allow the stately thirteenth-century vessels to come sailing in with their loads of supplies. A square tower was built down by the water to defend the dock and sluices.

144

Inner and outer views of the southern tower of the inner bailey at Rhuddlan. There was a cell below ground level, reached through a trapdoor, and three floors of living-rooms above.

The war against Llywelyn ended almost before it had begun. Edward had mustered the strongest army that had been seen since the time of the Conquest and, although Llywelyn had tried to bring his forces up to date with mounted soldiers and siege engines, he could not hope to withstand such an enemy. His southern territories were quickly overrun and by the end of 1277 the Welsh prince had come to Rhuddlan to swear fealty to the king, repeating the same ceremony at Westminster on Christmas Day.

In the settlement that followed, Wales continued to be a separate state and Llywelyn was still Prince of Wales, acknowledging Edward I as his overlord but holding a much smaller territory. Llywelyn's untrustworthy brother, David, who had plotted to kill him before the war started, was also given lands in Wales.

The northern and western parts of Wales, which had never been occupied by the Normans for any length of time, were full of small native strongholds which had been built on rocky heights, making the most of the natural defences. Throughout the thirteenth century the two Llywelyns had organized their courts on the same lines as their English overlords; but Wales was a poor country, and the castles were small; built out of the local stone which was unsuitable for elaborate decorations. The keeps were usually built on the old Norman pattern as stout rectangular towers; but some of the later ones were round, copied from Pembroke or Skenfrith.

After 1277 the masons carried on with the work at Flint and Rhuddlan, while the old eleventh-century castle at Builth, Powys, which had been destroyed by Llywelyn, had to be rebuilt. Another castle and town was under construction at Llanbadarn, Dyfed. Both of these last castles have since been destroyed. King Edward had also started to build a new castle at Ruthin, Clwyd; and in the peace settlement this was handed over to David ap Gruffydd, who was considered to be a safe ally. These five new castles were sited near the lands of Llywelyn, so that his activities could be watched for any signs of a further revolt (see map on page 53).

Things looked peaceful enough. By 1280 Rhuddlan was finished and the accounts mention the king's hall, chamber, kitchen and wardrobes, everything painted and plastered as usual. Edward's queen, Eleanor of Castile, had a chamber of her own, and there is mention of a timber building for her goldsmith to work in. The well was covered by a little roof and was encircled by a clay-lined pond, with seats at the edge so that people could sit and watch the fish swimming about. There was even a lawn, fenced round with the staves of old wine casks.

Meanwhile, Welsh feelings of unrest had been bubbling away under the surface. Although Llywelyn toed the line pretty well, his brother David stirred up trouble and broke out in open revolt in 1282; Llywelyn had to join in. Edward's reaction was swift and angry. He mustered his army at Chester once again and moved into Flint and Rhuddlan. The new plan was to attack the Welsh forces from all sides, including Anglesey; but on 11 December 1282, while Llywelyn was fighting in the south of Wales, he was killed by a soldier who failed to recognize him; the Welsh had lost their great leader and the war was over. David was captured soon afterwards and hanged.

WEST GATEHOUSE FROM THE INNER WARD

FOUNDATIONS OF HALF-TIMBER BUILDINGS

Half-timber buildings backed on to the walls and gatehouses of the inner ward, making the entrance passages twice as long. Their foundations can be seen above. Below is a view of Rhuddlan castle from the north-west. The low outer wall had little turrets with posterns leading down to the dry ditch.

POSTERN

WEST GATEHOUSE

REMAINS OF LITTLE TURRET AND POSTERN STEPS LEADING DOWN TO THE DRY DITCH

The Welsh castle of Dolwyddelan, which was used by both Llywelyn ab Iorwerth and his grandson, Llywelyn ap Gruffydd, was probably built in the early 13th century. It stands on the edge of a magnificent rocky site. The keep was a simple first-floor hall raised up on a store-room, with a small walled courtyard outside.

Edward was now free to sweep over the mountains and passes of Snowdonia and occupy all the royal strongholds of the Welsh princes. In January 1283 he captured Dolwyddelan, Gwynedd, which had been a residence of Llewelyn ab Iorwerth (the Great) and where Llywelyn ap Gruffydd had been living only a couple of years previously. It must have been easy work for Edward, with his vast army, to take this little castle: it is a primitive place. At that time it consisted of a two-storeyed keep, with the store-room below and hall above, entered through a small-scale forebuilding from a walled inner bailey. The second tower on the west side of the bailey appears to have been built by the English after their occupation, and the tower was heightened and a top room added considerably later.

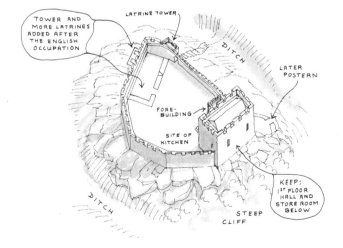

148

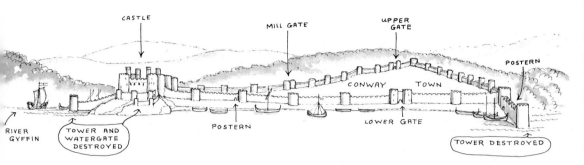

CASTLE   MILL GATE   UPPER GATE   POSTERN

CONWAY TOWN

RIVER GYFFIN   TOWER AND WATERGATE DESTROYED   POSTERN   LOWER GATE   TOWER DESTROYED

Edward moved north from Dolwyddelan and up the river Conway, until he came to the bay. Here the body of Llywelyn ab Iorwerth lay among the bones of earlier Welsh princes, in the Abbey of Aberconway, and Llywelyn's empty hall stood near by. Edward arranged to have the monastic community moved to another site, retained the church for the town and instructed Master James of St George to design the sort of castle and town that would clearly show that the next prince of all Wales was going to be an English one. Llywelyn's hall was retained and built into the new town-wall, and it would stay empty until such time as an English prince was old enough to use it.

Conway Castle, Gwynedd, therefore, was built as a symbol

The town walls of Conway were built at the same time as the castle, starting in 1283. Originally all the stonework was finished off with a coat of whitewash. An outer ditch was dug round the sides of the town not defended by the two rivers. All the towers, except one, were open backed, and the sentries walked over the gap on wooden planks, which could be removed in an emergency. Each stretch of wall could be defended separately. The nearest tower to the site of Llywelyn's timber hall was turned into living accommodation in 1302–6. The hall itself was finally dismantled in 1313 and shipped to Caernarvon.

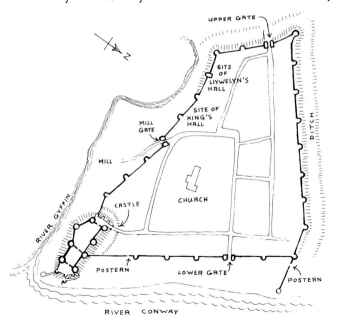

UPPER GATE

N

SITE OF LLYWELYN'S HALL

SITE OF KING'S HALL

MILL GATE

DITCH

MILL

CASTLE   CHURCH

RIVER GYFFIN

POSTERN   LOWER GATE   POSTERN

RIVER CONWAY

149

KING
T

GARRISON HALL

KING'S HALL

KING'S CHAMBER

BALCONY

TOWN WALL

GOODS COULD BE CARRIED FROM BOATS UP TO THE KING'S STORE ROOM

MODERN WALLS

Conway Castle, above, seen from the far side of the little river Gyffin. There were three sleeping-chambers in the king's tower, below left, and a store-room at the base, entered through a trapdoor. The king could have kept his treasure there.

WATCH TOWER

MACHICOLATION

KING'S TOWER

EAST GATE LEADING TO WATER GATE

of royal power; and it was designed in two parts: one for the garrison and one for the king. Instead of being a concentric castle, the walls follow the contours of the rock in a long, narrow, rectangular shape, defended by eight strong round-towers. The two entrances had the added protection of low-walled barbicans with open-backed towers. The usual timber hoarding jutted out round the rest of the castle; but the west gatehouse and the gatehouse to the east, both overlooked by men standing on top of the lofty corner-towers, were equipped with something quite new: a kind of stone hoarding. The parapet above the entrance arch was built to jut forwards on corbels, leaving square spaces between them through which missiles could be dropped on enemy heads. This stone *machicolation* was gradually to replace timber hoarding, and it was to become immensely popular in later centuries.

Originally there was timber hoarding all round Conway Castle; but – because wooden structures were easy to burn – the two vulnerable gateways were defended by machicolations, or stone galleries. The crenellated parapet jutted out, leaving holes through which water could be poured or missiles dropped.

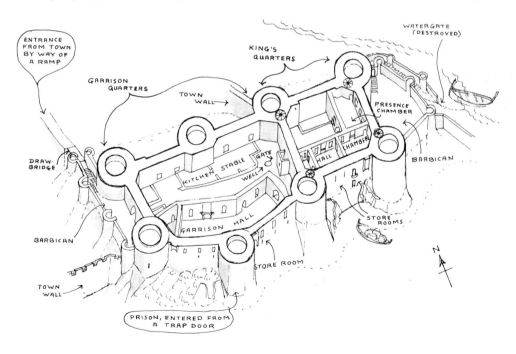

PINNACLES FOR ARCHERS TO STEADY THEIR AIM

The garrison hall, seen from the thick wall that divides Conway Castle in two. The photograph below shows the large windows, originally filled with fine stone tracery, of the king's apartments. The entrance to the presence chamber was by a timber stair from the courtyard, no longer there, and a similar upper doorway led to the hall.

PRISON TOWER

GARRISON HALL, CURVED TO FIT THE SHAPE OF THE ROCK

ENTR T H

The garrison-quarters were in the part of the castle that overlooked the town and, as usual, the constable and his family lived over the gate. In peacetime the garrison consisted of about thirty men: fifteen crossbowmen, a chaplain, a carpenter, a mason, a smith, porters and a watchman. Then there would be cooks, scullions and stableboys as well.

The royal apartments had the added distinction of watch-towers rising above the four main towers: they were arranged like a castle within a castle; cut off from the garrison-quarters by a ditch, wall, and entrance tower, so that they could be separately defended if necessary. The rooms were grouped round a courtyard, with the king's chamber, hall and audience chamber at first-floor level; and there was a tiny chapel in the north turret, with a round nave and the chancel built into the thickness of the wall.

When the castle was finished in 1297, it was painted white and the roofs were covered with lead. By that time Edward's much-loved queen, Eleanor of Castile, was dead, so she never used those splendid rooms. When staying at Conway, the royal couple had lodged in a hall in the town.

WINDOW AND ENTRANCE TO PRESENCE CHAMBER

KING'S CHAMBER (STORE ROOMS BELOW)

EAST GATEWAY

Such was the castle when it was built; but it was only at the planning stage when Edward left Conway in March 1283. From this secure base, which could be easily supplied from the sea, he led his army round the coast, along the banks of the Menai Strait to Caernarvon, down the west coast to capture the native castle of Criccieth and then on to Harlech – all in Gwynedd. With his usual energy, Edward arranged for a castle to be built at Harlech; for Llewelyn's castle at Criccieth (where the prince's father, Gruffydd, had once been held prisoner) to be occupied and strengthened; and for another castle and town, which would eventually be far more spectacular than Conway, to be built at Caernarvon.

The Romans had built a fort called Segontium near Caernarvon, and the place was important because it guarded the Menai Strait and the fertile island of Anglesey. But, to the Welsh, Caernarvon had another, special, significance: they

Criccieth Castle (see page 129) was occupied by King Edward's forces on 14 March 1283. The English twin-towered gatehouse, giving the castle it's striking silhouette, must have been built between 1285 and 1292.

In this map of Wales the boxed names are of castles built by Edward I after 1377; the underlined names are of castles that had been built by English barons; while the others are Welsh castles.

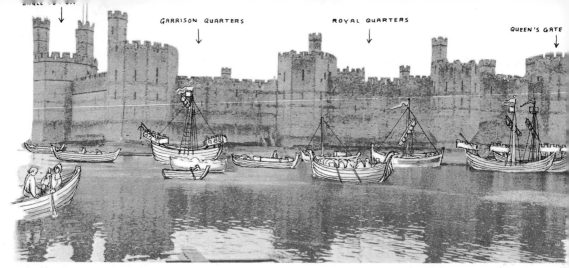

The south front of Caernarvon Castle is pierced by a multitude of arrow-loops. Arrows could be fired from the top of the battlements and the two tiers of loops in the walls during battle. The King's Gate, below, guarded the entrance from the town and was not completed until the early 14th century.

connected it with one of their greatest heroes – Magnus Maximus. Magnus had started off as an officer of the Roman army serving in Britain, and he married a British wife; but by 383 he had actually been made Emperor of Britain. He then led his British war bands right across Europe and became Emperor of Spain and Gaul as well. Wanting to become master of Rome itself, he gathered his forces together, crossed the Alps in 388, took Milan, and was then confronted by the great Theodosius I, Emperor of the East, who had marched from his capital at Constantinople. Magnus was defeated in the battle that followed and was promptly beheaded. However, by the twelfth century, the Welsh bards had woven a story, 'The Dream of Macsen Wledig', round Magnus Maximus, telling of how he came to Caernarvon to wed the maiden Ellen, whom he had seen in a dream.

Caernarvon had another, more recent, history as well. At the time of the Conquest, Hugh d'Avranches, a nephew of William I, had battled his way along the coast and built a motte-and-bailey castle there; but it was taken by the Welsh sometime before 1115. After that, the castle at Caernarvon was used as a royal residence by the Welsh princes. Now that the Welsh had been conquered again, Edward planned to make the place the centre of his administration.

Work on Caernarvon Castle commenced in the early summer of 1283 and went on until about 1327, which was right

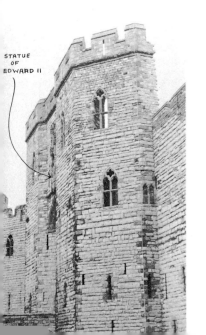

STATUE
OF
EDWARD II

154

at the end of the reign of Edward and Eleanor's son, Edward II; and it is the statue of Edward II which sits in the highly decorated niche over the main gate. When the baby was born at Caernarvon, they were still digging the foundations of the castle, and Queen Eleanor must have been living in an improvised hall, surrounded by the wooden lodges of the masons, and all the hoists, cranes, blocks of stone, barrows, piles of wood, sand, lime, and general overall mud of a busy building site. Edward of Caernarvon was not formally proclaimed the first English prince of all Wales – successor to Llywelyn ap Gruffydd – until 1301.

Caernarvon differs from Edward's other castles in two ways: the towers are many-sided instead of being circular, and they are decorated with bands of dark sandstone, very similar

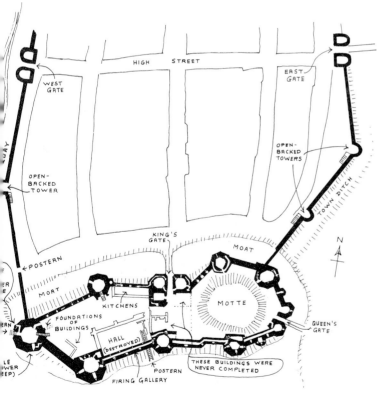

The Eagle Tower was the strongest building in Caernarvon Castle, with the water-gate at river level and three floors of living-rooms above. The battlements are original, with fine roll moulding round the top and sides of the merlons to deflect arrows, and arrow-loops in the middle. Like Conway, the castle was divided into garrison and royal quarters; but the range of rooms from the King's Gate to the opposite tower was never built.

155

The diagram, right, is of *Harlech Castle gatehouse. The entrance passage was defended with portcullises and two leaved doors. Drawbar holes were for the stout timber bars laid behind the shut doors, and the bars were pushed back into the guard-room walls when the doors stood open. There were murder-holes in the passage roof and it was overlooked by the arrow-loops of the guard-room. The rounded gatehouse towers jut well out from the curtain wall, with the guard-rooms below and chambers above.*

to the Land Wall of Theodosius II at Constantinople (see page 81). The three turrets at the top of the water-gate tower were eventually topped by three eagles: another reference to Imperial Rome. Eagles are also mentioned in 'The Dream of Macsen Wledig': they decorated the chair which the hoary-headed man, Ellen's father, sat in. Caernarvon Castle, therefore, was probably designed as a tribute to the Roman soldier-Emperor, Magnus Maximus, and some bones – presumed to be his – were discovered in 1283 and reverently reburied in the church.

Harlech was begun at the same time as Caernarvon; but did not take as long to build. It is a standard concentric castle, built on a high rocky site overlooking a sparkling bay; but now the sea has drained away and the bay has become dry land.

The strongest building was the three-storeyed gatehouse, with two rounded towers jutting well forward towards the ditch. There were guard-rooms at ground level with arrow-slits overlooking the passage, which was also defended by three portcullises, two pairs of doors and murder-holes in the roof. The upper rooms were used by the constable and his household, and each chamber had a huge fireplace. The chapel was placed directly over the entrance passage. As a reward for his great services, James of St George was appointed constable of Harlech in 1290, and it must have been an intense satisfaction to command a castle he had designed himself.

156

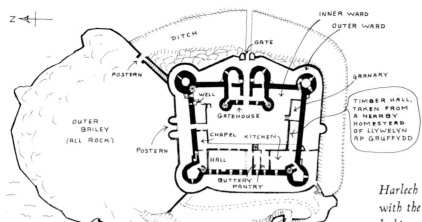

Z

DITCH

GATE

INNER WARD

OUTER WARD

POSTERN

WELL

GATEHOUSE

GRANARY

TIMBER HALL,
TAKEN FROM
A NEARBY
HOMESTEAD
OF LLYWELYN
AP GRUFFYDD

OUTER
BAILEY
(ALL ROCK)

CHAPEL KITCHEN

POSTERN

HALL

BUTTERY
PANTRY

WATER
GATE

UPPER GATE

SEA

Harlech is a concentric castle, with the high inner wall overlooking the low wall of the outer ward. Unlike the other Edwardian castles in Wales, it was not attached to a walled town. The gatehouse was the strongest part of the castle, with two suites of rooms, each with a chapel, on the two upper floors. The windows were small and narrow on the outside; but those facing the inner ward were once filled with fine stone tracery. The constable would have lived in the gatehouse. Another range of rooms, linked by a covered passage or pentice, was built against the high inner-bailey wall.

LATER
STAIRWAY

PROBABLE
WINDOW
DESIGN

NORTH WEST TOWER

PLATFORMS FOR WAR MACHINES

SEA GATE

Harlech stands on a magnificent rocky site which must have been even more spectacular before the bay was drained. Goods would have been carried up the winding path from the sea-gate, past the war machines poised ready to launch missiles at any enemy vessel that dared to approach too near.

A period of peace followed, during which time the king parcelled out slices of Welsh land and gave them to his barons; while existing Welsh castles, now in English hands, were strengthened. English law was enforced and resented, but King Edward was free to turn his mind to other matters. The years between 1286 and 1289 found him reorganizing the administration of Gascony. When he returned, he found that Gilbert de Clare and Humphrey de Bohun, both powerful barons with lands in south Wales, had reverted to the old border system of settling quarrels by private warfare. Then, in 1294, the new French king, Philip the Fair, tried to annex Guienne and Gascony; territories in the south-west part of France that had belonged to England ever since Henry II had married Eleanor of Aquitaine.

Accordingly, in 1294, King Edward raised an army to do service in Guienne and this included men from south Wales who were ordered to muster at Shrewsbury on 30 September. Reluctant to fight overseas, this new duty stirred up their simmering discontent. On 1 October, one of the officers commanding south Wales was murdered. Because the English soldiers had been called away and the Welsh castles were poorly garrisoned, the Welshmen, now liberally supplied with arms, took their chance to launch a full-scale revolt. The sheriff of Anglesey and many citizens were murdered at the new town of Caernarvon, while the half-finished castle was set ablaze. King Edward found he was forced to turn about, recall all the men who were not already at sea on their way to Gascony, and direct all his energies once more against Wales.

HARLECH IS A CONCENTRIC CASTLE

HIGH INNER WALL

LOW OUTER WALL

THE BAY IS NOW DRY LAND

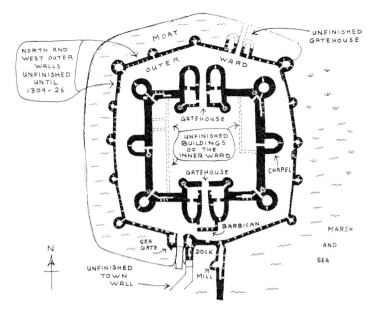

Diagram labels:
- MOAT
- UNFINISHED GATEHOUSE
- NORTH AND WEST OUTER WALLS UNFINISHED UNTIL 1309-26
- OUTER WARD
- GATEHOUSE
- UNFINISHED BUILDINGS OF THE INNER WARD
- GATEHOUSE
- CHAPEL
- BARBICAN
- SEA GATE
- DOCK
- MARSH AND SEA
- UNFINISHED TOWN WALL
- MILL
- N

Beaumaris Castle was started in 1295 and never finished. Work was stopped in 1300, when King Edward went to war with Scotland, and although building resumed between 1306 and 1330, the walls were never carried up to their full height. Less than half of the north outer gatehouse was built, and only the foundations of the south gatehouses laid. They would have been similar to the gatehouse at Harlech, with two suites of rooms on the upper floors. Together with the buildings of the inner ward, the castle would have accommodated five separate households.

The English armies were mustered at Chester, Brecon and Cardiff by the end of October; while the coastal castles had been provisioned by sea. The Welsh had caught the English napping and had the initial advantage; but Edward's army was fully prepared for the French war and was a formidable adversary.

King Edward made a rapid advance and spent Christmas at Conway. In January 1295, he decided to press on to Bangor, but the Welsh laid an ambush and captured his baggage, so he had to beat a retreat back to Conway Castle, where he was besieged. Supplies could not get through by land and the severe winter weather brought with it such high tides and floods that the ships could not sail on the sea: it looked as if the beleaguered garrison would run out of food. Wine was reduced to one small barrel, which the king refused to drink, declaring he was prepared to put up with honey and water like the rest of his men.

The Welsh spearmen were no match for the armed knights and the expert crossbowmen; Conway Castle was relieved and by April 1295 Edward had occupied Anglesey. He declared yet another castle to be necessary and chose a site overlooking the Menai Strait. The new castle was to be called Beaumaris.

OUTER WARD SOUTH WEST TOWER

INNER WARD SOUTH WEST TOWER

STONE-CUTTERS
AT WORK

Building methods appear to have been much the same in the medieval period as they are now; but the hoists lifting the huge blocks of stone were worked by tread wheels or hand winches instead of machines. Smaller stones were carted in wheelbarrows and carried up the ladders in baskets.

HOIST
OPERATED
BY A
TREAD-
WHEEL

Beaumaris, in Gwynedd, was the last of King Edward's castles in Wales. The building and repairing of so many fort-resses had proved to be enormously expensive and the royal coffers were empty.

In order to get some idea of what the conditions were like when a castle was under construction, and to glimpse the men working there, one can hardly do better than read this letter written by Master James of St George to the barons of the exchequer.

> Conway
> 27 February 1296

To their very dear lordships the Treasurer and Barons of the Exchequer of our lord the King, James of St George and Walter of Winchester send greeting and due reverence.

Sirs,

. . . we write to inform you that the work we are doing is very costly and we need a great deal of money.

You should know:

1 That we have kept on masons, stone cutters, quarrymen and minor workmen all through the winter, and are still employing them, for making mortar and breaking up stone for lime; we have had carts bringing this stone to the site and bringing timber for erecting the buildings in which we are all now living inside the castle; we also have 1000 car-penters, smiths, plasterers and navvies, quite apart from a mounted garrison of 10 men accounting for 70s. a week, 20 crossbowmen who add another 47s. 10d. and 100 infantry who take a further £6 2s. 6d.

2 That when this letter was written we were short of £500, for both workmen and garrison. The men's pay has been and still is very much in arrear, and we are having the greatest difficulty in keeping them because they simply have nothing to live on . . .

As for the progress of the work . . . We can tell you that some of it already stands about 28 feet high and even where it is lowest it is 20 feet. We have begun ten of the outer and four of the inner towers, i.e. the two for each of the two gatehouse passages. Four gates have been hung and are shut and locked every night, and each gateway is to have three portcullises. You should also know that at high tide a 40-ton vessel will be able to come fully laden right up to the castle gateway; so much have we been able to do in spite of all the Welshmen.

In case you should wonder where so much money could go in a week, we would have you know that we have needed – and shall continue to need – 400 masons, both cutters and layers, together with 2000 minor workmen, 100 carts, 60 waggons and 30 boats bringing stone and sea-coal; 200 quarrymen; 30 smiths; and carpenters for putting in the joists and floor-boards and other necessary jobs . . .

As to how things are in the land of Wales, we still cannot be any too sure. But, as you well know, Welshmen are Welshmen, and you need to understand them properly; if, which God forbid, there is war with France and Scotland, we shall need to watch them all the more closely . . .

PS. And, Sirs, for God's sake be quick with the money for the works, as much as ever our lord the king wills; otherwise everything done up till now will have been to no avail. (*The History of the King's Works*, p. 398.)

DOCK

The castle dock, where ships could tie up and unload their cargoes of timber and stone. The goods could then be floated round the walls on boats or rafts. Other supplies arrived on carts. James of St George died in 1309, when the castle was half built. Had it been finished, it would have been the best concentric castle of all.

NORTH GATEHOUSE

HIGH INNER WARD WALL

LOW OUTER WARD WALL

CASTLES BEGIN TO LOSE THEIR IMPORTANCE

I I

The plan of Kildrummy Castle is on page 164. The first-floor chapel was built to face east and is out of line with the curtain wall.

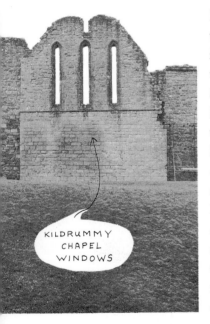

KILDRUMMY CHAPEL WINDOWS

THE END OF THE BRILLIANT REIGN OF EDWARD I WAS clouded by troubles, disappointments and shortage of cash. Sending a large army overseas to defend Guienne and Gascony was expensive and so was the war against the Welsh. The royal coffers were empty and Edward's subjects always complained loudly about having to raise more money. Then, as a final straw, the king of Scotland joined Philip of France in league against him.

This was a new problem for Edward. Relations between England and Scotland had been friendly all through the thirteenth century and the Scottish lords, who often held lands in England, were familiar figures at King Edward's court. The way of life in the north was much the same as in the south. Scottish castles tended to follow the same pattern as the English ones, timber fortresses being rebuilt in stone as time went by. For example, there was a motte-and-bailey castle at Kildrummy, Grampian; then, sometime before 1249, a stone castle was built near by, while the old timber castle was allowed to fall into decay. Kildrummy Castle was dominated by a fine cylindrical keep, which – as at Flint – must have been copied from a French prototype, with a smaller round tower at the opposite end of the bailey, D-shaped mural towers and a good gateway. It was an extremely strong castle which would not have looked out of place in the south: the three lancet chapel windows have a decidedly English look about them.

The quarrel with Scotland was rooted in the past. In the time of Henry II, the Scottish king, William the Lion, had been taken prisoner and forced to swear fealty to the King of England for himself and his country. However, when Richard I was trying every means in his power to raise money for his crusade, he had allowed the Scottish people to buy back their freedom by paying a large quantity of silver. After a period of disagreement the two countries had been drawn together when Alexander II had married Joan, the sister of Henry III, in 1221; and then, to strengthen the ties, Alexander III had married Margaret, the sister of Edward I. The two royal houses being so closely related, no one had bothered to define the ancient rights between England and Scotland. Then, Alexander III fell from his horse and died, in 1286, leaving his throne

These family trees, showing the relationships between the kings of England and Scotland, read from the roots upwards. All the children of Alexander III died before him: David in 1281, Margaret in 1283, and Alexander in 1284, leaving Margaret's daughter, the little maid of Norway, to inherit the throne.

163

NORTH-EAST TOWER

CHAPEL

LATER CHAMBER

HALL

The finest building in Kildrummy Castle must have been the strong round keep to the west, but only its foundations remain. The eastern tower at the opposite corner of the bailey stands almost to its full height, with a dark prison below and living-rooms on the upper floors. The gatehouse, built by the English after the castle had been taken in 1306, is similar to the one at Harlech.

to his little granddaughter, the Maid of Norway, who was only three years old at the time. The Maid of Norway died in 1290 when she had got as far as the Orkneys on her voyage to Scotland, and the throne was left empty. Many men put themselves forward, claiming to be descended from the Scottish kings, but the most serious contestants for the throne were John Baliol, Robert Bruce (an old man of eighty and grandfather of the future king), and John Hastings; all three were closely related, having David of Huntingdon, the brother of William the Lion, as their common ancestor. Edward I was invited in a friendly way to act as judge and he selected John Baliol to be the Scottish king.

After this, relations between England and Scotland began to turn sour. There was a general misunderstanding. The people of Scotland had not forgotten the high price they had paid for their freedom, while Edward had always considered

LATRINE HOLES

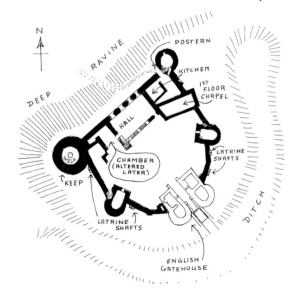

N

RAVINE

POSTERN

KITCHEN

DEEP

1ST FLOOR CHAPEL

HALL

CHAMBER (ALTERED LATER)

LATRINE SHAFTS

KEEP

LATRINE SHAFTS

DITCH

ENGLISH GATEHOUSE

himself to be their feudal overlord and insisted on imposing his will with a heavy hand. King John Baliol was reluctant to obey the English king and preferred to act on the advice of his Scottish ministers. Things came to a head when Edward was raising an army to defend his lands in France and the Scottish lords flatly refused to serve overseas. Then a marriage was arranged between Baliol's son and a niece of Philip the Fair, the French king. This meant that Scotland and France were now allied against England: France could carry on with the war in the south, while the Scottish armies would be free to sweep down and harry the north of the country.

Caught between two fires, Edward I mustered his forces at Newcastle, massacred the people of Berwick, shipped John Baliol and the coronation stone of the Scottish kings – the Stone of Scone – back to England, and proclaimed himself overlord of all Scotland.

Although Edward fortified the burnt-out town of Berwick and turned it into a secure base for his army, he saw no chance of building a string of castles along the coast as he had done in Wales: there was too much coast and not enough money. Successive English parliaments had refused to supply him with funds or, if they did, demanded all kinds of hard concessions in return. Edward did what he could afford to do. James of St George was summoned to strengthen some of the existing Scottish castles; but he was forced to use timber instead of stone: timber palisades and even timber gatehouses were built. The men were reluctant to work because the wages never seemed to arrive on time.

Contemporary documents refer to the English work force digging ditches and constructing peels to strengthen existing castles. A *peel* is an enclosure of stakes, like a bailey enclosed by a palisade: in fact, a poor man's castle. Ordinary people often built peels to protect their goods and cattle, and these were sometimes defended by square towers called *peel towers*. These were especially common in the border country in later centuries.

165

MACHICOLATIONS   CHAMBER

HALL

STORE
ROOM

*A good example of a peel
tower is the early 14th-century
Vicar's Pele, which is merely
a fortified priest's house. The
vulnerable corners were
defended by machicolations
jutting out from the parapet
above.*

Because so many of the Scottish castles have been so
repeatedly knocked down and rebuilt, it is hard to tell what
they originally looked like. For example, Edinburgh Castle
has a chapel that dates from about 1100 but most of the buildings are of the fifteenth century or later. Alexander I and William the Lion both died in Stirling Castle, Central, but no one
knows what kind of halls and chambers the kings used. A
fortress of some kind, probably timber, had stood high up on
the rock overlooking the crossing of the River Forth from the
very earliest times; while the ornate buildings of the present
castle belong to the fifteenth and sixteenth centuries.

The Scottish people found a champion in William Wallace
who, together with Andrew Moray, rose up at the head of a
Scottish army and defeated the English forces at the battle of
Stirling Bridge in 1297. From now on, England and Scotland
were almost continually at war.

King Edward patched up his quarrel with Philip the Fair
by marrying Philip's young sister, Margaret; then he betrothed
his son, Edward of Caernarvon, to Philip's daughter, Isabella.
This double alliance between England and France meant that
Scotland had been deserted and was left to carry on her fight
alone.

Edward's army included men from south Wales who carried
long supple bows which were roughly the same height as a
man, with arrows that measured about a yard along the shaft.
A *longbowman* could fire six arrows in the time it took a cross-
bowman to wind up his weapon; and these arrows were capable
of penetrating a door that was four inches thick, they could
pierce mail armour and pin a man's leg to his horse. When
William Wallace's pikemen made their firm stand at Falkirk
in 1298, they had no protection against such rapid and deadly
showers of arrows. The Welsh longbow was to win many
battles for England on the fields of France.

STIRLING
CASTLE

GOODS WERE
CONVEYED BY CARTS
AND
PACK-HORSES

GATEHOUSE REBUILT IN THE 15TH CENTURY

17TH CENTURY HOUSE

15TH CENTURY MACHICOLATIONS

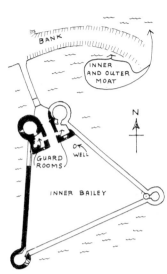

BANK

INNER AND OUTER MOAT

N

GUARD ROOMS

WELL

INNER BAILEY

Caerlaverock, Dumfries and Galloway, built sometime before 1290 on a site close to the Solway Firth, was one of the castles that was besieged by King Edward. It was to the usual English pattern, with a strong gatehouse and round corner-towers, but the bailey was shaped like a triangle. In 1300 it received a great battering from Edward's siege engines and when he took the castle, he gave orders for it to be slighted. Therefore, only about a third of the gatehouse and the lower parts of the walls are original, the other buildings being later additions.

Edward I, splendid and chivalrous in his youth, had become bitter in his old age. His Scottish campaigns were hard and cruel and not to his credit. William Wallace was captured and brutally executed in 1305. Robert Bruce, crowned king of Scotland in 1306, was defeated at Methven and managed to escape; but twelve of his knights were hanged. Bruce had sent his queen and her ladies to Kildrummy Castle where she was quickly besieged by Prince Edward of Caernarvon. The garrison put up a stout defence, but their blacksmith was bribed with 'as much gold as he could carry' to set fire to the buildings and the flames forced them to surrender. The blacksmith

Caerlaverock Castle, built sometime before 1290, was besieged and taken by Edward I in 1300. It remained in English hands until 1312 when the castellan transferred his allegiance to Robert Bruce and destroyed the castle rather than allow the English to take it again. The west gatehouse tower is original almost up to the level of the later machicolations, and so are the lower parts of the west wall; the rest belongs to a later period.

167

received his reward when the gold was melted and poured down his throat. The queen was treated honourably; but Bruce's sister was displayed in a wooden cage outside Roxburgh Castle for the people to stare at, and the Countess of Buchan was treated in a similar fashion at Berwick. Several bishops were imprisoned in irons, and some Scottish lords were ignobly executed in London. It was a sad end to Edward's career that such brutalities were permitted. He died near the Scottish border in 1307.

The architecture of English castles had always been one step ahead of those in Scotland and Ireland; and there had been improvements towards the end of the thirteenth century. The round towers at the angles of curtain walls were often built on square bases with *pyramid spurs* at the corners. These sharp edges provided acute angles from which to bounce stones or other missiles, while at the same time the towers stood on such solid foundations that it was almost impossible to undermine them.

By now, the merlons on the parapet were smaller and more regularly spaced than before. Occasionally, as in the Eagle Tower at Caernarvon which was not finished until 1327, the merlons were surrounded by a roll moulding which allowed arrows to glance off more easily than from a straight edge. In other cases, the roll moulding merely ran along the top. A hole at either side of a crenel shows where a wooden shutter once hung across the gap, suspended from an iron bar which allowed it to swing out, shielding the archer from enemy arrows.

In previous times, the roofs of important buildings had been covered with oak shingles, stone, slate or earthenware tiles, and they had been set at a steep pitch to allow the rain to run off easily. Lead, however, being watertight, was found to be a better material to use, but lead tended to creep downwards under a hot sun when laid on a steeply sloping surface, so the pitch of the roofs had to be lowered. This posed a tricky problem of design, because low roofs did not harmonize well

Pyramid spurs, like those built about 1300 at Goodrich Castle below, are made by setting a round tower on a square base. The solid masonry prevented undermining and if stones or other missiles were dropped from above, they would bounce off into the ranks of the enemy.

PYRAMID SPURS

168

with tall buildings, so it became the fashion towards the end of the thirteenth century to carry the walls up to crenellated parapets which matched the outer curtain walls. These parapets were never intended to be used for defensive purposes and were purely decorative. The rain now trickled into lead box-gutters, hidden away behind the parapet, and came out through a series of spouts.

English castles had always been designed for military reasons; but now the barons seemed to be more concerned about elegance than about defence. They wanted to improve their living standards. Some of them resented having to mix with the hired soldiers and servants in the common hall and built themselves a second hall where they could live and entertain their guests in private. Here's what Langland had to say about it a century later in his *Piers Plowmen*.

Desolate is the hall each day in the week
Where neither lord nor lady delights to sit.
Now has each rich man a rule to eat by himself
In a privy parlour, because of poor men
Or in a chamber with a chimney and leave the chief hall
That was made for meals and men to eat in . . .
(*English Historical Documents*, vol. IV, p. 138.)

Soon after 1270, a descendant of old Hugh Bigod of Framlingham, Roger Bigod, lord of Chepstow Castle, left the

The complete plan of Chepstow is on page 170. The old Norman stronghold was enlarged and another storey added to the hall in the 13th century under the ownership of William Marshal and his sons. A member of the Bigod family (married to William Marshal's grand-daughter) built the east corner-tower above, and the domestic range in the lower bailey below.

LORD'S HALL

SMALL CHAMBER OVER PORCH

LARGE CHAMBER

SERVANT'S HALL (WINDOW GREATLY RESTORED)

UPPER CHAMBER

LOWER CHAMBER

THE INNER PART OF THE GATEHOU[SE] HAS BEEN DESTROY[ED]

Roger Bigod's halls and chambers were built on sloping ground and his hall was about a storey higher than that of his servants. The buttery and pantry for the upper hall were directly above those of the lower hall. Food must have been carried into the passage from an outside kitchen; while visitors, alighting from their horses and carriage, would have used the entrance (now blocked) at the side of the two-storeyed porch. Clothes were becoming more elaborate: heads being carefully draped with the veil and wimple, and a wife would often have her husband's coat-of-arms embroidered on her gown.

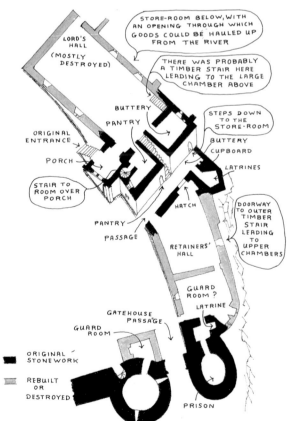

LORD'S HALL (MOSTLY DESTROYED)

STORE-ROOM BELOW, WITH AN OPENING THROUGH WHICH GOODS COULD BE HAULED UP FROM THE RIVER

THERE WAS PROBABLY A TIMBER STAIR HERE LEADING TO THE LARGE CHAMBER ABOVE

BUTTERY

PANTRY

ORIGINAL ENTRANCE

PORCH

STAIR TO ROOM OVER PORCH

STEPS DOWN TO THE STORE-ROOM

BUTTERY CUPBOARD

LATRINES

HATCH

DOORWAY TO OUTER TIMBER STAIR LEADING TO UPPER CHAMBERS

PANTRY PASSAGE

RETAINERS' HALL

GUARD ROOM ?

LATRINE

GATEHOUSE PASSAGE

GUARD ROOM

ORIGINAL STONEWORK

REBUILT OR DESTROYED

PRISON

170

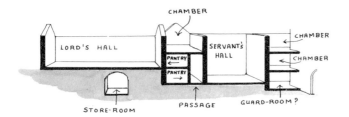

LORD'S HALL · CHAMBER · CHAMBER · CHAMBER · SERVANT'S HALL · PANTRY · PANTRY · STORE-ROOM · PASSAGE · GUARD-ROOM?

ancient Norman hall, which had been heightened and altered during the course of the thirteenth century, for others to use, and erected a new range of domestic buildings down by the main gatehouse. Here there were two halls, one at either end, with two sets of service rooms sandwiched, one above the other, in the middle. The lord's hall has been partly demolished; but the two-storeyed entrance porch still stands.

Prince Edward of Caernarvon had become Edward II in 1307, and by that time the admirable restraint of the thirteenth century had disappeared, and the more flamboyant *Decorated period*, which speaks for itself, was well under way. It lasted roughly from 1307 until the death of Edward III in 1377. Doorways and windows were often heavily ornamented and so were the fireplaces. A good example of the domestic architecture of this period is at Ludlow.

The old Norman stronghold at Ludlow had come into the hands of Roger Mortimer of Wigmore through his marriage with Joan de Geneville. It was Joan's father, a friend of

Above, servants are carrying bread trenchers from the pantry and fish from the outer kitchen (through the passage and up the stairs) into the lord's hall at Chepstow. Left, above and below, are sections through the domestic buildings at Chepstow and Ludlow. Below is a fireplace from Roger Mortimer's large upper chamber at Ludlow.

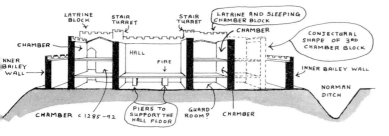

CHAMBER · INNER BAILEY WALL · LATRINE BLOCK · STAIR TURRET · STAIR TURRET · LATRINE AND SLEEPING CHAMBER BLOCK · CHAMBER · CONJECTURAL SHAPE OF 3RD CHAMBER BLOCK · HALL · FIRE · INNER BAILEY WALL · NORMAN DITCH · CHAMBER c 1285-92 · PIERS TO SUPPORT THE HALL FLOOR · GUARD ROOM? · CHAMBER

SLOT FOR A ROOF BEAM SUPPORTED BY A QUEEN'S HEAD · SLOT FOR A ROOF BEAM SUPPORTED BY A KING'S HEAD

The plan of Ludlow Castle is on page 74. The late 13th-century hall and chambers were built on level ground against the north length of the old Norman inner bailey wall. The hall, raised over a store-room, was entered from a flight of steps that passed through a porch (since demolished). The original chamber block was built alongside this busy entrance; but it was altered when the second chamber block was added to the dais end.

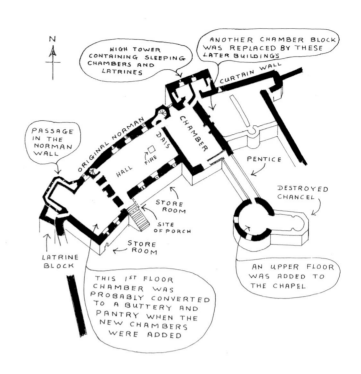

N

HIGH TOWER CONTAINING SLEEPING CHAMBERS AND LATRINES

ANOTHER CHAMBER BLOCK WAS REPLACED BY THESE LATER BUILDINGS

CURTAIN WALL

PASSAGE IN THE NORMAN WALL

ORIGINAL NORMAN

CHAMBER

DAIS

HALL

FIRE

PENTICE

DESTROYED CHANCEL

STORE ROOM

SITE OF PORCH

STORE ROOM

LATRINE BLOCK

THIS 1ST FLOOR CHAMBER WAS PROBABLY CONVERTED TO A BUTTERY AND PANTRY WHEN THE NEW CHAMBERS WERE ADDED

AN UPPER FLOOR WAS ADDED TO THE CHAPEL

UPPER CHAMBER

LATER WINDOW

Edward I, who had built the spacious hall, raised up on a basement with a chamber block at the screens end. Sometime before 1320 Roger Mortimer built a similar, and larger chamber block at the dais end of the hall. Any building of this date seems to be riddled with huge fireplaces, which suggests that they liked to keep the rooms well heated. The scars on the walls show that the open timber roof was almost flat, while the beams were supported on large stone corbels which were carved with decorative crowned heads.

Edward II never built a castle in all the twenty years of his disorderly reign and so it is not necessary to give the details of the scandals and intrigues that surrounded him. Froissart, writing his chronicles towards the end of the fourteenth century, explains what the situation was like in the north.

172

Soon after he [Edward II] had been crowned, Robert Bruce, King of Scotland, who had given so much trouble to the gallant King Edward I, reconquered the whole of Scotland and the city of Berwick as well, twice burnt and ravaged a large part of England stretching as far as four or five days' ride beyond the border, and defeated this king and all the barons of England at a place in Scotland called Stirling. [The Battle of Bannockburn.] (Froissart, *Chronicles*, Penguin, p. 39.)

The years passed and matters went from bad to worse: by 1320 Edward had completely fallen out with his wife, Isabella, to whom, as mentioned before, he had been betrothed in his father's time. In 1324 her brother, Charles IV, who had been king of France for two years, started invading the English possessions of Guienne and Gascony, and Isabella was sent on a peace mission to Paris to try to patch matters up. Her eldest son, Prince Edward, followed shortly after, to swear fealty to the French king for the disputed lands. In Paris, Isabella had met Roger Mortimer, the owner of Ludlow Castle; she fell in love and shocked everyone by her scandalous behaviour. So much so, that Charles IV was pleased to see the last of his sister when, together with Mortimer and Prince Edward, she left Paris for Hainault. The English prince was betrothed to Count William of Hainault's daughter, Philippa, and in return Count William promised to raise a small army. On 23 September 1326, Isabella, Mortimer, Prince Edward and the Count's brother, John, landed at the head of their forces near Harwich.

Edward II had never been popular and the barons flocked to join the invaders. Chased by his wife and her ever-increasing army, the king flew westwards from one castle to the next, trailing his possessions behind him. Contrary winds did not allow his little boat to carry him to the comparative safety of Ireland and he was finally captured, taken to Berkeley Castle, Avon, and imprisoned in the keep.

As was the case at Farnham, Berkeley was a Norman motte-

The barons had acquired a taste for privacy and wanted more, and larger, chambers than before. There were further chambers in the latrine block behind Roger Mortimer's spacious new chambers, above. Below, one of the late 13th-century hall windows, seen from the inside.

A motte-and-bailey castle was built at Berkeley in 1067; the shell keep enclosed the motte (as at Farnham) about 1153; and inner-bailey walls were added 1160–90. The lord Berkeley, who had held Edward II in custody, replaced most of the buildings of the inner bailey before he died in 1361. Below is the forebuilding enclosing the steps leading up to the keep, with the 14th-century pointed doorway built into the old round Norman archway. A sentry is spinning yarns about the wars.

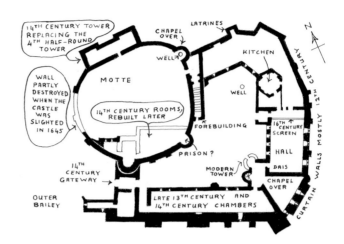

and-bailey castle where a shell wall had been built round the outside of the motte, starting at the original ground level. This high wall was supported by pilasters and four semi-circular towers, while the entrance stairs went through a square tower facing the inner courtyard. The castle prison, where ordinary law-breakers were thrown, was at the base of the semicircular tower next to this entrance.

The law of the land was brutal. A suspected criminal had the choice of being tried by a jury and hanged if found guilty; or of refusing trial and being starved to death in a prison. The advantage of refusing trial was that, his guilt never having been proved, all his goods and chattels could be kept by his family.

The customary punishment, indeed, for those mute of malice is carried out thus throughout the realm. The prisoner shall sit on the cold, bare floor, dressed only in the thinnest of shirts, and pressed with as great a weight of iron as his wretched body can bear. His food shall be a little rotten bread, and his drink cloudy and stinking water. The day on which he eats he shall not drink, and the day on which he has drunk he shall not taste bread. Only super-human strength survives this punishment beyond the fifth or sixth day. (*English Historical Documents*, p. 566.)

This inhuman method of putting people to death was described by the author of *The Life of Edward the Second*, who was probably a monk at Malmesbury. It was the sheriff's duty to see that the punishment was duly carried out, and the prisoners were often incarcerated in his castle. It appears to have been the custom at Berkeley to throw the rotting carcasses of animals among the starving prisoners, and tradition has it that Edward II was held in the room directly above this grisly cell, so that the stench of the decomposing corpses underneath would eventually kill him. However, Edward had inherited his father's fine physique and he survived. Two attempts were made to rescue him and, although nothing is known for certain, Mortimer seems to have decided that the king was too dangerous a person to be left alive and arranged to have him murdered in September 1327. William Ogle, Thomas Gurney – a Somerset knight – and Sir John Maltravers, who had been left in charge of the royal prisoner, were later accused of the crime.

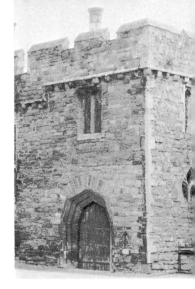

The travelling musicians are standing just inside the gateway leading to the inner bailey, giving someone a noisy welcome. Berkeley Castle has been inhabited ever since the motte was first dug, and it has been necessary to insert other doorways and windows into the walls of the mid 14th-century domestic buildings, which is confusing. However, the unfamiliar 'Berkeley arch' seen in the entrance to the screens passage above is absolutely authentic: a shape only used in this castle and the surrounding district. Wooden screens separating the passage from the hall were introduced in the 15th century (the one at Berkeley is slightly later).

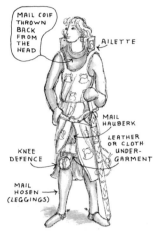

The tiny rings of mail armour could not stop the deadly arrows of the longbows, so plate armour was strapped to the warriors' arms and legs. A garment fitted with metal plates was worn under the surcoat. A knight's arms were displayed on his shield, his surcoat and on strange shoulder decorations: ailettes.

As if to blot out the stain of the king's murder, a complete new range of domestic buildings was put up at Berkeley about the middle of the fourteenth century: a splendid example of the Decorated style.

Prince Edward was crowned king while his father was still imprisoned at Berkeley; but in reality it was Isabella and Mortimer who ruled. Mortimer was greedy and had acquired such a wealth of lands and goods that people whispered that his ambition was to sit on the throne itself. Edward III was no fool and he realized that his only chance of survival lay in getting rid of his mother's paramour: he himself helped to arrest Mortimer in Nottingham Castle. Convicted for his 'notorious crimes', Mortimer was hanged, drawn and quartered at Tyburn in November 1330. The king told his parliament that from now onwards it was he who would rule.

Isabella was sent to live alone with her uncomfortable memories at Castle Rising. Instead of lodging in the massive Norman keep, she occupied a range of half-timbered buildings which had been crammed into the southern part of the small bailey, the foundations of which have only recently been discovered.

When Isabella's brother, Charles IV, had died in 1328, there were only daughters left to succeed him, so the crown of France went to his cousin, Philip VI. Edward III declared that he had a much better right to the throne through his mother, and in 1337 he decided to press his claim, quartering the arms of France with his own on his shield as an act of defiance. Throughout his reign the small population of England was caught up in a struggle against the vast resources of France, always hampered by the Scottish armies, making the most of the situation, and attacking from the north.

By this time a new weapon had appeared on the scene. No one knows who invented gunpowder, but it appears to have been used in ancient China. The first recipe for an explosive mixture – seven parts saltpetre to five of charcoal and sulphur – appeared in 1240, when an English monk, Roger Bacon, wrote it down in a secret code. After that, various texts men-

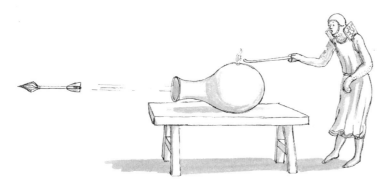

tioned gunpowder and explosives. A manuscript dated 1326, written by Walter de Milemete for his pupil Prince Edward, is decorated with two drawings of men firing a primitive cannon and in the same year it is known that cannon were being manufactured in Florence.

The English drawings show an object which looks like a brass vase, laid on its side, and with a gigantic arrow flying out of the neck. A tube was soon found to be a more efficient shape than a vase; but both forms were probably used by the English at the sea battle of Sluys, at Crécy, and at the siege of Calais, which was taken in 1347. The explosion of a cannon would have been demoralizing for the enemy; but the range was short and the firing was not very accurate: they did little damage. It was the skill of the English longbowmen, with their volleys of arrows fired in quick succession, that won the day at Crécy; not the newly invented cannon.

There were many changes about this time. The appalling disaster of the Black Death in 1348 and succeeding years, caused a serious shortage of manpower. The old feudal system was slowly breaking up. Serfs had always been forced to live out their lives in the villages where they were born, owing allegiance to the lords who lived in the manor houses or castles. Now things were different. Many serfs escaped to the cities to work for wages; or slipped through the dark forests to other parts of the country where landlords would employ them on reasonable terms.

The man touching off the 'pot de fer' with a heated iron rod is taken from a manuscript drawing. This fails to explain how the brass vase was fixed to the table. The armour is old-fashioned for 1326. Edward III, below, drawn from a brass of 1347, is up to date. His arms and legs are partly protected by plate armour and under his short surcoat, decorated with the arms of England quartered with the arms of France, are metal plates.

177

In 1067 William I built a castle on high wooded land overlooking the river Thames; calling it Windlesora after the near-by Saxon settlement and royal hunting lodge. This view of Windsor Castle shows its strong position: the round tower standing on the original motte; the two baileys on either side; and the steep bank dropping down to the river. Edward III, who was born at Windsor, spent the enormous sum of £51,000 converting the old fortress into one of the finest palaces in Europe.

In the old system of warfare, the barons at the head of their untrained men had rallied round the king to serve the required forty days. However, professional soldiers were more efficient and better trained; so the later kings only called up the old feudal levies when they ran short of cash. If a knight preferred not to fight, he could pay a fine and this would pay for the mercenaries. Many noblemen had been captured in the French war and ransom money was pouring into England, so Edward could well afford to pay for professional soldiers.

With all the new changes in the system, castle owners did not hold their villagers in the same vice-like grip as before, and they did not have the same duty to protect them. Castles were starting to lose their importance.

When existing castles were being improved in the middle of the fourteenth century, it was usually the domestic buildings which needed to be replaced. Edward III did this on a grand scale. He set his masons to work on the old Norman castle at Windsor, Berkshire, and turned it into the sort of palace that was fit for a king.

178

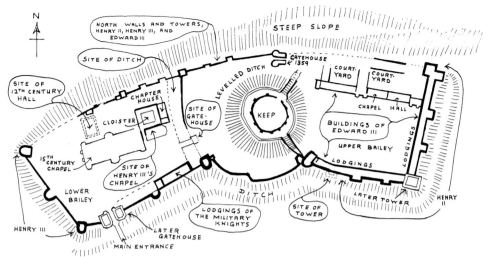

Windsor Castle had been laid out by William I with a motte between two baileys, although there is the possibility that one of the baileys was added slightly later. Henry I held court at Windsor in 1110, so there must have been a hall in the upper bailey at this time, though there is no trace of it now. The authorities are not sure if the original shell keep was built in the time of Henry I or Henry II: there is no mention of it in the records and the stonework is hard to date. Henry II built a curtain wall, with square towers, round the upper bailey and there was a stone hall standing in the lower bailey by the end of the twelfth century. Richard I left the castle alone; while John levelled the ditch round the motte – probably to make it easier to get from one bailey to the other – and carried out a few repairs. With his usual enthusiasm, Henry III filled the upper bailey with pleasant half-timbered houses for the use of his growing family. Queen Eleanor's apartments were built round a square herb garden and there was a second courtyard; all the buildings were linked with *pentices*, or covered ways. Henry III also built a church in the lower bailey alongside the existing hall, started to replace the old original palisade with a stone curtain wall with rounded towers, and added a barbican to the main gate. A fire had destroyed some of the buildings in the lower bailey and the whole castle was starting to fall into decay when Edward III turned his thoughts towards Windsor in 1344.

Windsor Castle has been repeatedly altered to suit the needs of the times, but the existing layout is basically the same as that planned by Edward III. His new buildings are mentioned in contemporary accounts. Those in the upper bailey included a hall, chapel, four chambers for the queen. The old hall was converted to a large chamber and there were kitchens, a larder, a salting house and a pastry house. In the lower bailey there was a hall, lodgings, a chapter house, vestry, treasury, warden's lodge, kitchen, roasting house, brewhouse, bakehouse and a horse mill. The present Chapel of St George was built towards the end of the 15th century.

The young king had a romantic turn of mind and he and his glittering court took a great interest in the half-legendary dark-age hero, Arthur. Already, people had been trying to find out if he had really existed or not. In 1190, it was claimed that the two ancient coffins dug up in the burial ground at Glastonbury belonged to Arthur and Guinevere. In 1278, Edward I had opened these coffins and, according to Adam of Domerham, a monk of Glastonbury, 'found separately the bones of the said king, which were of great size, and those of Queen Guinevere, which were of marvellous beauty'. So Arthur had already been promoted from the rank of a war leader to that of a king. Edward imagined him to be a man like himself:

Men's tunics tended to become shorter as the 14th century progressed, but women's skirts were as voluminous as ever. Long white streamers hanging from the elbows were popular and the complicated head-dresses, like the one below, were made by pleating layers of veiling into zigzag patterns. Bodices and sleeves were tightly buttoned.

'At that time King Edward of England conceived the idea of altering and rebuilding the great castle of Windsor, originally built by King Arthur, and where had first been established the noble Round Table, from which so many fine men and brave knights had gone forth and performed great deeds throughout the world.' (Froissart, *Chronicles*, p. 66.)

Froissart was stretching a point here because King Arthur did not really build Windsor Castle; but fiction is often as effective as fact. Because Edward III wanted to surround himself with enthusiastic high-minded young men who would help him to win battles in France, he decided to imitate Arthur's court. In 1344 he held a tournament in honour of the knights of the round table. A timber hall was built in the upper bailey, in which to put the round table, but this was pulled down again in order to make way for Edward's more ambitious alterations.

Edward's next idea was to found an order of chivalry. The exact reason why he chose a blue garter for his symbol is not known. Legend has it that the king was dancing with a lady – possibly the Countess of Salisbury, whom he loved passionately at the time – when her garter worked loose and dropped to the floor. To cover her embarrassment, the king gallantly held up the garter and proclaimed: 'Honi soit qui mal y pense.' (Evil be to him who evil thinks.) Then, to remove all traces of smiles, he added, 'I will make it ere long the most honourable garter that ever was worn.' As knights often wore women's favours in the form of ribbons and sleeves at tournaments, it was not out of place to found a new order of chivalry with a lady's blue garter.

The lower bailey of the castle at Windsor was to be the spiritual home of the Order of the Garter. Henry III's chapel was repaired and reconsecrated in honour of St George – another of Edward's heroes – and the buildings for a College of Priests were ranged round a cloister alongside. Twenty-five old and battle-scarred knights were to be given food, lodging and an honourable retirement.

Unfortunately, all the magnificent royal apartments set up against the twelfth-century wall in the upper bailey were demolished in 1660, and they have been built and rebuilt time and again since then. Many of the Gothic windows look medieval, but they were inserted in Regency times, when the Round Tower was also heightened and altered.

The Round Tower is basically the old original shell keep; and it had been used by Edward III and Queen Philippa, his wife from Hainault, while they waited for their new apartments to be ready. A timber hall, chambers, and probably a chapel, were fitted inside the old roughly circular wall at

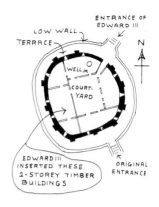

The shell keep at Windsor would have been considerably lower in the 14th century than it is now. It was raised in Victorian times. The Norman foundations were laid in a rough circle to suit the shape of the top of the mound, and Edward III ordered his carpenters to set up two-storey timber buildings inside the wall as temporary accommodation for himself and his queen while waiting for the royal apartments to be finished in the upper bailey.

Queenborough Castle, built 1361–77 to defend the south bank of the Thames against the French, was a concentric castle. The outer bailey enclosed the circular inner bailey which was virtually a keep. The entrance to this keep was not, as would be expected, in front of the gatehouse, but on the opposite side, subjecting the enemy to showers of arrows from the six tall towers. Royal lodgings were built against the inner wall of the keep, leaving a stone-paved court and well in the middle. This sketch, taken from a 17th-century drawing, gives some idea of what the castle looked like before it was demolished.

first-floor level, with a small courtyard in the middle. They installed the first clock ever to be seen in England: it was operated by means of weights and struck the hours on a bell.

The alterations at Windsor were more or less complete by 1365; which was about the time that King Edward built Queenborough Castle, Kent, overlooking the busy waters of the Thames estuary, on the Isle of Sheppey. The design was based on a circle. There was a circular keep in the middle, enclosing a circular courtyard and defended by six semi-circular towers. This inner building was reached by means of two passages which divided the outer area into two semi-circular baileys. A moat encircled the outside.

It is a great pity that this unusual fortress was destroyed in the seventeenth century: as it happened, it was the last royal English medieval castle ever to be built.

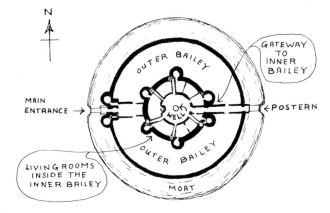

182

THE RETURN OF THE GREAT SQUARE KEEP

12

THE CASTLE ERA WAS ALMOST OVER IN ENGLAND BY the end of the fourteenth century; but the Scottish lords were just starting to break away from English traditions and build their own types of fortresses. These had no unnecessary trimmings: they were thick-walled, austere, and built for defence.

King Robert Bruce had married twice. The son of his second marriage, David II, died in 1371 and he was succeeded by the grandson of the first, Robert the Steward – the first of the Stewarts. Robert II was old and had a weak character. His barons did as they liked and were soon building strong castles in order to increase their power. As with the old Norman keeps, most of the Scottish castles of this period had all the domestic rooms packed into one rectangular stone tower, but there was usually a short wing attached to the main block which contained a kitchen and several extra chambers up above. These buildings are called *tower houses*.

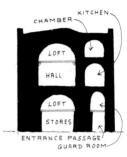

Above is the north–south section through Craigmillar tower house. The hall is below. Corbels running along the two walls supported the floor of the loft over the hall, where servants slept.

HALL FIREPLACE

CORBELS TO SUPPORT THE LOFT FLOOR

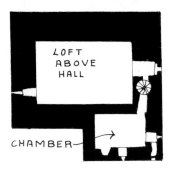

LOFT ABOVE HALL

CHAMBER

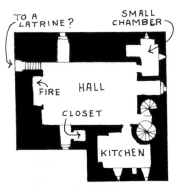

TO A LATRINE?

SMALL CHAMBER

FIRE HALL

CLOSET

KITCHEN

LOFT ABOVE STORE-ROOMS

MURDER-HOLE

GUARD-ROOM

N

STORE ROOMS

DRAWBRIDGE (PIT FILLED IN)

DOOR BACKED BY A YETT (SEE GLOSSARY)

PEASANT WOMAN AND HER HUT

TOWER HOUSE

LATER BUILDINGS

THIS LATER ROOM HAS ALTERED THE ROOF LINE

MACHICOLATED PARRAPET

OUTER WALL ADDED 1427

Craigmillar tower house is basically a two-storey building, but each main room was divided into upper and lower parts by the wooden floors of the lofts. The wing has four floors. The view of the castle above is taken from the south-east.

The castle at Craigmillar, Lothian, just south of Edinburgh, was built about 1375, and the main building is a typical tower house: two storeys high, with massive vaulted ceilings and an attached wing. The two main floors were subdivided with timber floors set high on the walls, just below the vaults, making low lofts. The top of the keep was stone vaulted as well, so that a war machine could be mounted on the roof – war machines always needed a solid foundation to stand on. Craigmillar has none of the complicated window-tracery found in contemporary English buildings, and the entrance doorway is a simple arch. Stone machicolation, now firmly established in the south, was rarely seen in Scotland until after 1400; so the outer curtain at Craigmillar, which has machicolations all round, was built as late as 1427.

184

Dunnottar, perched on a gigantic rock jutting out into the North Sea off the Grampian coast, is a late fourteenth-century tower house that was built on a smaller scale. There were store-rooms and a small prison at ground-floor level; a hall, kitchen and minute chamber on the first floor, with two similar shaped rooms up above; and garrets fitted under the gabled roof. The wall-walk had round watch-towers, or *bartizans*, jutting out at the corners, overlooking the sea and the solitary track winding up to the castle from the mainland. The track is carefully cobbled and passes through two tunnels. Dunnottar had been a Pictish stronghold and was in constant use from roughly A.D. 300 right up to the sixteenth and seventeenth centuries, when a palace was built on the far side of the rock.

The entrance to most tower houses was in the angle between the main block and the wing; but, at Dunnottar, the entrance was at first-floor level and on the other side. There were store-rooms below the hall, a great chamber above, and garrets under the roof. A sentry could walk behind the parapet and keep watch from the bartizans *(or watch-towers).*

The lord of Doune Castle lived in the massive keep-gatehouse. It had its own entrance in the courtyard. This tower had a hall over the passage, the chamber above, and four small chambers in the half-round turret with the well-chamber at the base. There were more sleeping-rooms at the top of the tower under the roof. Soldiers and servants kept to their own quarters alongside, with no communicating door.

Not all Scottish castles of this period were standard tower houses. Robert Stewart, Duke of Albany, was the brother of Robert III; but his power far exceeded that of the king. Sometime after 1381 he built a castle at an ancient site called Doune, in Central near Stirling. The strongest part of this fortress was the tower, which served as both gatehouse and keep. It is a four-storeyed tower, with the entrance passage running through it at ground level, and containing the lord's hall, his chapel, several chambers, a guard-room, store-rooms, a well-chamber and a prison; added to which, there were garrets under the roof. The tower was completely self-contained and could be defended from the courtyard side as well as from the outside: because unreliable bands of mercenary troops were often employed, there was the threat of revolt from within as well as from without. A solid wall divided the lord's hall from the garrison hall alongside.

Over the border in England, money from the French wars was still plentiful in the 1370s and the barons could well afford to improve their strongholds. The old Norman motte-and-bailey castle at Warwick, Warwickshire, was almost

STAIR TURRET HAD A BEACON PLATFORM AT THE TOP

SLEEPING ROOMS

BARTIZAN

CHAMBER

MODERN LOUVER

LATRINE SHAFT

RETAINERS' HALL

STORE-ROOMS

LORD'S HALL

PRISON

WELL CHAMBER

BARTIZAN
(WATCH TOWER)

RAINWATER
SPOUTS

WINDOWS FOR
VANISHED BUILDINGS

SLEEPING
ROOM

FIRE

CHAMBER

LATRINE

CHAPEL

ACCESS TO
WALL-WALK

The buildings of Doune Castle were grouped
round a courtyard, with the gatehouse and
retainers' hall defending the entrance. Each hall
has a music gallery on the side facing the dais.
Originally there were more buildings, including
a chapel, standing against the east and south walls.

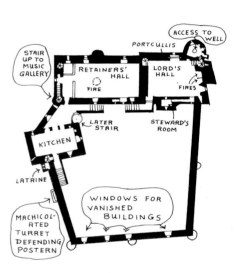

ACCESS TO
WELL

PORTCULLIS

STAIR
UP TO
MUSIC
GALLERY

RETAINERS'
HALL

FIRE

LORD'S
HALL

FIRES

LATER
STAIR

STEWARD'S
ROOM

KITCHEN

LATRINE

MACHICOL-
ATED
TURRET
DEFENDING
POSTERN

WINDOWS FOR
VANISHED
BUILDINGS

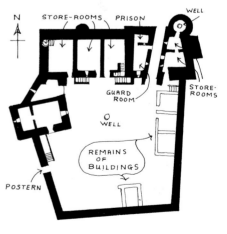

N

STORE-ROOMS

PRISON

WELL

GUARD
ROOM

STORE-
ROOMS

WELL

REMAINS
OF
BUILDINGS

POSTERN

RETAINERS'
HALL

RETAINERS'
ENTRANCE

RD'S ENTRANCE
NDED BY A WALL
D IRON GATE

MACHICOLATIONS
GUARD-ROOM
TURRETS CONNECTED BY BRIDGES
GATEHOUSE
GUARD-ROOM
MACHICOL-ATIONS
PRISON
BARBICAN

A motte-and-bailey castle had been standing at Warwick since 1068, and was badly damaged by Simon de Montfort in the reign of Henry III. The castle was rebuilt on a grand scale towards the end of the 14th century, with a new domestic range, a water-gate, and superb line of fortifications defending the entrance. These consisted of a square gatehouse with a long barbican before it, and two tall towers at the angles of the bailey wall. Any attacking force would have to endure a hail of arrows from the high towers, from the barbican walls and from the top of the gatehouse.

entirely rebuilt at this time, with a domestic range and a fine new gatehouse, with long barbican attached, and two tall towers at the angles of the curtain. Small rooms were packed one on top of the other inside the towers, and there were guard-rooms at the top leading out to the machicolated parapets. These little rooms provided comfortable lodgings for visitors in times of peace; while the entrance to the castle could be well defended in the event of an attack.

The tide of war had finally turned against Edward III. By 1370 he was in his dotage, while the French army, led by the brilliant commander, Bertrand du Guesclin, recaptured castle after castle. By 1375 Edward had lost all the territories he had won in France; his heir, the Black Prince, was dead, leaving

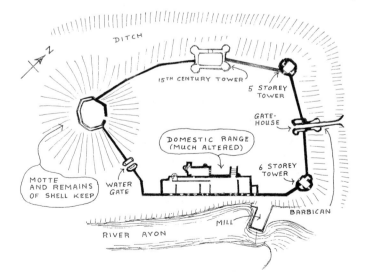

DITCH
15TH CENTURY TOWER
5 STOREY TOWER
GATE-HOUSE
DOMESTIC RANGE (MUCH ALTERED)
6 STOREY TOWER
MOTTE AND REMAINS OF SHELL KEEP
WATER GATE
BARBICAN
MILL
RIVER AVON

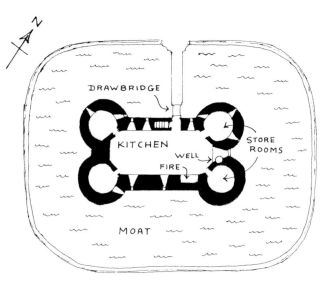

WINDOW IN THE PHOTOGRAPH BELOW

CHAPEL

DRAWBRIDGE

KITCHEN

WELL

FIRE

STORE ROOMS

MOAT

KNIGHT ABOUT TO ATTEND A TOURNAMENT

his small son, Richard, to take his place; and the French army was massed on the far side of the Channel, ready to invade England. Because Scotland and France were in sympathy with each other, the Scottish armies were likely to come sweeping over the border once the French had landed, and England was in danger of being attacked from two sides at once. In view of this general situation, it is not surprising that the English barons who were granted permission to fortify their homes should be living either in the north or the south of the country.

Broadly speaking, two types of castles were being built in England at the end of the fourteenth century. There were huge tower houses like Nunney Castle, which was erected in Somerset after 1373, similar in principle to the ones in Scotland, but built on a rather grander scale. Then there were castles which had the rooms ranged round a square courtyard, and these provided a larger and more comfortable place to live in. One of the best examples is at Bodiam in East Sussex.

In 1377 – the year in which the old king was buried and was succeeded by his grandson, Richard II – the French overran the Isle of Wight and set fire to the ports of Hastings and Rye. All the south-coast defences had to be strengthened because invasion was expected hourly. A veteran soldier from the

The great tower is all that is left of Nunney Castle. The plan shows the kitchen at ground-floor level. Servants' quarters were directly above and the lord's hall and chamber were on the third and fourth floors. The north wall was destroyed when the castle was slighted by Oliver Cromwell in 1645.

189

French war, Sir Edward Dalyngrigge, was called upon to inspect the walls of Winchelsea and to fortify Rye against a further attack. Several years later, in 1386, the same knight was given a licence to 'strengthen his manor with a wall and stone and lime, and crenellate and construct and make into a castle his manor house at Bodyham, near the sea, in the county of Sussex, for the defence of the adjacent country and resistance to our enemies.' (*Calendar of Patent Rolls 1385–9, p. 42.*)

Bodiam was some way inland, up a navigable river; and Sir Edward Dalyngrigge made more than full use of his licence, because he abandoned his old manor altogether and set up a completely new castle on a near-by site.

All the domestic buildings at Bodiam are carefully packed inside the high curtain wall, with the two tall gateways facing each other across the courtyard. The wide moat was crossed by a bridge that stood at right angles to the main approach, so that the invaders were forced to show the side of

This is the south wall of Bodiam Castle, with the postern tower which had a platform before it to support the vanished bridge over the moat. The window of Sir Edward Dalyngrigge's hall is to the right of it. The round tower would have been reserved for his own use or as lodgings for his intimate friends. In their memorial brass, Sir Edward (above) wears armour, while his wife (right) has her feet on a little dog. The pigeon loft is out of the picture at the top of the left-hand tower.

MACHICOLATED PARAPET

BARBICAN TOWER

OILETTE

PRISON

their advancing force, rather than the front: a wider target. There was a postern bridge leading over the moat from the far gateway.

By this time, firearms were being used for defence. Until about 1370 the cannon had been made of brass or copper; but now wrought iron was found to be a more suitable material. *Cannon* comes from the word 'cane', meaning a reed or tube. The weapons were now being made in the form of iron tubes, blocked at one end, reinforced with strong iron rings, and firing stone balls or lead shot. The various types of cannon were given different names: from the larger *bombards*, down to the thin iron tubes which were strapped to poles and operated by one or two men, called *handguns*. These are the ancestors of our modern rifles.

If these new weapons were to be used to defend a building, the walls had to be pierced with round holes to take the ends of the iron tubes, and slits were needed to see through. The *gun-loops* on the gatehouse at Bodiam have vertical slits and holes at the bottom. Similar ones had already been used in the west gate at Canterbury, which had been built by 1380, and in the new defences at Southampton. They are also called *oilettes* or *keyhole gunports*.

Bodiam gatehouse was equipped with keyhole gunports, or oilettes, so that the primitive tube-shaped guns could be poked through the round hole. The gunner could sight his gun by peering through the slit. Below is an oilette from the city gatehouse at Canterbury.

191

Bodiam Castle is the result of centuries of experience. All the necessary rooms were symmetrically packed inside the curtain wall facing the square courtyard. Protected by the moat, the round corner-towers could not be undermined and the rectangular gatehouse and postern tower had machicolations at the top. The retainers' quarters were well away from Sir Edward's lordly apartments where there was one chamber for formal occasions and another for family use, with two extra rooms above, probably reserved for the ladies of the household. The west side of the castle is below.

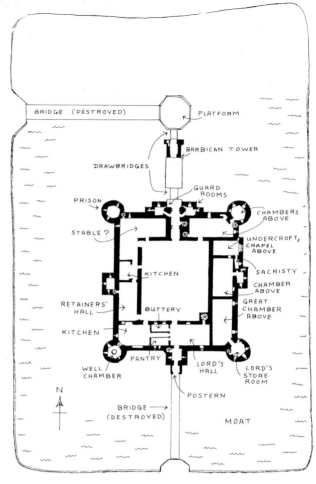

BRIDGE (DESTROYED)   PLATFORM
BARBICAN TOWER
DRAWBRIDGES
GUARD ROOMS
PRISON   CHAMBERS ABOVE
STABLE?   UNDERCROFT, CHAPEL ABOVE
SACRISTY
KITCHEN   CHAMBER ABOVE
RETAINERS' HALL   BUTTERY   GREAT CHAMBER ABOVE
KITCHEN
PANTRY
WELL CHAMBER   LORD'S HALL   LORD'S STORE ROOM
N   POSTERN
BRIDGE →
(DESTROYED)   MOAT

PIGEON LOFT (300 NESTS)

WELL CHAMBER

Although it had been built for defence during a state of emergency, Bodiam made an extremely comfortable home for Sir Edward Dalyngrigge. There were two halls: one for his own use and the other for the servants and mercenary troops; each with its own kitchen, and with the well-chamber leading off the larger one. The great chamber was at the dais end of the hall, with a second chamber adjoining and the chapel beyond. There was plenty of space at ground level for the workshops, smithies and store-rooms; while many guests could be lodged in the numerous little chambers fitted into the gatehouses and turrets. There was a prison and a pigeon loft: all that a man could desire if he wanted to live in style.

A similar castle was built at Bolton, North Yorkshire, sometime after 1378 by Lord Scrope, who was chancellor to

MACHICOLATION

CHAPEL WINDOWS

Bolton is more massive than Bodiam, with square corner-towers and tall three-storey buildings surrounding the courtyard. It is dark and austere. Below is the outside of the main entrance: a porter would wait just inside the passage where he had his lodge, ready to question strangers visiting the castle. Each of the four doorways leading from the courtyard to the interior rooms had a machicolation in the angle above. The way to the hall was through the north-west doorway, along a passage to a left-hand turn, and up the stairs.

Richard II. In this romantic ruin all the doorways leading from the central courtyard to the interior rooms were defended by portcullises which had machicolations above. If an enemy managed to fight his way through the main gate, he would have been trapped in the yard and have become a standing target for the men shooting from the windows, unable to force a way into the building and, if the entrance was subsequently barred, unable to get out again.

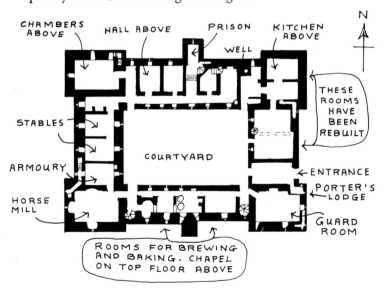

CHAMBERS ABOVE   HALL ABOVE   PRISON   KITCHEN ABOVE

N

WELL

THESE ROOMS HAVE BEEN REBUILT

STABLES

COURTYARD

ARMOURY

←ENTRANCE

←PORTER'S LODGE

HORSE MILL

GUARD ROOM

ROOMS FOR BREWING AND BAKING. CHAPEL ON TOP FLOOR ABOVE

PORTER'S LODGE

193

NORTH-WEST TOWER CONTAINING 4 CHAMBERS

GREAT CHAMBER

SOUTH-WEST TOWER CONTAINING 4 CHAMBERS

SOUTH-EAST TOWER USED BY THE RETAINERS AND CONTAINING THEIR HALL

CHAPEL

New castles of this size and scale were extremely rare. The king built no new fortresses and the barons had plenty of castles already; all they needed was larger and better living accommodation. It may have been because it was hard to fit beds and other pieces of furniture into circular rooms that, by the end of the fourteenth century, square towers and turrets had definitely come back into fashion. The gatehouses and some of the towers round the courtyard at Bodiam are basically square and there are square corner-towers at Bolton. The same can be said about the outer defences. When the ancient castle at Rochester was repaired between 1367 and 1370 to prepare for the anticipated French invasion, two small square towers were built on the curtain wall. These are so exactly like early Norman towers that at first glance they appear to be original; and, in fact, the northern tower stands on earlier foundations which may possibly have been laid in Gundulf's time.

The flamboyant decorations used in the first three-quarters of the fourteenth century had now given way to the formal patterns of the *Perpendicular period*, which is usually considered to start with the reign of Richard II and continue until the death of Richard III in 1485. Fine cathedrals and churches, with enormous windows, were built at this time; but for reasons of defence, the castles reserved their larger openings for the inner walls which overlooked the courtyard. Not only were the parapets crenellated inside and outside the buildings, but toy merlons and crenels ornamented everything: they ran along the tops of wooden screens and pieces of furniture. The patterns made by the windows were echoed in miniature on the stone panelling of the walls.

Chaucer gives a good account of the way fourteenth-century people lived and one can imagine some of his wealthier characters sweeping through the palatial apartments built at Kenilworth by his patron John of Gaunt, the great Duke of Lancaster.

NORTH-EAST MURAL TOWER c1370

FOUNDATIONS MAY BE c1087

Square shapes returned to fashion in the 14th century, and some of the smaller towers look like the old Norman ones. This is one of the towers built to defend Rochester Castle at the time of the threatened French invasion. Chaucer describes what life was like in the latter years of the 14th century, and a manuscript painting (left) shows members of Richard II's court sitting on the grass in their magnificent clothes, listening to him telling one of his stories. The knight riding past Bolton Castle, opposite, is the kind of man Chaucer had in mind for his knight.

GEOFFREY CHAUCER TELLING HIS STORIES

EAST ORIEL

HALL BUILT OVER A STORE ROOM

A PORCH STOOD HERE

REMAINS OF THE GREAT CHAMBER, BUILT OVER A STORE ROOM

ENTRANCE TO HALL

Kenilworth Castle had been growing ever since the early 12th century (see page 125). At the end of the 14th century John of Gaunt, the great Duke of Lancaster, transformed the inner bailey by fitting a magnificent range of domestic buildings inside the old curtain wall. The hall and chambers were built over low store-rooms; the hall was entered from a long flight of steps that were originally partly covered by a porch – as at Chepstow. The great chamber would have been used for formal occasions, with a private chamber beyond.

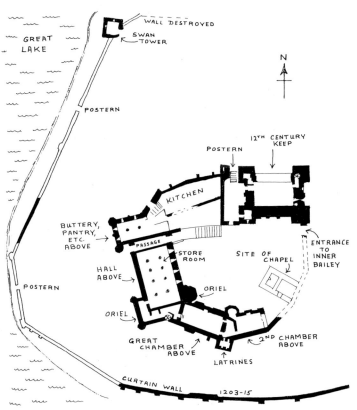

GREAT LAKE

WALL DESTROYED

SWAN TOWER

POSTERN

N

POSTERN

12TH CENTURY KEEP

KITCHEN

BUTTERY, PANTRY, ETC. ABOVE

PASSAGE

STORE ROOM

SITE OF CHAPEL

ENTRANCE TO INNER BAILEY

HALL ABOVE

ORIEL

POSTERN

ORIEL

GREAT CHAMBER ABOVE

LATRINES

2ND CHAMBER ABOVE

CURTAIN WALL

1203-15

196

John of Gaunt was the most powerful man in the land while his nephew, Richard II, was young; and the extensive range of domestic buildings he set up in the inner bailey at Kenilworth show it. They were built between 1390 and 1393. The huge first-floor hall had the usual store-rooms underneath; while the buttery, pantry and other service rooms were in a tower at the screens end of the hall. There was another tower at the dais end, with an oriel on either side of the high table. An *oriel* is like an outsize bay window, and the western oriel is almost as large as a room, while the one at the east was smaller, but had the advantage of a fireplace.

The duke would have held audience, dined, danced and carried out public business in the great hall; while a passage led from the larger oriel to his private apartments, where there was a great chamber and a lesser chamber. There were further small chambers over the buttery and pantry at the far end of the hall, and this would have been the sort of place where Chaucer might have lodged. The following excerpt from *The Book of the Duchess* was written soon after 1369, which was before the new range at Kenilworth had been built, so he therefore had some other place in his mind's eye.

Above: The inside of the smaller oriel, looking towards the inner bailey: the centre window is a reconstruction. The large oriel, below, is a rectangular shape, to fit the base of the tower that stood above it. Both oriels were entered from the dais of the hall.

And, sooth to seyn, my chambre was
Ful wel depeynted, and with glas
Were all the windowes wel y-glased,
Ful clere, and nat an hole y-crased,
That to beholde hit was gret joye.
For hoolly al the storie of Troye
Was in the glasing y-wroght thus,
Of Ector and king Priamus,
Of Achilles and Lamedon,
Of Medea and of Jason,
Of Paris, Eleyne, and Lavyne.
And alle the walles with colours fyne
Were paynted, bothe text and glose,
Of al the Romaunce of the Rose.

My chamber (it had come to pass)
Was brightly painted; there was glass
In all the windows, clear and fair,
– Not a hole broken anywhere –
So looking at it was a joy,
For the entire Tale of Troy
Was pictured in the glazing thus:
Sir Hector and King Priamus,
Achilles and Laomedon,
Medea and Jason; further on
There was Lavinia to be seen
And Helen, Menelaus' Queen,
With Paris; there were paintings too
On all the walls – their colours new –
With text and commentary prose
Of the whole Romance of the Rose.
(*A Choice of Chaucer's Verse*, Faber &
Faber, p. 25.)

This hall window is intact, apart from a few missing pieces of carved stone on the right-hand side. It has the usual seats at the bottom. The two fireplaces stand between the windows opposite each other: the simple rectangular shapes hinting at the Tudor fireplaces to come.

Interior decoration would have been much the same as before, and coloured glass of the kind that Chaucer describes would still have been an expensive luxury. Sometimes the glass was fixed into wooden frames so that the windows could be removed and fitted into the next castle that the household visited. Walls were covered with lively paintings illustrating heroic or romantic events, such as the Tale of Troy; and subjects to do with the stories of King Arthur were extremely popular, as were tournaments, battle scenes and shields displaying the owner's arms. Artists were busily employed painting patterns on the wooden wainscoting that covered the lower part of some of the walls; while painted woven cloths were hung round less important rooms. Tapestries had been introduced to England by Eleanor of Castile; but only the very rich could afford them. A whole set of tapestries would almost certainly have been used at Kenilworth, pegged to the wall, then taken down, rolled up and carted along in the wake of the duke as he travelled round the country from castle to castle.

ONE OF THE TWO HALL FIREPLACES

198

Richard II went to Ireland in 1394 and received the homage of four Irish kings, whom he dubbed knights. There was an immense difference between the knights of the king's court and these rough chieftains, wrapped in their woollen cloaks, who were given lessons on how to behave at the king's table. The Irish kings still liked to live in their timber fortresses (which have disappeared, leaving few traces). They ate their meals in the open air, sharing their plates and cups with their minstrels and servants.

The Normans had defended their lands against the Irish with numerous motte-and-bailey castles and impressive stone keeps. Round and many-sided keeps had been introduced at the beginning of the thirteenth century, and also a type of keep that was built in Ireland and nowhere else in the British Isles (except, possibly, at Nunney). This was a *turreted tower*: a rectangular building of two or three storeys, but with a round tower at each of the four corners, rising from the foundations up to parapet level. An example of one of these is at Ferns in County Wexford.

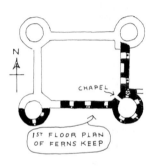

Richard II was on his second visit to Ireland, in 1399, when he heard the unwelcome news that his cousin, Henry of Bolingbroke, had landed on the Yorkshire coast, and had come to claim his estates. Henry's father, John of Gaunt, had died in February, and the king had taken the old man's great possessions into his own hands. Henry had always been popular, while the king, who was extravagant and high-handed, was greatly disliked. The people of London flocked to Bolingbroke's banner while the men of Richard's army slipped

The ruined three-storey keep is all that remains of the castle at Ferns. It was built either by William Marshal in the early years of the 13th century, by his son, or by William de Valence, who married the Marshal heiress, in the middle of the century. It is an example of an Irish turreted tower: basically a rectangular keep with round corner-turrets.

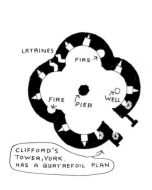

LATRINES · FIRE · FIRE · WELL · PIER

CLIFFORD'S TOWER, YORK, HAS A QUATREFOIL PLAN

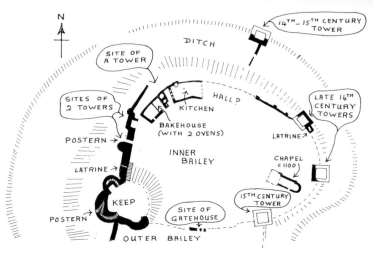

N

14TH–15TH CENTURY TOWER

DITCH

SITE OF A TOWER

SITES OF 2 TOWERS

HALL?

KITCHEN

LATE 14TH CENTURY TOWERS

BAKEHOUSE (WITH 2 OVENS)

POSTERN →

LATRINE ↗

← LATRINE ↗

INNER BAILEY

CHAPEL c 1100

KEEP

15TH CENTURY TOWER

SITE OF GATEHOUSE

POSTERN

OUTER BAILEY

A motte-and-bailey castle was built at Pontefract in 1080 and a keep of trefoil or quatrefoil plan was built on the motte top about 1230: it is hard to tell the exact shape from the ruined foundations. A similar 13th-century keep, standing on a motte at York, is quatrefoil, but has only two storeys whereas a picture painted before the castle was slighted in 1646 shows the keep at Pontefract to have been exceptionally tall. Perhaps the original tower was heightened by John of Gaunt when he strengthened the castle at the end of the 14th century.

KEEP ↓

OUTER BAILEY WALL

quietly away. By the time Richard had crossed over to Wales, most of his soldiers had deserted. The king's uncle, Edmund, Duke of York, who had been appointed 'keeper of the realm' during Richard's visit to Ireland, shut himself up in Berkeley Castle and then joined forces with Bolingbroke. Next, Bristol surrendered. Richard hurried northwards, only to discover that the forces he had expected to be waiting for him at Caernarvon had been disbanded before he arrived. He then moved on to Conway at the head of his diminished army, while Henry's forces were massed at Chester. It would have been in the royal apartments in Conway Castle that Richard received Henry Percy, the Earl of Northumberland, who had given his powerful support to Bolingbroke. The earl made the suggestion that Richard should meet Henry at Flint Castle, just along the coast, in order to talk things over and come to a peaceful settlement. By the time Richard had entered the town of Flint, he was surrounded by armed men and already a prisoner.

Richard II was taken to London and formally resigned his throne on 30 September 1399. Henry Bolingbroke then became King Henry IV and Richard ended his life, or had it ended for him, in Pontefract Castle early the following year. Once one of the strongest fortresses in the land, only the foundation stones are left of this castle where King Richard II dragged out the last of his days. The exact cause of his death has always been a mystery.

200

13 ENDING THE STORY

PRIMITIVE CANNON HAD BEEN MUCH IMPROVED BY THE start of the fifteenth century and as early as 1405 Henry IV was using them to good effect against the strongholds of Henry Percy, the same earl of Northumberland who had helped him to overthrow Richard II.

The Earl of Northumberland had been complaining that the king owed him some money. He had also protested that the man he had joined forces with in 1399 had only been Henry of Bolingbroke, who was fighting to claim his rightful inheritance: he had not expected Henry to overstep the bargain and take the throne. Northumberland's son, 'Harry Hotspur', had led a rebellion and been slain two years previously; but in 1405 Northumberland himself had joined a further conspiracy and was declared a traitor: Henry marched northwards to take Northumberland's castles of Alnwick, Prudhoe and Warkworth – all in Northumberland – into his own hands. The garrison at Warkworth had been prepared to hold out for some time; but after seven ponderous shots from Henry's cannon, the men changed their minds and surrendered. Prudhoe fell and Alnwick withstood the attack.

At this period heavy guns were usually mounted on wooden bases and fired from a fixed position, though some of the lighter pieces were equipped with wheels. In the distance is Alnwick Castle, ancient stronghold of the Percy family. It was restored and altered in the 18th and 19th centuries, but has many interesting early buildings, including a shell keep.

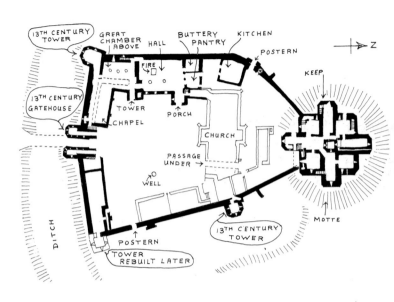

The plan shows the original domestic buildings placed against the west wall of the bailey. When the tower house was erected on the motte top, the old hall was given a new porch, below. A huge church was planned at the same time, with an entrance at the side of the porch and running right across the bailey, but it was probably never finished.

A motte-and-bailey castle had been established at Warkworth before 1158 and there would always have been a keep of some kind on top of the motte. There was a ground-floor hall in the bailey and the entrance was protected by an exceptionally strong thirteenth-century gatehouse, which had been heightened in the early years of the fourteenth century. Sometime before the siege of 1405, the old tower on top of the motte had been demolished and an up-to-date tower house had been built in its place. The Percy family spent much of their time at Warkworth and the new keep had been designed to add to their prestige and comfort, rather than to their defence. It is basically a square tower with the angles cut off and a bay projecting out from each of the four sides; the hall, chamber, chapel and kitchens were all on the first floor. This keep had all the latest innovations – including latrine shafts that were flushed from a rainwater tank in the north wall – but the lower windows were too large and the outer walls too thin for the building to be of much use against a determined attack.

202

As the fifteenth century progressed, so the pieces of artillery became heavier and more cumbersome; but they were still unreliable, inaccurate and likely to explode the wrong way. It was popularly thought that the men who operated these infernal machines must be in league with the Devil. On the whole, they were too unwieldy to be of much use in battle, despite the impressive roar and flash of the explosion, which must have alarmed the enemy and terrified their horses; they could not be fired more than about seven times a day because the iron had to be given time to cool off. Handguns were also being used; but battles were still won by longbowmen, soldiers with pikes, and knights on their heavy chargers, not by an artillery force.

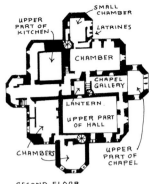

SECOND FLOOR

The tower house at Warkworth stands almost as it was, although some of the windows were inserted later. The square area in the centre of the building, rather like a lift shaft, allowed daylight to filter down from the lantern on the roof and light the rooms below. The entrance was on the ground floor (see plan opposite).

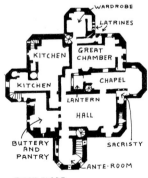

FIRST FLOOR

Dress became increasingly elaborate as the 15th century progressed. Skirts grew to such a length that the heavy folds of a great lady's train had to be carried by a handmaiden following behind. Guests always washed their hands before a meal and the hall in the tower house at Warkworth (above) shows the usual three doorways leading to the kitchen, pantry and buttery.

However, the tube-shaped bombards and short stocky mortars, with their high-flying tracery, were the standard weapons to use on the walls of towns and castles. Soon, small wheels were being fitted to the wooden stands and, instead of having to be dismantled, loaded on waggons, and carted from one siege to the next, the cannon could be dragged along the muddy roads behind teams of horses or oxen. It was becoming increasingly obvious that no castle, however strong, would be able to withstand an artillery bombardment for long.

Henry IV died in 1413, and two years later his illustrious son, Henry V, was invading France in pursuit of Edward III's claim to the French throne. Henry used artillery to destroy enemy defences; and after ten cannon had been trained on the walls of Harfleur, the barbican and gatehouse were quickly reduced to rubble.

Having fought his way through France and up to the walls of Paris, Henry V clinched his conquest by marrying Catherine, daughter of the mad French king, Charles VI. Although Catherine's brother, the Dauphin, was next in line to the throne, it was decided to cut him out of the succession so that Henry could be king when Charles finally died. It so happened that Henry died first, and in 1422 Catherine's baby, Henry VI, became monarch of the two countries before he was a year old.

The king's uncles acted as regents. Humphrey, Duke of Gloucester, took over affairs in England; while John, Duke of Bedford, ruled in France; but a large section of the French people ignored the treaty that had given them an English king and continued to support the Dauphin, who held court at Bourges, just south of Orléans. War was resumed and, in October 1428, the Duke of Bedford was leading his armies towards Bourges in order to attack the enemy's base, when he laid siege to Orléans which stood in his way. It was at this time that Joan of Arc appeared on the scene to rekindle the spirit of French resistance: she succeeded in raising the siege of Orléans the following year. The Dauphin was crowned king of France at Rheims; but Joan eventually fell into English hands and was burnt as a heretic. The Duke of Bedford died in 1435, the Dauphin – now Charles VII – came to terms with the Burgundians who had hitherto been staunch allies of the English; and the French were well on their way to recovering their lost territories. By 1453 they had occupied the whole of France, apart from the Channel Islands and the small patch of land occupied by the port of Calais.

Hardly any new castles had been built in England during the whole of this period, although a great many tower houses were being put up in Scotland and Ireland. Life in these territories was still being lived on feudal lines; but the feudal system in England was breaking up, and with it the need for strong castles. Anyway, the English lords possessed as many castles as they could afford to keep in repair, and these were already outdated because they were no longer proof against cannon: it was far more convenient to live in an unfortified manor house. If an Englishman started to build a castle at this time, it was because he was romantic, chronically conservative, or wanted to show off his wealth and position.

Knights only wore armour (without a cloth covering) at the very end of the medieval period. The early 15th-century warrior, above, still has the iron plates covered with cloth. Opposite, Henry V probably wore a polished breastplate between the mail shirt and tabard decorated with the arms of England and France. By the 1470s, below, every knight riding to battle would be encased in glittering armour and only occasionally wore a cloak or tabard.

SEVERAL GUNS COULD BE FIRED AT THE SAME TIME

TAR

The 13th-century castle at Tattershall had a hall surrounded by a curtain wall defended at intervals by round towers, traces of which have survived. Owing to lack of space, the 15th-century tower was built with its foundations in the moat, outside the line of the old curtain wall. This was immediately behind the hall, and the two buildings were linked by a double-storey passage.

Perhaps the most magnificent example of a castle built for good looks, rather than defence, is Tattershall Castle in Lincolnshire. Ralph, Lord Cromwell, had been treasurer to the infant Henry VI, had fought for the king's father at Agincourt, and spent much of his time in France. When he started building the huge tower house in 1433, it was in the French style, with high pointed roofs to the corner-turrets. The tower was placed in line with the curtain wall of the earlier, thirteenth-century castle, so that the massive building actually had its foundations in the moat. Although there were two water-filled ditches, one inside the other, and numerous gatehouses, there is not much evidence of an outer curtain wall, and the windows of the keep were too large on the lower floors for serious defence. From the viewpoint of a beleaguered garrison, this was not a patch on the earlier castles.

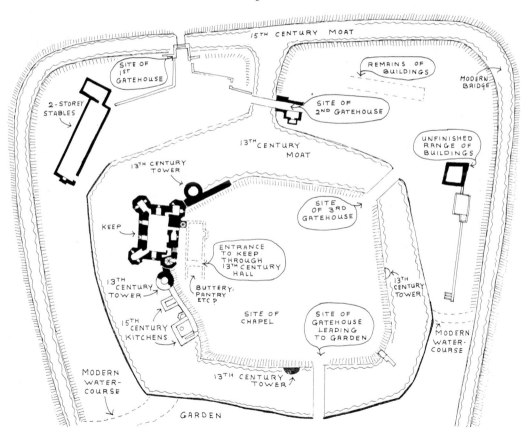

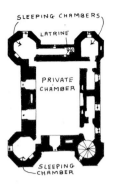

SLEEPING CHAMBERS
LATRINE
PRIVATE CHAMBER
SLEEPING CHAMBER

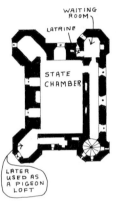

WAITING ROOM
LATRINE
STATE CHAMBER
LATER USED AS A PIGEON LOFT

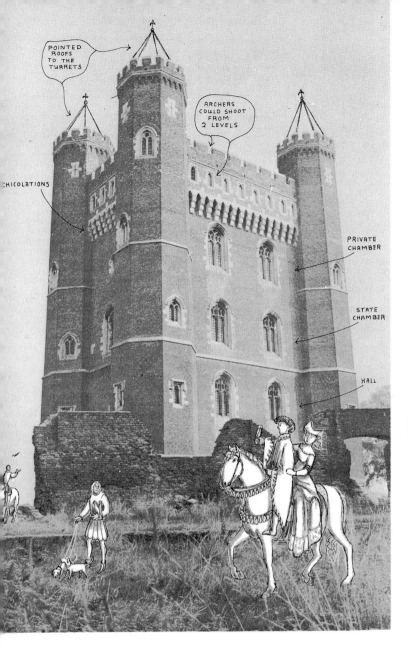

POINTED ROOFS TO THE TURRETS

ARCHERS COULD SHOOT FROM 2 LEVELS

CHICOLATIONS

PRIVATE CHAMBER

STATE CHAMBER

HALL

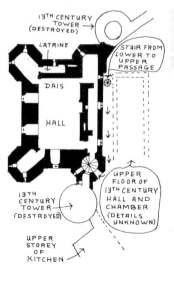

13TH CENTURY TOWER (DESTROYED)

STAIR FROM LOWER TO UPPER PASSAGE

LATRINE

DAIS

HALL

UPPER FLOOR OF 13TH CENTURY HALL AND CHAMBER (DETAILS UNKNOWN)

13TH CENTURY TOWER (DESTROYED)

UPPER STOREY OF KITCHEN

Tattershall keep from the far side of the outer moat, approaching the entrance gatehouse. The old hall and buildings of the inner bailey would have been hidden away on the other side. The ruined stables are in the foreground. The plan of the keep at ground-floor level is opposite. The first, second and third floors are on the right.

In fourteenth-century England bricks were being more widely manufactured, and the city of Hull was fortified with a brick wall and towers by about 1380. Tattershall Castle, built some fifty years later, is a superb example of the way they could be used. The outer walls are decorated here and there with over-baked black bricks placed end-on in diamond patterns called *diaper work*; while the window recesses and corridors are covered with carved brick vaulting. Unlike most tower houses the kitchens were outside the building – the food being carried into the tower at first-floor level. The main entrance was through the old hall which still stood in front of the new building and was connected to it by passages at two levels. The arrangements inside the keep were much the same as in Norman times: store-rooms below; garrison-quarters on the first floor; the hall on the second; the great chamber, where Lord Cromwell gave audience to his humble petitioners, on the third; and an extra chamber, possibly for the use of the ladies of the household, on the fourth. The roof was up above. The corner-turrets were used for small private rooms and there is a pigeon loft in one of them, put in at a later date. The machicolated parapet would have allowed three tiers of archers to fire all at once; but it also gave a smart finish to the top of the building. The machicolations round the turrets are pure decoration. All in all, Tattershall Castle was the kind of place that a successful man could be proud of, not because it made him secure against attack, but because it showed off his position and power.

The window and machicolations are in the firing gallery at roof level, and the stair runs from top to bottom of the south-east turret. The fireplace in Lord Cromwell's state chamber is decorated with shields and purses because Cromwell was treasurer to Henry VI. Here he is giving money to a petitioner.

MACHICOLATIONS

HOLES FOR GUNS

From this time onwards there were many large buildings made of brick. One of them, Herstmonceux Castle, was built in East Sussex by Sir Roger Fiennes soon after 1441, to strengthen the defences of the south coast. The gatehouse towers were fitted with the usual late-medieval cross-slits for arrows, but they also have the round holes for cannon underneath. Caister Castle in Norfolk, begun sometime after 1432 by Sir John Fastolf, was also fitted with gunports.

Shakespeare made fun of this knight and altered the spelling to Falstaff; but in fact John Fastolf had carved out quite a respectable career for himself and had been dubbed a knight because of his success in the French war. His greatest exploit was winning the battle of the Herrings. In the spring of 1429, he was at the head of a small company of archers, escorting a convoy of provisions from Paris to the soldiers encamped outside the besieged city of Orléans, when he was attacked by a superior force of Frenchmen. The barrels of herrings appear to have been used as some sort of defensive barrier for Sir John and his archers to fight behind. Sir John Fastolf became extremely rich because he was a shrewd businessman, and he had just finished building Caister Castle when he died, in 1459.

Herstmonceux Castle has been heavily restored; only the gatehouse and outer walls are original. Little more than a corner-tower is left of Caister Castle. Both were brick buildings surrounded by moats, and designed on the same courtyard principle as Bodiam and Bolton.

CORNER TOWER

HOLES FOR GUNS

209

TURRET

REMAINS OF THE MACHICOLATED PARAPET

GREAT CHAMBER

HALL

KITCHEN

STORE ROOM

The 12th-century castle at Ashby-de-la-Zouche had a first-floor hall and a chamber near the entrance. Alterations were made in the 14th century when the earth level was slightly raised, and the hall became a ground-floor aisled hall. A new great chamber was added at the dais end. A kitchen was built on the far side of the old chamber which then became a buttery and pantry. The Hastings tower and an impressive chapel were built in the 15th century to give the castle status and security. Only half of the Hastings tower remains because the castle was slighted in 1648.

After 1455, the English nobles were too preoccupied with the Wars of the Roses to worry about building projects. Some men supported the descendants of John of Gaunt (the house of Lancaster); while others upheld the descendants of Gaunt's elder brother, Lionel, Duke of Clarence (the house of York). Lord Hastings was chamberlain to the Yorkist king Edward IV when in 1474 he added a huge tower house to his castle at Ashby-de-la-Zouche, and he also laid plans for a stately new castle at Kirby Muxloe – both fortresses in Leicestershire. Lord Hastings probably did not live to see either of them finished, as he was beheaded by the brother of Edward IV, Richard III, in 1483. Richard himself was slain two years later at the battle of Bosworth, and the opposing sides came to terms when the wise Henry VII of Lancaster married Elizabeth of York. So started the Tudor dynasty, and with it the Tudor period in architecture, which was influenced by the Italian Renaissance.

All kinds of new ideas had been fermenting in Europe throughout this period. People had begun to inquire more closely into history and to break away from the hidebound teachings of the Church. There was renewed interest in the

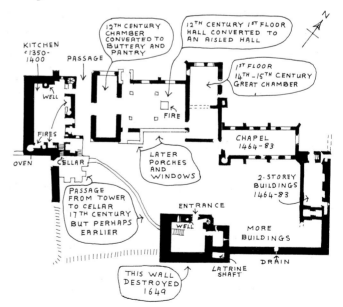

KITCHEN c1350-1400

PASSAGE

12TH CENTURY CHAMBER CONVERTED TO BUTTERY AND PANTRY

12TH CENTURY 1ST FLOOR HALL CONVERTED TO AN AISLED HALL

1ST FLOOR 14TH-15TH CENTURY GREAT CHAMBER

WELL

FIRE

FIRES

OVEN   CELLAR

LATER PORCHES AND WINDOWS

CHAPEL 1464-83

2-STOREY BUILDINGS 1464-83

PASSAGE FROM TOWER TO CELLAR 17TH CENTURY BUT PERHAPS EARLIER

ENTRANCE

WELL

MORE BUILDINGS

DRAIN

THIS WALL DESTROYED 1649

LATRINE SHAFT

210

writings of the pagan Greeks and Romans. From the start of the fifteenth century, the Italians had been taking a fresh look at the architecture of ancient Rome. They studied the crumbling ruins and then began to copy them in their own way, not using the heavy forms of the old Romanesque buildings, but making the most of their advanced technology. By the time that the disputes of the Wars of the Roses had been settled, some of the ideas of the Italian Renaissance had filtered across Europe to England. The *Tudor period*, lasting from about 1485 to 1558, was the English version of Renaissance architecture. This did not affect the design of castles as much as churches, university buildings, and the great country houses. No new castles were being built in England now; but when an extra wing was added, or alterations were made to an existing fortress, the windows, doorways and fireplaces were designed with the wide flat Tudor arch, usually placed under a square hood-mould, and with the corners filled in with leaf shapes or some geometric pattern.

Handguns, which had been used with little or no effect from about 1350, became far more efficient when an automatic firing mechanism, the matchlock, was introduced towards the end of the fifteenth century. The handgun was now made with a short wooden butt to rest against the shoulder and was renamed the arquebus. The design of cannon had also been improved: they were lighter and mounted on gun carriages, which made them more mobile; they could also be raised and lowered, to alter the angle of fire. By 1494 the French had equipped themselves with such a splendid artillery train that they were able to march across Italy and destroy fortress after fortress with their guns. The new invention had given the foot-soldier the power to overcome the man on a horse. Medieval ideas about individual valour and chivalry had been blown away. Accepted methods of warfare were out of date and military engineers had to think again about matters of defence.

Henry VIII succeeded his father, Henry VII, to the throne

By the beginning of the 16th century castles were no longer being built in England. Although the gun-forts of Henry VIII are called castles, they are only soldiers' forts, having no living accommodation for the owner and his family. These photographs are of the fort at Deal built in 1540: the Tudor doorway from the interior of the keep; and the soldier with musket and rest (to steady his aim) in the narrow ward between the inner and outer curtain wall.

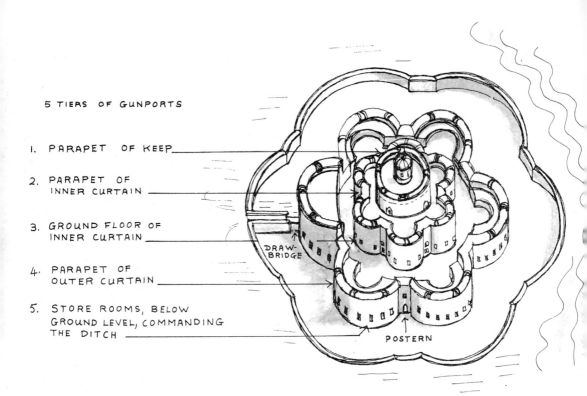

The gun-fort at Deal is a series of circular bastions: the inner ones are higher than the outer ones to allow the cannons to be fired from five different levels. The captain and twenty-four men lived in the central keep. There were store-rooms below; the hall, kitchen and living-rooms on the ground floor; and chambers, probably reserved for the captain, on the first floor. The rooms were partitioned by wattle-and-timber walls. The central spiral stair – directly over the well – had a lantern above to illuminate it.

of England in 1506. Henry quarrelled with the Pope when he divorced his wife, Catherine of Aragon, in 1533; and again, when he cast the monks and nuns out of their monasteries. In retaliation, the Pope invited the Holy Roman Emperor, Charles V (who was also king of Spain), and the French king, Francis I, to join him in league against Henry and by 1538 England was again threatened with invasion. Using some of the money he had taken from the Church, Henry decided to build a series of gun-forts all along the south coast: the largest defensive work since the time of Edward III.

Although Henry's buildings are referred to as castles, they are not really so in the strict sense of the word. They had some of the features of castles: the central keeps where garrison-commanders and their men were quartered, thick outer walls and moats, but there were no domestic apartments for the lord's family and household. They were, in fact, military forts. The king's courtiers and friends had outlived the castle

212

system: the old halls and chambers were dark and inconvenient, and they preferred to live in more spacious buildings where plenty of daylight could enter through the large square Tudor windows. By the time Henry had built his gun-forts, in the middle of the sixteenth century, the split was complete: barracks and forts were being erected for the use of the soldiers; while the English gentlemen enjoyed their high standard of living in their great stately houses.

This is where *The Castle Story* ends; although it must be remembered that some of the castles continued to be inhabited, besieged, knocked down and rebuilt until the time of the Civil War in the seventeenth century, when a great many of them, such as Corfe and Pontefract, were blown up by order of Oliver Cromwell. Other castles, like Windsor, Berkeley and Warwick, have been used as royal or family homes right up to the present day. The rest of the fortresses were turned into prisons, used as store-rooms, or simply abandoned and allowed to fall to ruin, after which, farm workers and local cottagers would cart away the old stones and use them to repair barns and cowsheds.

Because so many of the castles were built over a long period of time and were constantly being altered and brought up to date, it is often hard work trying to sort them out. All castles are different and the only way to understand them properly is to study the official guidebooks.

PART OF THE ORIGINAL PARAPET

GUNPORTS OVERLOOKING THE DITCH

Deal is the largest and most complete of Henry VIII's gun-forts; but the parapets were replaced in 1732 and the crenellations are not part of the original design. This is a section of the original parapet: massive, rounded, and built to withstand the shock of an enemy cannon ball. Below, as it is today.

INNER CURTAIN

OUTER CURTAIN

LANTERN (LATER RECONSTRUCTION)

KEEP

PARAPETS 1732

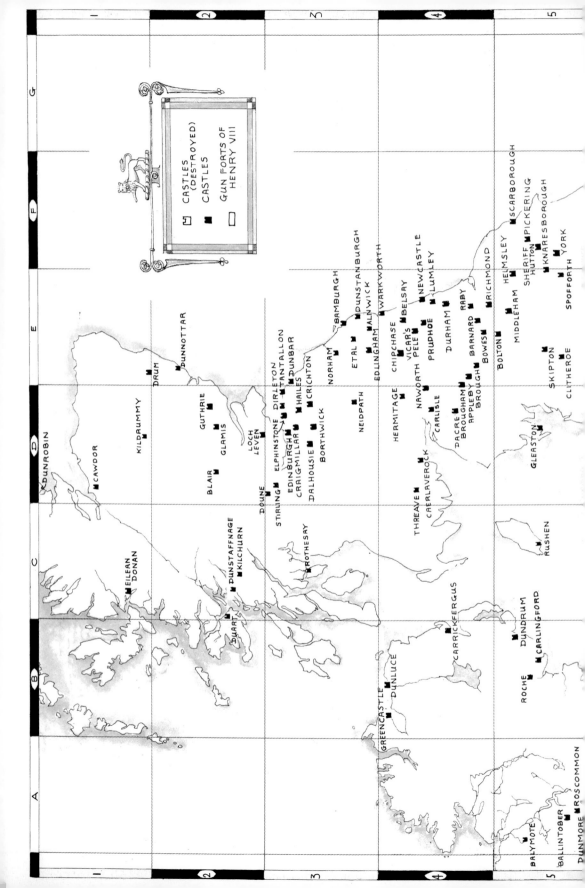

CASTLES (DESTROYED)

CASTLES

GUN FORTS OF HENRY VIII

DUNROBIN

CAWDOR

KILDRUMMY

DRUM

DUNNOTTAR

GUTHRIE

BLAIR

GLAMIS

LOCH LEVEN

DOUNE

EILEAN DONAN

DUART

DUNSTAFFNAGE

KILCHURN

ROTHESAY

STIRLING

ELPHINSTONE

DIRLETON

TANTALLON

EDINBURGH

CRAIGMILLAR

HAILES

DUNBAR

DALHOUSIE

CRICHTON

BORTHWICK

NORHAM

BAMBURGH

DUNSTANBURGH

ETAL

ALNWICK

WARKWORTH

EDLINGHAM

NEIDPATH

CHIPCHASE

VICAR'S PELE

BELSAY

NEWCASTLE

HERMITAGE

NAWORTH

PRUDHOE

LUMLEY

THREAVE

DACRE

CARLISLE

DURHAM

RABY

CAERLAVEROCK

BROUGHAM

BARNARD

RICHMOND

APPLEBY

BOWES

BROUGH

BOLTON

MIDDLEHAM

HELMSLEY

SCARBOROUGH

PICKERING

SHERIFF HUTTON

KNARESBOROUGH

GLEASTON

SKIPTON

YORK

SPOFFORTH

RUSHEN

CLITHEROE

GREENCASTLE

DUNLUCE

CARRICKFERGUS

DUNDRUM

CARLINGFORD

ROCHE

BALYMOTE

ROSCOMMON

BALLINTOBER

DUNMORE

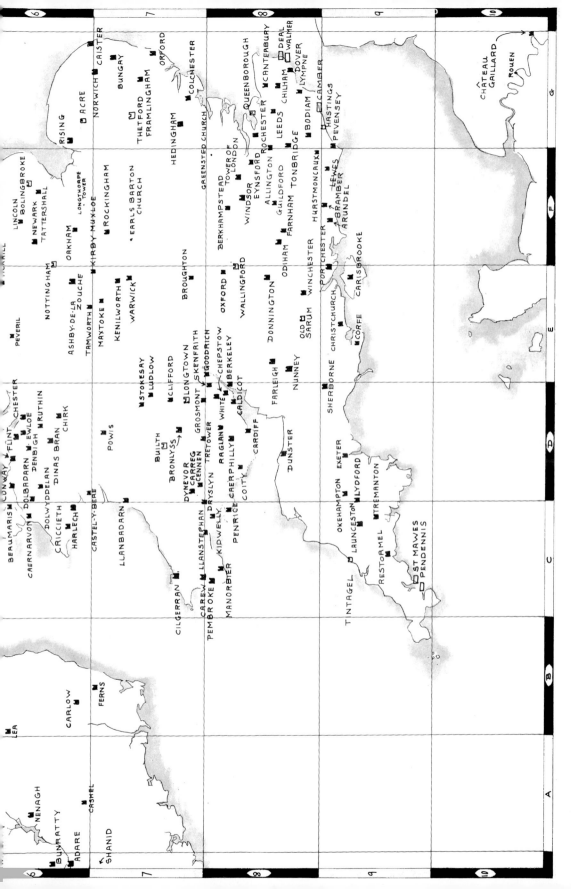

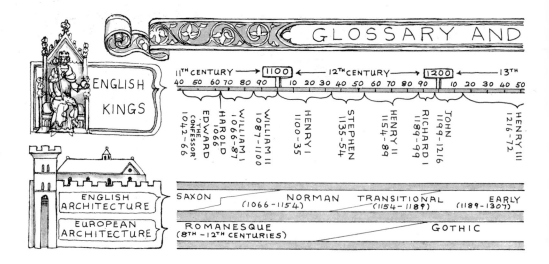

GLOSSARY AND

ENGLISH KINGS

| 11TH CENTURY → | 1100 | ← 12TH CENTURY → | 1200 | ← 13TH |

EDWARD 'THE CONFESSOR' 1042–66
HAROLD 1066
WILLIAM I 1066–87
WILLIAM II 1087–1100
HENRY I 1100–35
STEPHEN 1135–54
HENRY II 1154–89
RICHARD I 1189–99
JOHN 1199–1216
HENRY III 1216–72

ENGLISH ARCHITECTURE

SAXON — NORMAN (1066–1154) — TRANSITIONAL (1154–1189) — EARLY (1189–1307)

EUROPEAN ARCHITECTURE

ROMANESQUE (8TH–12TH CENTURIES) — GOTHIC

The above dates are taken from page 624 of Sir Banister Fletcher's A History of Architecture on the Comparative Method *(18th edition); but it was Thomas Rickman who first thought of dividing medieval building periods into the reigns of kings, publishing* An Attempt to Discriminate the Styles of Architecture in England *in 1817. These divisions are only intended as rough guide-lines: architectural design did not change all at once on the death of a king, and the slanted lines on this chart indicate the length of time it would have taken for new ideas to be universally adapted.*

ALURE: The path running behind the parapet at the top of a wall or tower. A wall-walk. It can also be the path running in front of the parapet if there is a timber hoarding.

APSE: The semicircular or polygonal end to a church or other building.

ASHLAR: Stone that has been cut and worked to a smooth regular shape.

AUMBREY: Cupboard.

BAILEY: The area of ground enclosed by a wall or palisade on which the domestic buildings of a castle stood. A courtyard. Also, in a concentric castle, the area of ground between two encircling walls. A WARD means the same thing.

BARBICAN: A wall, or other kind of structure, built to protect the outside of an entrance. Also called a HORNWORK. A barbican sometimes also refers to a special kind of towered gatehouse, built in two parts, as at Ludlow and Exeter.

BARTIZAN: A watch-tower or turret jutting out from the top of a building, more frequently found in the later castles of Scotland and Ireland.

BASTION: A solid tower or gun platform.

BATTERED: Sloping.

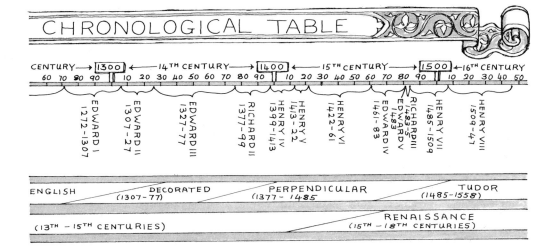

| CENTURY → | 1300 | ← 14ᵀᴴ CENTURY → | 1400 | ← 15ᵀᴴ CENTURY → | 1500 | ← 16ᵀᴴ CENTURY |

60 70 80 90 ‖ 10 20 30 40 50 60 70 80 90 ‖ 10 20 30 40 50 60 70 80 90 ‖ 10 20 30 40 50

EDWARD I 1272-1307
EDWARD II 1307-27
EDWARD III 1327-77
RICHARD II 1377-99
HENRY IV 1399-1413
HENRY V 1413-22
HENRY VI 1422-61
EDWARD IV 1461-83
RICHARD III 1483-5
EDWARD V 1483
HENRY VII 1485-1509
HENRY VIII 1509-47

ENGLISH

DECORATED (1307-77) PERPENDICULAR (1377-1485) TUDOR (1485-1558)

(13ᵀᴴ – 15ᵀᴴ CENTURIES) RENAISSANCE (15ᵀᴴ – 18ᵀᴴ CENTURIES)

BAYS: Compartments into which a building is divided; the size of each section being decided by the roofing system.

BLIND ARCADE: A series of shallow arches used to decorate a wall.

BUTTERY: From the French 'bouteilerie', meaning a room where the drinks were kept.

BUTTRESS: Projecting masonry, built against a wall to strengthen it.

CAPITAL: A block of stone, usually ornamented, at the top of a column.

CAUSEWAY: A bank which has a path or road running along the top, built across water or marshy ground.

CHANCEL: The part of a church which is used by the priest.

CLERESTORY: Literally, a clear storey. Windows, or openings, set high in a wall in order to illuminate the area below.

COLUMN: From the Latin 'columna' meaning 'post'. Usually with a base, circular shaft and capital, and built to support the weight above.

CONCENTRIC: With a common centre. One line of defences enclosing another.

CORBEL: A stone jutting out from a wall in order to support a roof beam or some other weight.

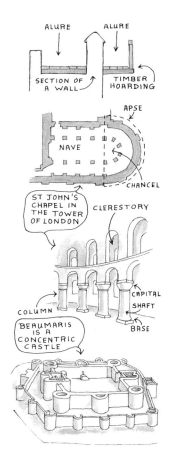

ALURE ALURE

SECTION OF A WALL   TIMBER HOARDING

APSE

NAVE

CHANCEL

ST JOHN'S CHAPEL IN THE TOWER OF LONDON

CLERESTORY

CAPITAL
COLUMN
SHAFT
BASE

BEAUMARIS IS A CONCENTRIC CASTLE

217

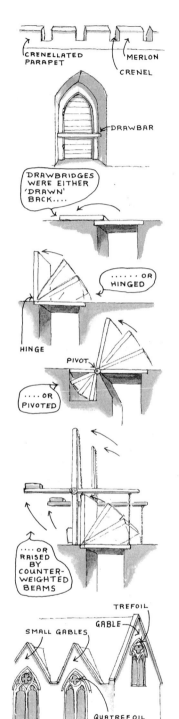

CRENELLATED PARAPET

MERLON

CRENEL

DRAWBAR

DRAWBRIDGES WERE EITHER 'DRAWN' BACK....

.....OR HINGED

HINGE

PIVOT

....OR PIVOTED

....OR RAISED BY COUNTER-WEIGHTED BEAMS

SMALL GABLES

GABLE

TREFOIL

QUATREFOIL

COUNTERSCARP: The outer slope of a ditch.

CRENELLATED (Also EMBATTLED): Where a parapet is built with gaps (CRENELS) at regular intervals. This allowed the defenders to shoot through the gaps and shelter behind the solid parts (MERLONS).

CRYPT: The area directly under the CHANCEL.

CURTAIN WALL: The wall enclosing a bailey.

DAIS: The raised floor area at the upper end of a hall where the lord's table or chair was placed.

DIAPER WORK: A pattern, usually in the form of lozenges or squares, which decorated a wall.

DRAWBAR: A stout wooden bar which could be slotted into the stonework and laid behind a door in order to stop anyone opening it from the outside.

DRAWBRIDGE: The end part of a bridge, which could be raised up or removed altogether, leaving a gap over the ditch which prevented an enemy from reaching the entrance.

FOIL: Little arc-shaped patterns of window-tracery. QUATREFOIL has four arcs; TREFOIL has three arcs etc.

FOREBUILDING: A small building tacked on to the side of a larger building to defend the entrance.

GABLE: The triangular upper part of the end wall of a building, so formed because the side roofs slope up and meet at the top. Small GABLES can be found at the side of a building where each window is covered by a little pitched roof.

GATEHOUSE: Literally the house over a gate. A tower defending an entrance.

GREAT CHAMBER: Also SOLAR. A bedroom and living-room combined for the use of the lord and his family.

GUN-LOOPS (OILETTES): Openings in walls with round holes, to take the muzzles of the guns, and slits to see through.

HALL KEEPS: Keeps where the hall and chamber are placed alongside each other at the same level and which tend to be wider than they are high.

HERRINGBONE WORK: Walling where stones or tiles are laid slantwise in alternating rows, giving a pattern like the bones of a herring.

218

HOARDING (Also BRATTICE, or BRETASCHE): A timber gallery built out at the top of a wall or tower. BRETASCHE can also apply to a timber tower.

TIMBER HOARDING

JOGGLED ARCH: An arch which is kept in position by the shape of the jagged overlapping stones.

JOIST: The beam supporting a floor.

KEEP (Also DONJON): The strongest building in a castle.

LANCET WINDOW: A narrow pointed window, used mainly in the thirteenth century.

JOGGLED ARCH

LANTERN: A small hut-like structure (looking much the same as a louver) with openings or windows at the sides, set on the roof of a building in order to allow daylight to filter down to the area below.

LATRINE (Also PRIVY and GUARDEROBE): A lavatory. GUARDEROBE is occasionally used to describe the small room between the latrine and the great chamber which is more generally called the WARDROBE.

LANCET WINDOW

LANTERN

LOUVER

CINQUEFOIL

MULLION

LINTEL

LINTEL: A horizontal stone slab laid across the top of a doorway, window, etc.

LOUVER: A small hut-like structure, with openings at the sides, built on the roof of a hall to cover the smoke-hole.

MACHICOLATIONS: The openings in the floor of a projecting stone gallery which allow missiles to be dropped on the enemy below. A stone version of timber hoarding.

MERLON: A solid part in a crenellated parapet.

MOAT: A water-filled ditch defending a castle, manor, settlement, etc.

MOTTE: A large earth mound.

MULLION: An upright division of a window.

MURAL: To do with a wall. A MURAL tower is a tower standing on a wall. A MURAL stair is a stairway that is built into the thickness of a wall.

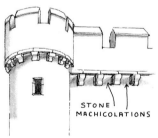

STONE MACHICOLATIONS

MURDER-HOLE: An opening in the roof of an entrance passage which allows the defenders standing in the room above to drop missiles on to enemies passing below. Alternatively, water could be poured through the hole in order to extinguish any fires that had been lit. Sometimes called MEURTRIERE.

MURDER HOLES IN THE ROOM OVER THE ENTRANCE PASSAGE IN GOODRICH CASTLE

PORTCULLIS SLOT

LATE 14TH CENTURY ORIEL IN LINCOLN CASTLE

PIER

QUOIN

PLINTH

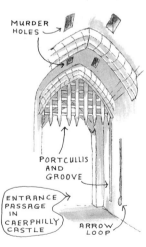

MURDER HOLES

PORTCULLIS AND GROOVE

ENTRANCE PASSAGE IN CAERPHILLY CASTLE

ARROW LOOP

NAVE: The part of a church used by the congregation.

OGEE ARCH: An arch which curves from the concave (hollow) shape to a convex (bulging) shape. Popular in the Decorated period.

ORIEL: A kind of bay window, usually jutting out from an upstairs room.

OUBLIETTE: From the French 'l'oublier', to forget. A prison. A cell where prisoners could be held and forgotten about.

PALISADE: A wooden wall or fence.

PANTRY: A store-room for bread.

PARAPET: The part of a wall that rises above roof level at the top of a building.

PEEL TOWER: A square tower built to defend a PEEL, or small palisaded enclosure. Usually found from the fourteenth century onwards in country near the Scottish border.

PENTHOUSE (Also PENTICE): A covered passageway of one or two storeys, often running alongside a building, with a lean-to roof. (PENT means sloping.) A shelter for a war machine, battering-ram, etc.

PIER: A support of solid masonry, usually rectangular, built to hold up an archway or upper floor. Performs the same function as a column.

PISCINA: A wash-basin; especially one of the little basins in churches used for rinsing out the sacred vessels.

PLINTH: The area of stonework (or brickwork) that projects at the base of a building because the foundations are wider than the wall-thickness of the building as a whole.

PORTCULLIS: A wood-and-metal trellis-work gate running up and down in grooves cut into the sides of a passage.

POSTERN (Also SALLYPORT): A small doorway let into the side of a tower or curtain wall. A means of getting in and out of a castle when the main gateway is out of use.

PUTLOG HOLES: A PUTLOG was a length of timber scaffolding and the little holes were left in the outer walls of buildings in order to take the ends of the putlogs whenever the building had to be painted or repaired.

PYRAMID SPUR: A sharp-angled sloping plinth, usually

formed when a round tower is built on a square base.

QUOINS: Cut stones used at the corners of buildings.

REVETMENT: A wall built into the side of a bank.

RUBBLE: Building material of rough uncut stones or flints.

SACRISTY: A tiny room next to the chapel, where the priest kept his vestments, sacred vessels, etc.

SCARP: The steep slope of a hill. To SCARP a hillock into shape is to cut away the unwanted rocks and bumps.

SCREENS PASSAGE: The passage directly before the entrance door of a hall, where the hall is on one side and the doorways to the buttery, kitchen and pantry on the other. It did not become a complete passage until about the fifteenth century: previously the hall had been only partially screened off.

SHELL KEEP: A keep built in the form of a high, circular or many-sided wall which encloses the area at the motte top and which has the domestic buildings leaning up against the inside of the wall. The wall can also enclose the whole of the motte if the masonry is built on the solid earth of the original ground level.

SHELL WALL: The wall itself, as above, without the interior buildings.

SHINGLES: Little oak roofing-tiles.

SIEGE CASTLE or TOWER: A timber tower standing on a mound, which enabled the besiegers to see into the bailey of the castle under attack. Alternatively, a SIEGE TOWER or BELFRY could be fitted with wheels or rollers and, after part of the ditch had been filled in, it could be hauled up to a castle wall in order to launch an attack.

SQUINT: A tiny window which enabled a person to see from one room into the next. Usually placed between the chamber and the hall.

TOWER HOUSE: A large rectangular building which usually had one short wing attached in order to add extra chambers and a kitchen. Introduced in the fourteenth century.

TOWER KEEP: A strong rectangular tower where the hall is usually on one floor and the chamber on the floor above. A keep which is higher than it is wide.

221

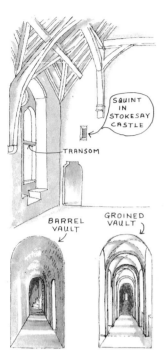

SQUINT IN STOKESAY CASTLE

TRANSOM

BARREL VAULT

GROINED VAULT

RIBBED GROINED VAULT

YETT IN GLAMIS CASTLE

TRANSOM: The horizontal division of a window.

TURRETED TOWER: A rectangular keep which has round turrets at each corner. Usually found only in Ireland.

UNDERCROFT: A solidly built stone-vaulted room which supports the room above.

VAULT: A means of covering an area with a stone ceiling. A BARREL VAULT is a simple tunnel shape, semicircular in the Romanesque period and pointed in the Gothic period. A GROINED VAULT is where two barrel vaults cross at right angles, forming diagonal edges called GROINS. A series of GROINED VAULTS was often used to cover a passage. A RIBBED GROINED VAULT is where the groins are covered with stone ribs. A RIBBED VAULT, introduced in the twelfth century, is a framework of ribs which take the weight of thin stone slabs fitted into the spaces between.

WAINSCOT: Wooden boarding, usually pine, covering the lower parts of the walls of a room. The boards, placed horizontally or vertically, were often painted and decorated.

WARDROBE: A small room, usually placed between the chamber and the latrine, used for storing clothes, as a changing-room, for sewing, or as a place for a clerk to work out the household accounts. Because the state accounts were done in the king's WARDROBES, and the CLERKS OF THE WARDROBE handled not only the king's private money, but the finances of the army etc. as well, WARDROBE also refers to the huge separate organization of the medieval civil service.

WATTLE AND DAUB: The filling between the timber frame of a building, made up of wood, clay, straw and animal hair and finished off with plaster.

YETT: An iron door made in the form of a grille. Usually placed just inside the main door, so that if the outer door was burnt down the yett was still in place to keep the enemies out. Generally found in Scottish castles.

INDEX

Italic references are to map pp. 214–15

Aberwystwyth – *see* Llanbadarn
Adelize, queen of Henry I, 76
Alexander II, King of Scotland, 163
Alexander III, King of Scotland, 163
Alexander, Bishop of Lincoln, 71
Alfred the Great, 17, 45
Alnwick Castle, 20, *E3*
Arthur, 13–14, 180
Ashby-de-la-Zouche Castle, 210, *E6*
Baliol, John, King of Scotland, 164–5
Bamburgh Castle, 15–16, *E3*
Beaumaris Castle, 159–61, *C6*
Bede, the Venerable (Saint), 15–16
Berkeley, Lord, 174
Berkeley Castle, 173–6, 200, *D8*
Berkhampstead Castle, 26, 27–9, 30, *F8*
Bigod, Hugh, 86–7
Bigod, Roger (died 1221), 86–8
Bigod, Roger (died 1270), 169–71
Bodiam Castle, 189–92, 194, 209, *G8*
Bolton Castle, 192–4, 209, *E5*
Bruce, Robert, of Annandale, 164
Bruce, Robert, King of Scotland, 167, 173, 183
Builth Castle, 146, *D7*
Cadbury Castle, 10, 14–15
Caerlaverock Castle, 167, *D4*
Caernarvon Castle, 149, 153–6, 158, 168, 200, *C6*
Caerphilly Castle, 130–5, *D8*
Caister Castle, 209, *G6*
Canterbury Castle, 52; town gate, 191, *G8*
Cardiff Castle, 53, 130, *D8*
Carrickfergus Castle, 98–9, *B4*
Carrisbrooke Castle 65–7, *E9*
Castle Hedingham, 61–2, *G7*
Castle Rising, 76–8, 176, *G6*
Charles IV, King of France, 173, 176
Charles VII, King of France (as Dauphin), 204–5
Château Gaillard, 101, *G10*
Chaucer, Geoffrey, 195, 197–8
Chepstow Castle, 32, 38–40, 44, 169, *D8*
Chilham Castle, 92, *G8*
Clare, Gilbert de, 130–3, 158
Clare, Richard de, (Strongbow), 97
Colchester Castle, 45–6, 50–1, 54, *G7*
Conisbrough Castle, 98–100, *E6*
Constance, tower of (Aigues-Mortes), 143
Constantinople, land wall of, 80–1
Conway Castle, 149–53, 159, 200, *D6*
Corfe Castle, 104–6, *E9*
Craigmillar Castle, 183–4, *D3*
Criccieth Castle, 129, 153, *C6*
Dalyngrigge, Sir Edward, 190–2
David ap Gruffydd, 141, 146–7
David ap Llywelyn, 129–30

David of Huntingdon, 164
Deal Castle, 211–13, *G8*
Deganwy Castle, 129–30, 141
Dolwyddelan Castle, 148–9, *D6*
Doué-la-Fontaine, 23, 38
Doune Castle, 186–7, *D3*
Dover Castle, 92–7, 106, 109; Constable's tower, 110–11
Dunnottar Castle, 185, *E2*
Dyserth Castle, 129, 130, 141
Earl's Barton church tower, 18
Edinburgh Castle, 166, *D3*
Edward the Confessor, 19, 21, 23
Edward the Elder, 17
Edward I, 125, 141–60, 162–8, 180
Edward II, 155, 166–7, 171–6
Edward III, 171, 173, 176–82, 188–9, 204
Edward IV, 210
Eleanor of Castile, queen of Edward I, 147, 152, 155, 198
Ethelfleda, Lady of Mercia, 17
Ewyas Harald, 21
Exeter Castle and town, 32–3, 64–5, *D9*
Eynsford Castle, 87, *F8*
Farnham Castle, 80, 91–2, *F8*
Fastolf, Sir John, 209
Ferns Castle, 199, *B7*
Fiennes, Sir Roger, 209
Flint Castle, 142–3, 146–7, 200, *D6*
Framlingham Castle, 86–9, 95, 169, *G7*
Fulk Nerra, Count of Anjou, 22–3
Greenstead-Juxta-Ongar church, 34, 37
Gruffydd ap Llywelyn (killed 1064), 21–2
Gruffydd ap Llywelyn (died 1244), 129–30, 153
Guildford Castle, 53, *F8*
Gundulf, Bishop of Rochester, 45–6, 50, 54, 56
Hamelin Plantagenet, 99–100
Harlech Castle, 153, 156, *C6*
Harold, King, 26, 93
Hastings, Lord, 210
Hastings Castle, 24–5, *G9*
Hereford Castle and town, 21–2
Herstmonceux Castle, 209, *F8*
Henry I, 51–4, 62–3
Henry II, 79–80, 83, 86, 92–3, 97, 179, 104, 158, 163
Henry III, 62, 107, 110, 116–20, 123–7, 129–33, 140–1, 179
Henry IV, 199–200, 201, 204
Henry V, 204
Henry VI, 204, 206
Henry VII, 210–11
Henry VIII, 211–13
Henry of Blois, Bishop of Winchester, 79, 91
Henry de Ferrers, 102
Henry of Huntingdon, 74–5

Hubert de Burgh, 110–12
Isabella, queen of Edward II, 166, 173, 176
James of St George, 144, 149, 156, 160–1, 165
John, King, 61–2, 104–10, 124, 179
John of Gaunt, Duke of Lancaster, 195, 199, 210
Kenilworth Castle, 92, 109, 124–5, 196–8, E7
Kildrummy Castle, 162, 164, 167, D1
Kirby-Muxloe Castle, 210, E7
Langeais, 22, 23, 38
Launceston Castle, 114, C9
Lawrence de Ludlow, 136
Lewes Castle, 30, F9
Lincoln Castle, 30, F6
Llanbadarn Castle (Aberwystwyth), 146, D7
Llywelyn ab Iorwerth, 128–9, 148, 149
Llywelyn ap Gruffydd, 130–1, 146–8, 155
Longthorpe Tower, 140, F6
Louis VIII, King of France, 109, 117
Louis IX (Saint), King of France, 124
Ludlow Castle, 44, 74, 87, 95, 171–3, D7
Magnus Maximus (Prince Maxim), 154, 156
Maid of Norway, 163–4
Manorbier Castle, 120–3, C8
Marshal, William (William the Marshal), 107–8, 110
Matilda, Empress, 54, 63, 69–70, 79
Montfort, Simon de, 123–5, 127, 130, 188
Mortimer, Roger, 171, 173, 176
Newark Castle, 71, 110, F6
Nigel, Bishop of Ely, 71
Norwich Castle, 53–4, G7
Nottingham Castle, 176, F6
Nunney Castle, 189, 199, E8
Oakham Castle, 102–3, F6
Odiham Castle, 104, 106, F8
Offa's Dyke, 16–17
Old Sarum Castle (Old Salisbury), 72, E8
Orford Castle, 83–6, 92, G7
Oxford Castle and town, 18, 26–7, 69–70, E8
Pembroke Castle, 107–9, 146, C8
Percy, Earl of Northumberland, 200, 201
Pevensey Castle, 12, 24–5, G9
Philip the Fair, King of France, 158, 162, 165–6
Philippa, queen of Edward III, 173, 181
Pontefract Castle, 200, F5
Portchester Castle, 13, 58–61, E9
Prudhoe Castle, 201, E4
Queenborough Castle, 182, G8

Ralph, Lord Cromwell, 206
Ralph the Timid, Earl of Hereford, 21–2
Ranulf Flambard, Bishop of Durham, 51–2
Redvers, Baldwin de, 64–6
Rhuddlan Castle, 143–7, D6
Richard I, 101, 104, 163, 179
Richard II, 189, 193, 195, 197, 199–201
Richard III, 195, 210
Richard's Castle, 21
Richmond Castle, 41–4, 74, 75, 87, E4
Robert, Count of Mortain, 27–9
Robert, Duke of Normandy, 52–3
Robert's Castle (Clavering?), 21
Robert d'Oilgi, 27
Rochester Castle, 54–8, 61–2, 194–5, G8
Roger, Bishop of Salisbury, 71–2
Rouen, 23, 45, G10
Ruthin Castle, 146, D6
Scarborough Castle, 92, F5
Scrope, Lord, 192
Sherborne Castle (Old), 72–3, 76, D9
Skenfrith Castle, 112–13, 146, D8
Stephen, King, 63–4, 69, 74–5, 78–9, 86, 107
Stewart, Robert, Duke of Albany, 186
Stirling Castle, 166, D3
Stokesay Castle, 135–40, D7
Tamworth Castle and town, 17, E6
Tattershall Castle, 206–8, F6
Thetford Castle, 31, G7
Tower of London, 45, 50, 101, 120, 123, 126–7, 129, 133, F8
Tretower Castle, 114, D7
Trim Castle, 97–8, B5
Wallingford Castle, 26, E8
Warkworth Castle, 201–4, E4
Warwick Castle, 186–8, E7
Westminster Abbey, 19, 45, 116, 120
Westminster Hall, 51
White Castle (Llantilio), 112, D8
William I, the Conqueror, 24–7, 44–5, 50, 56, 63, 93
William II, Rufus, 50, 56
William de Corbeil, Archbishop of Canterbury, 54
William Fitz Osbern, 38
William the Lion, King of Scotland, 163, 166
Winchester Castle, 101, 117–19, 136, E8
Windsor Castle, 26, 30, 178–82, F8
York Castle (Clifford's tower), 200, F5